TOXIC MIX?

TOXIC MIX?

A Handbook of
Science and Politics

Herbert N. Foerstel

GREENWOOD PRESS

An Imprint of ABC-CLIO, LLC

A B C ☰ C L I O

Santa Barbara, California • Denver, Colorado • Oxford, England

Copyright 2010 by Herbert N. Foerstel

Library of Congress Cataloging-in-Publication Data

Foerstel, Herbert N.
   Toxic mix?: a handbook of science and politics / Herbert N. Foerstel.
     p. cm.
   Includes index.
   ISBN 978-0-313-36234-7 (alk. paper) — ISBN 978-0-313-36235-4 (ebook) 1. Science and state—United States. I. Title.
   Q127.U6F57 2010
   338.973'06—dc22   2009041623

14 13 12 11 10   1 2 3 4

This book is also available on the World Wide Web as an eBook.
Visit www.abc-clio.com for details.

ABC-CLIO, LLC
130 Cremona Drive, P.O. Box 1911
Santa Barbara, California 93116-1911

This book is printed on acid-free paper. ∞
Manufactured in the United States of America

Contents

Introduction   vii

1. Atomic Politics   1

2. The Politics of Space Science   25

3. The Politics of Sexual Reproduction   49

4. The Politics of Stem Cells   65

5. The Heated Politics of Global Warming   83

6. The Politics of Nature   105

7. The Politics of Public Health   129

8. The Politics of Evolution   153

9. Science and the Politics of Xenophobia   173

10. The Promise of Political Change and Scientific Redemption   191

Appendix   A Survey of Private Organizations Involved
in Science and Politics   215

Index   233

Introduction

Critics of President George W. Bush charge that he has introduced an era in which science is dominated by politics, reversing years of productive and respectful cooperation between the scientific community and the federal government. In his book, *The Republican War on Science,* Chris Mooney writes, "For anyone who doubts the crisis over science politicization today, let me take you back to a very different era: the 1940s."[1] Mooney describes the "strong partnership between science and our political leaders" during the Roosevelt and Truman administrations. In reality, that partnership was quite one-sided.

American scientists became virtual wards of the state during World War II, and the link between scientific research and the military remained even after the war. In September 1946, the popular financial magazine *Business Week* appraised America's postwar science as follows: "Partly by design, partly by default, federal support of pure science is today almost completely under military control. Its general direction is being set by military needs; its finances are coming from military funds. The odds are getting better all the time that pure scientific research will become, permanently, a branch of the military establishment."[2]

In a 1946 lecture, award-winning physicist Philip Morrison urged scientists not to cede their independence to the military: "The armed forces are always, sooner or later, concerned with secrecy, and with the restrictions such concerns imply on the travels, publications, and even the characters and background of their research workers. Such restrictions will greatly harm our science. It will become narrow, national, and secret."[3]

The inadequate demobilization of science following World War II not only compromised the independence of scientific research but also imposed unprecedented secrecy on that research. The Atomic Energy Act of 1947 introduced massive censorship and federal control of science, including bizarre new notions like "born classified," which imposed national security classification over scientific *ideas* before they were even conceived. (See Chapter 1.)

Historian J. W. Grove would later warn, "There are no limits in principle to the power of the state to declare the open communication of *any* scientific knowledge contrary to the interests of national security. . . . Yet the unrestricted use of this power would do irremediable harm to the progress of science, and it is scientific progress on which, paradoxically, the welfare and security of nations now increasingly depend."[4]

Facing criticism and concern from the scientific community, the federal government weaned most scientists off of direct military funding, replacing that link with "soft" federal money. Soon, most researchers were maintained by the government as an elite reserve labor force that would provide the nation's authoritative voice on scientific ideas and advise politicians on all technical matters. Chandra Mukerji, author of *A Fragile Power: Scientists and the State,* writes, "[L]ike the unemployed on welfare, scientists on research grants are kept off the streets and in good health because of the interests and investments of the elites."[5]

In 1945, President Roosevelt's director of the Office of Scientific Research and Development issued a report, *Science: The Endless Frontier,* that called upon the federal government to invest heavily in the funding of scientific research at American universities. The National Science Foundation Act of 1950 subsequently authorized the National Science Foundation (NSF) to initiate and support basic scientific research, and although the NSF was intended to restrain the military domination of science, it often functioned as a middleman for the military. Still, postwar American scientific research seemed robust and internationally respected. Then came a shocking scientific event that caused the United States, and the world, to reevaluate the health of American science.

On October 4, 1957, the Soviet Union successfully launched its space capsule, *Sputnik,* into orbit, commanding the attention and respect of the world and jolting America's presumed scientific preeminence. Moved to action by national pride and Cold War politics, President Dwight Eisenhower convened a star-studded President's Science Advisory Committee (PSAC) and appointed the first White House Science Adviser, MIT president James Killian. With the full cooperation of the American scientific community, an ambitious space program was begun, mobilizing scientific talent and funding to an extent unseen since the Manhattan Project developed the atomic bomb. (See Chapter 2.)

A close association had already developed between the military, private industry, and the scientific community. As a result, university-based scientific research boomed. By 1961, that connection became so powerful that President Eisenhower, America's most famous World War II general, issued a stark warning in his farewell address to the nation.

"[W]e have been compelled to create a permanent armaments industry of vast proportions. . . . In the councils of government, we must guard against the acquisition of unwarranted influence, whether sought or unsought, by the military-industrial complex. The potential for the disastrous rise of misplaced power exists and will persist. We must never let the weight of this combination endanger our liberties or democratic processes. We should take nothing for granted."[6]

Following the Eisenhower Administration, President John Kennedy established the White House Office of Science and Technology and made his science adviser, Jerome Wiesner, a part of his inner circle. Perhaps the earliest example of a president ignoring his science adviser for political reasons occurred when Kennedy pushed for a manned lunar exploration despite Wiesner's advise that a "crash program aimed at placing a man into orbit . . . cannot be justified solely on scientific or technical grounds."[7]

Kennedy believed that a manned lunar exploration would serve the vital interests of the United States during the Cold War by demonstrating this nation's scientific prowess and resolve. He reached an agreement with his science adviser that the manned lunar probe would proceed, but with no public claim that significant amounts of scientific knowledge would result from the program. In retrospect, Kennedy's handling of this scientific dispute can be distinguished from the current politicization of science insofar as it studiously avoided dressing up a political decision in scientific garb.

The emergence of strong environmental and consumer movements during the late 1960s and 1970s brought expanded federal regulations on industry. This, in turn, led companies to sponsor their own "science" to refute proposed regulatory plans. Some businesses began funding research organizations that would promote their goals and interests. Even the Heritage Foundation, today's most prominent conservative "think tank," was created in 1973 as a response to the earlier Senate vote to cut funding for the supersonic transport (SST) program, which lost its support after critics warned of "sonic boom" noise pollution and atmospheric pollution.

The Nixon Administration argued forcefully for the SST, despite public concerns expressed by its Council on Environmental Quality and a critical report prepared by the President's Science Advisory Council (PSAC). Enraged by the unwillingness of his science advisers to fall in line, Nixon suppressed the advisory council's report, dissolved the PSAC, and abolished the office of the presidential science adviser. Throughout his second term, Nixon maintained an adversarial relationship with the scientific community, which not only opposed the SST, but criticized the proposed antiballistic missile system and the Vietnam War.

President Ronald Reagan carried forward the national security science agenda of previous administrations, but magnified its effect by cloaking almost all government-produced or government-funded scientific and technical information in secrecy. In 1982, Reagan issued Executive Order 12356, under which national security classifiers were no longer required to weigh the public's need to know against the need to classify information. Instead, they needed only to have a "reasonable expectation of damage" to national security. Classifiers were now told: "if there is a reasonable doubt about the need to classify information, it shall be safeguarded as if it were classified . . . and if there is a reasonable doubt about the appropriate level of classification it should be safeguarded at the higher level of classification."

Unlike previous executive orders, which prevented the reclassification of information already released to the public, E.O. 12356 specified that "information may be classified or reclassified after an agency has received a request for it under the Freedom of Information Act or the Privacy Act." In effect, Reagan decided that the classification of information would be triggered whenever the public showed an interest in it.

All previous classification orders had limited the scope of secrecy to "official information" in which the government held some proprietary interest. But Reagan's E.O. 12356 extended classification to any information that "is owned by, produced by, produced for, or is under the control of the United States Government." As a result, E.O. 12356 set an all-time record for newly classified documents, including a significant amount of academic scientific research. In the prestigious journal *Physics Today*, Harvard's John Shattuck noted that E.O. 12356 "appears to allow classification to be imposed at any stage of a research project and to be maintained as long as government officials deem prudent."[8]

Reagan's national security obsession went beyond the formal classification system when he signed National Security Decision Directive 145 (NSDD-145), creating a category called "unclassified but sensitive national security-related information." Enforcement authority for this new secrecy order was assigned to the highly secretive National Security Agency, which was to exercise control over all computers and communications security for the federal government and private industry.

Late in the Reagan administration, a front-page story in the *New York Times* revealed a secret FBI program called the Library Awareness Program (LAP), which sought to recruit librarians around the country to restrict access to publicly available science collections and conduct surveillance on their users. I had already experienced the heavy hand of the LAP in 1986 when the FBI visited two science libraries that I managed at the University of Maryland. An agent came to the Engineering and Physical Sciences Library and the Chemistry Library, flashed a badge, and asked that we report to the FBI anyone with "a foreign-sounding name or foreign-sounding accent."

My subsequent book, *Surveillance in the Stacks,* describes the LAP in detail, tracing its origins in the 1970s through its full bloom during the Reagan administration, during which it intruded on public libraries such as the New York Public Library, academic libraries such as Columbia University and the University of Maryland, and even corporate and government libraries. In 1988, Dr. Robert Park, public affairs director for the American Physical Society, decried the FBI's "attempts to recruit snitches at scientific and technical libraries," but the Bureau continued to warn that allowing foreigners to use our unclassified science libraries would result in "illegal technology transfer." The prestigious journal *New Scientist* observed, "How consulting information held in a public library for anyone to see can be described as 'stealing' it is an FBI secret."[9]

In addition to expanding federal controls over scientific information, President Reagan introduced a new political force, the "religious right," that has vexed science advisers in every subsequent administration. Influenced by domestic policy advisor Gary Bauer, who would later become a national leader of the religious right, Reagan turned a blind eye to the beginning of the AIDS epidemic. Educating children about safe sex and condoms was too much for Reagan to countenance, even in the face of a devastating AIDS epidemic. Indeed, Reagan forbade his Surgeon General, C. Everett Koop, from even mentioning AIDS during his entire first term. (See Chapter 7.)

Reagan's opposition to the teaching of evolution preceded his presidency. During his 1967–1975 governorship of California, his appointed state board of education endorsed creationism and attempted to limit the teaching of evolution. During his 1980 campaign for president, Reagan maintained this position, declaring that great flaws existed in evolutionary theory and advocating the teaching of creationism alongside evolution. Even Reagan's science adviser, George Keyworth, refused to repudiate the teaching of creationism in public schools. (See Chapter 8.)

As much as Reagan courted the religious right on matters of "creation science," he was even more aggressive in seeking the support of industry by opposing federal regulations. James Watt, Reagan's secretary of the interior, and Anne Gorsuch, his head of the Environmental Protection Agency (EPA), were avowed anti-environmentalists. In the summer of 1981, Reagan's EPA held private "science forums" to allow industry representatives to rebut scientific evidence that two chemicals, formaldehyde and DEHP, were carcinogens. These one-sided proceedings were successful in fending off tough regulations on both chemicals.

The Reagan administration was also responsible for the unprecedented politicization of the appointment process for federal scientific advisory committees. Indeed, Reagan's EPA prepared a "hit list" of scientists to be excluded from advisory committees because of their environmental concerns or liberal politics. After the "hit list" was made public, the scandal led to the resignation of Anne Gorsuch, Reagan's first EPA administrator. In the journal *Science*, Gorsuch's successor, William Ruckelshaus, declared, "There will be no hit lists. . . . I intend that EPA will operate forthrightly and honestly."[10]

The Reagan administration also clashed with the scientific community over the environmental effects of "acid rain," the acidic precipitation caused by the emission of sulfur dioxide and nitrogen oxides from power plants, auto exhausts, and similar sources. The White House sided with the coal and electric power industries, challenging the connection between acid rain and environmental damage as well as industry's role in causing the problem. In 1983, two events undercut the White House's position on acid rain. First, a panel of scientists convened by the White House Office of Science and Technology Policy

(OSTP) recommended immediate action to curb acid rain, and then a report by the National Academy of Sciences directly linked acid rain in the northeastern United States to industrial pollution and car exhaust. In response, the White House delayed and watered down the OSTP's report, and Reagan's staff recommended that the OSTP be abolished.

The next quantum leap in the politicization of science came in 1994, when conservative representative Newt Gingrich (R-GA) ushered in the "Republican Revolution" and immediately abolished the congressional Office of Technology Assessment (OTA). The OTA had been created in the wake of the SST scandal to provide members of Congress more impartial and independent scientific analysis. Now Congress would have no bipartisan arbiter on scientific matters. Gingrich claimed that members of Congress could instead contact individual scientists and inform themselves, with no expert "filter" interposed. Representative George Brown, the senior Democrat on the House Science Committee, said the OTA had been Congress's "defense against the dumb," and he concluded, "[I]t is shameful that OTA was defenseless against a very dumb decision by Congress."[11]

In the absence of the OTA, conservative Republicans located their own experts to challenge the scientific mainstream on matters like global warming, while pushing a regulatory reform bill through Congress. It was during the Gingrich ascendancy that the term "sound science" was introduced as a supposed alternative to mainstream science. The tobacco industry and its allies helped to popularize the term in support of their agenda to block federal controls on tobacco by challenging the medical data arrayed against smoking.

In an attempt to justify its rejection of mainstream science, the Gingrich Congress arranged a series of hearings by the Energy and Environment Subcommittee of the House Committee on Science entitled "Scientific Integrity and Public Trust." Chaired by Representative Dana Rohrabacher (R-CA), the hearings covered three environmental issues of great interest to industry: global warming, ozone depletion, and dioxin hazards. The methodology of these hearings was unique, eschewing peer-reviewed scientific consensus in favor of self-styled "science courts" that pitted industry scientists against the mainstream. After the adversarial proceedings, members of Congress, not scientists, would exercise the final judgment. These "scientific integrity" hearings, as they were called, produced a demand for "sound science" in the making of public policy. That term would resonate within conservative ranks from the Gingrich era to the administration of George W. Bush, who invoked "sound science" on issues ranging from global warming to unsafe drinking water.

Actually, the earliest presidential invocation of "sound science" came during the administration of the elder Bush, George Herbert Walker Bush, who used the term to denigrate claims of growing environmental threats. The elder Bush's EPA administrator, William Reilly, also used the term frequently to rebut critics of his environmental policy. Shortly after the 1994 elections, the Gingrich Republicans adopted "property rights" and "sound science" as their environmental buzzwords. A Knight Ridder news story explained that the goal of the "sound science" coalition was deregulation: "'Sound science' is short-hand for the notion that anti-pollution laws have gone to extremes, spending huge amounts of money to protect people from minuscule risks."[12]

The "sound science" movement closely accompanied Newt Gingrich's wildly successful "Contract with America," which enshrined regulatory reform as its crown jewel. Reform bills were introduced in both houses of the Republican-controlled Congress, prescribing rigid rules for assessing risk before requiring federal regulation. Agencies would also be required to submit their scientific studies to "peer review" panels that could be dominated by industry scientists. In addition, the regulatory reform bills would have created new opportunities for federal court challenges to the validity of scientific studies.

As they pushed for regulatory reform, the Gingrich Republicans not only sought to slash funding for federal scientific research but also proposed closing the U.S. Geological Survey, the essential agency for tracking earthquakes, volcanic eruptions, and other geologic cataclysms. A new conservative group, The Advancement of Sound Science Coalition (TASSC), attacked federal regulation, releasing a report protesting alleged negative media coverage of the regulatory reformers.

If the notion of "sound science" were to be taken seriously and treated respectfully, it would be interpreted as a demand for a higher burden of scientific proof before taking action to protect public health and the environment. This is a debatable political proposal, but it is not a scientific position. As the conservative Annapolis Center for Science-Based Public Policy explains, "sound science" functions as a counterpoint to the precautionary principle, the regulatory principle that recommends erring on the side of caution when faced with an environmental or public-health risk. Clearly, such "counterpoint" must occur within the public-policy sphere, not within science. Science must be used to inform political leaders, who are always free to ignore scientific advice, but not to alter, distort, or redefine science in the process.

The growing political movement to create a new science wedded to an antiregulatory and pro-business agenda is antithetical to the very basis for scientific inquiry. It proposes a partisan science—a them-versus-us, conservative-versus-liberal science—an ideological science. This brave new science has been embraced by the administration of President George W. Bush. In the recent words of Thomas McGarity, president of the conservative Center for Progressive Regulation, "Our science is sound science and their science is junk science."[13]

The Bush administration's application of national security controls on scientific research and communication, though frequent and often severe, does not represent a significant increase over past administrations. It is on domestic issues affecting education, environment, public health, and corporate prerogatives that the Bush administration has mobilized a newly politicized scientific arsenal. What the Bush administration has introduced is not political domination of science—that was accomplished years ago—but religious and corporate domination of politics, resulting in a bureaucratic mistrust of the scientific method itself. World War II permanently linked science and national security, but the Bush administration has distorted science beyond the military, serving a domestic agenda that intrudes on the social attitudes and intellectual judgments of private citizens.

The National Coalition Against Censorship (NCAC) says, "The use of scientific research to serve illegitimate ends is obviously a serious concern, but hardly a new one. . . . Censoring science to promote a political or ideological agenda is a different matter. Whatever justifications may be advanced where national security is involved have no bearing on this phenomenon."[14]

In response to this phenomenon, NCAC initiated The Knowledge Project: Censorship & Science, which Executive Director Joan Bertin said "will call attention to the erosion of our country's knowledge base and the rise of anti-intellectualism as a national credo. . . . [W]e are also witnessing a wholesale loss of respect for the power of rational analysis based on scientific research and information."[15]

In an article in the *Legal Times,* Bertin wrote: "Censoring science is bad, not just as a matter of principle, or because the Constitution prohibits it. It's bad because suppressing and distorting science keeps us from responding to a reality that won't change just because we ignore it. It makes us a nation of the ignorant, uninformed, and just plain stupid."[16]

Congress has made some attempts to limit the administration's war on science, but for the most part it has been reduced to sideline criticism. Representative Henry Waxman (D-CA), the ranking minority member on the House Committee on Government Reform, generated a report titled "Politics and Science in the Bush administration," which remains an important primer on the dangers of politicized science. The report concludes, "The Administration's political interference with science has led to misleading statements by the President, inaccurate responses to Congress, altered web sites, suppressed agency reports, erroneous international communications, and gagging of scientists. The subjects involved span a broad range, but they share a common attribute: the beneficiaries of the scientific distortions are important supporters of the President, including social conservatives and powerful industry groups."

The Waxman report concludes with a set of findings:

"First, the Administration has repeatedly manipulated the composition of scientific advisory committees. . . . Second, the Administration has suppressed or distorted scientific information on a wide range of topics. . . . Third, the Administration has interfered with scientific research." The report declares that the Bush administration "has repeatedly suppressed, distorted, or obstructed science to suit political and ideological goals. These actions go far beyond the traditional influence that Presidents are permitted to wield at federal agencies and compromise the integrity of scientific policymaking."[17]

In May 2008, the first World Science Festival opened in New York with a panel of scientists who criticized America's science policies. Nobel laureate David Baltimore, board chairman of the American Association for the Advancement of Science (AAAS), said, "I think there's a loss of American power and prestige that came about as a result of our anti-science policies. . . . What we need is leadership that respects science."[18]

Late in 2008, James McCarthy, AAAS president, complained about the outgoing Bush administration's attempt to transfer political appointees into permanent federal positions with scientific responsibilities. "It's ludicrous to have people who do not have a scientific background, who are not trained and skilled in the ways of science, make decisions that involve resources . . . [and] facilities in the scientific infrastructure," said McCarthy. He warned that such actions would "leave wreckage behind with these appointments."[19]

The Union of Concerned Scientists agreed, declaring, "Across a broad range of issues—from childhood lead poisoning and mercury emissions to climate change, reproductive health, and nuclear weapons—political appointees have distorted and censored scientific findings that contradict established policies. In some cases, they have manipulated the underlying science to align results with predetermined political decisions."[20]

This brief introduction to modern science and politics demonstrates the dangerous consequences that result whenever the federal government, often allied with big business, distorts or misrepresents scientific evidence to advance a political agenda. The chapters that follow document particular fields of science that have been compromised or corrupted by political influence.

Chapter 1 examines the heavy-handed federal control of nuclear science, which has left the American public essentially ignorant of all things nuclear. The Atomic Energy Act of 1946 established almost total secrecy over all atomic research, introducing such bizarre concepts as "born classified," which applied national security secrecy to scientific concepts not yet conceived. After America's use of atomic weapons against Japan at the end of World War II, a combination of public ignorance and political hysteria cloaked nuclear research, particularly weapons research. The result was a political witch hunt of scientists who were considered insufficiently supportive of the American program to develop a new "super bomb," the hydrogen or fusion bomb. One of these scientists, J. Robert Oppenheimer, the father of America's atom bomb, was actually stripped of his security clearance and denied access to the very research that he created. Chapter 1 describes the enforced ignorance of the American public on nuclear issues, which allowed the government to freely manipulate the public debate on everything from domestic weapons production to the foreign threat of weapons of mass destruction (WMDs).

Chapter 2 describes the politics of aviation and space science. America was the home of humankind's first flight, and this country dominated the air in peacetime and war until 1957, when the Soviet Union's *Sputnik* orbited the earth, challenging not only America's supremacy in space, but its Cold War politics as well. The "space race" that followed was politically motivated, and in the process science was often prostituted. The explosion of NASA's *Challenger* spacecraft in 1986 shortly after liftoff is described in Chapter 2 as a failure of politics and the managerial culture, not science. Despite a scathing report from a blue-ribbon science review panel, NASA failed to learn its lessons, and the *Columbia* disaster soon followed.

The Reagan Administration's "Star Wars" missile defense program, plagued to this day by technical failures and cost overruns, is also described in Chapter 2 as an unfortunate triumph of politics over science. Two decades of seemingly unlimited funding and political support in the face of scientific skepticism and technical malfunctions has characterized the "Star Wars" missile defense program.

Chapter 3 documents the uneasy role medical science has played in the raging political debate over abortion, abstinence, and family planning. The recent emergence of the "religious right" as a prominent force in American politics has produced federal policies designed to discourage, or even criminalize, abortion and family planning. This chapter reveals the medical science used to support these policies to be shoddy at best, yet federal funding has been consistently withheld from medical programs that do not comport with the political or religious views of the Bush administration. In addition, the administration has resorted to heavy-handed censorship to suppress criticism of the "abstinence-only" programs supported by religious organizations.

Chapter 4 examines what is surely the most politicized area of modern science, stem-cell research. Stem-cell research promises revolutionary cures for the most intractable maladies known to humankind, yet political opposition has left this important medical field in stagnation. On August 9, 2001, President Bush announced that federal research on stem cells would be restricted to a small number of already existing cell lines. It would soon be discovered that most of these "existing" lines were contaminated or otherwise not viable for research. As a result, American research on stem cells came to a virtual halt.

In 2006, after Congress passed a bill to increase the number of stem-cell lines eligible for federal funding, President Bush vetoed it, bringing human embryonic stem-cell research to life as a political issue for federal and state candidates for office. In Missouri, Republican senator John Danforth, an Episcopal priest and abortion opponent, nonetheless cited the New Testament in supporting a state constitutional amendment protecting the legality of human embryonic stem-cell research. "I find nothing in the Bible that tells me that cells in a lab dish are people," said Danforth. "What I do find in the Gospels is an emphasis on healing—relieving people of their suffering."[21] Around the country, in state capitols and on Capitol Hill, the political battles over stem-cell research continue.

Chapter 5 presents the most publicized area of conflict between scientists and politicians: the issue of global warming. Since refusing to sign the Kyoto treaty on emissions, the Bush administration has denied the dangers of global warming and silenced officials who disagreed. The process of political denial has not only put America at odds with a global scientific consensus, but has left the federal government unprepared for domestic environmental threats such as rising sea levels and increasingly severe storms. Everything from poor design of New Orleans levees by the Army Corps of Engineers to the inadequate federal response to the Katrina disaster indicates political indifference to scientific evidence.

Because of the international threat posed by global warming, the eyes of the entire world have been focused on America's response. Former vice president and presidential candidate Al Gore won a Nobel Prize for his effective work in bringing world attention to the threat of global warming, and he has galvanized a coalition of scientists and environmentalists in an effort to identify the human causes of climate change and reverse their effects. Chapter 5 examines this ongoing environmental struggle and the corporate and political opposition to any change that might have adverse economic effects.

Chapter 6, "The Politics of Nature," examines the threat to our environment represented by government corruption and cultivated ignorance. The continuing pollution of our air, land, and water is documented in the context of a politicized Environmental Protection Agency. Similar threats to our wilderness and wildlife are described, particularly as the result of political manipulation of the Endangered Species Act. The work of the Union of Concerned Scientists (UCS) is documented, including its recent revelation that the Department of the Interior has "systematically distorted, manipulated, and misused the scientific process prescribed by the Endangered Species Act."[22] Such political tampering with objective environmental science has compromised America's precious natural resources: its land, air, water, and wildlife.

Chapter 7 documents the growing public-health crisis in the United States and the reluctance of the federal government to take ameliorative action. Indeed, public-health policy in the United States may have been more disastrously politicized than any other federal area. Among the specific public-health problems examined are HIV/AIDS, smoking, and obesity. The federal government's willingness to sacrifice public health for political purposes can be seen in the congressional testimony of America's Surgeons General, detailed in Chapter 7. In an amazing display of scientific solidarity, the Surgeons General from both Republican and Democratic administrations told Congress of politically manipulated science by successive administrations from Reagan to Bush.

Chapter 8 presents the science and politics of evolution, creationism, and Intelligent Design. While campaigning for the presidency in 1999, George W. Bush advocated the teaching of creationism alongside evolution in public schools. Because creationism is, by definition, a religious concept, this would be an unconstitutional violation of the Establishment Clause of the First Amendment. However, seizing on the legitimacy accorded to creationism by Bush, a group of political and religious leaders propounded the concept of "Intelligent Design," a pseudo-scientific notion that an unspecified intelligent force must have designed the more-complex life forms on Earth. Chapter 8 examines the landmark 2005 court case, *Kitzmiller v. Dover Area School District,* that declared the teaching of Intelligent Design to be an unconstitutional endorsement of religion. Because the *Dover* decision did not carry legal precedent outside the local school district, many state and federal officials continue to oppose the inclusion of evolution in public school science curricula or, like President Bush, insist that Intelligent Design be taught alongside evolution.

Chapter 9 examines the political exploitation of visa restrictions and export control to restrict or manipulate scientific communication. The federal government continues to use visa restrictions and export controls to prevent foreign scientists from attending conferences and speaking engagements in the United States and to restrict the number of foreign students who may attend American universities. The primary justification given for such policies is national security, including the desire to reduce so-called "technology transfer," the process by which foreign nations, adversaries or friends, acquire *unclassified* scientific and technical information through the open literature or collegial exchanges. But the seemingly irrational exclusion of badly needed scientific expertise from American universities and laboratories defies any explanation other than politically stoked xenophobia.

Chapter 10 describes the political transition from the Bush administration to the Obama administration. The Bush administration's frenzied, eleventh-hour administrative changes to environmental regulations are documented. President Barack Obama's inauguration brought explicit and implicit promises of increased support for science and its integrity, and the scientific and environmental communities were quick to communicate their agendas to the new administration. Chapter 10 presents the specific recommendations of these organizations and describes the Obama administration's response during its first year.

Appendix A lists and annotates the major private organizations, think tanks, and research institutes that influence American science policy. The annotated list of organizations includes: The Advancement of Sound Science Center, the American Association for the Advancement of Science, the American Civil Liberties Union, the American Enterprise Institute, the Annapolis Center for Science-Based Public Policy, the Center for Regulatory Effectiveness, the Discovery Institute, the Federation of American Scientists, the Frontiers of Freedom Institute, the George C. Marshall Institute, the Guttmacher Institute, the Heritage Foundation, the Institute for Creation Research, the National Center for Science Education, the National Coalition against Censorship, the Natural Resources Defense Council, OMB Watch, the Pacific Legal Foundation, the Rutherford Institute, and the Union of Concerned Scientists.

NOTES

1. Chris Mooney, *The Republican War on Science*, New York: Basic Books, 2005, p. 7.
2. "Science Dons a Uniform," *Business Week*, September 14, 1946, 19.

3. Philip Morrison, "The Laboratory Demobilizes," *Bulletin of Atomic Sciences*, November 1, 1946, 5–6.

4. J. W. Grove, *In Defense of Science: Science, Technology, and Politics in Modern Society* (Cheektowaga, N.Y.: University of Toronto Press, 1989), 67.

5. Chandra Mukerji, *A Fragile Power: Science and the State* (Princeton, N.J.: Princeton University Press, 1989), 7.

6. Quoted in McGeorge Bundy, *Dangers and Survival: Choices about the Bomb in the First Fifty Years* (New York: Random House, 1988), 201.

7. Chris Mooney, *The Republican War on Science*, New York: Basic Books, 2005, 28.

8. Irwin Goodwin, "Reagan Issues Order on Science Secrecy," *Physics Today*, November 1985, 56.

9. Quoted in Herbert Foerstel, *Secret Science: Federal Control of American Science and Technology* (Westport: Praeger, 1993), 179, 181.

10. Marjorie Sun, "Ruckelshaus Promises EPA Cleanup," *Science* 220, May 20, 1983, 801.

11. House Science Committee, press release, September 29, 1995. www.house .gov/science_democrats/releases/95sep29.

12. Heather Dewar, "GOP Ready to Dilute Environmental Laws: New Buzzwords Target Property Rights," *Houston Chronicle*, November 12, 1994.

13. Thomas McGarity, "Our Science Is Sound Science," *Kansas Law Review* 52 (2004): 897.

14. "National Coalition Against Censorship Program Description 2003," NCAC, November 2003, 5.

15. "NCAC Initiates The Knowledge Project: Censorship & Science," *Censorship News*, Fall 2005, 1.

16. "Censoring Science: Politics Trumps Knowledge," *Legal Times*, December 11, 2006.

17. U.S. House of Representatives, Committee on Government Reform, Minority Staff, "Politics and Science in the Bush Administration," August 13, 2003, prepared for Rep. Henry A. Waxman, http://www.reform.house.gov/min.

18. Keith Richburg, "U.S. Experts Bemoan Nation's Loss of Stature in the World of Science," *Washington Post*, May 29, 2008, A4.

19. Juliet Eilperin, "Top Scientist Rails Against Hirings," *Washington Post*, November 22, 2008, A3.

20. Union of Concerned Scientists, "Political Interference in Science," http://www.ucusa.org/scientific_integrity/interference/.

21. Susan Okie, "Stem-Cell Politics," *New England Journal of Medicine* 355, no. 16 (2006): 1633.

22. Union of Concerned Scientists, "Systematic Interference with Science at Interior Department Exposed," http://www.ucusa.org/scientific_integrity/abuses_of _science/political-interference-in.html.

I

Atomic Politics

A "mushroom cloud" hovers over Nagasaki, Japan, three minutes after the second atomic bomb ever to be used in warfare struck the city, August 9, 1945. (AP Photo/USAF)

ORIGINS OF ATOMIC SECRECY

Nuclear science is the only area of scientific research over which the U.S. federal government exercises full statutory authority. This heavy-handed federal control began during World War II, as the United States worked feverishly to develop an atomic bomb predicated on the process of nuclear fission. The act of splitting the atom would release vast amounts of energy with devastating explosive effect.

The top-secret American program to build an atomic bomb, code-named the Manhattan Project, required unprecedented federal control of the media, including scientific publications. Scientists and researchers understood the need for control over the technology of nuclear weapons, but they were skeptical of the advisability and effectiveness of controls over pure research. After all, they argued, one cannot hide the secrets of nature, which are available to anyone with an inquiring mind.

Despite their concerns, American scientists complied voluntarily with the code of censorship applied over nuclear science throughout World War II. Indeed, the federal controls extended beyond scientific papers to cover popular fiction and even comic strips. On April 11, 1945, the popular newspaper comic strip *Superman* showed the "Man of Steel" in a university physics lab, being addressed by an arrogant professor.

"The strange object before you is the cyclotron—popularly known as an 'atom smasher,'" declares the professor. "Are you still prepared to face this test, Mr. Superman?"

"Why not?" answers Superman, whose assembled friends are horrified by the dangers he would face.

"No, Superman, wait!" shouts one of the friends. "Even you can't do it. You'll be bombarded with electrons at a speed of 100 million miles per hour and charged with three million volts! It's madness!!"[1]

Upon seeing this comic strip displayed in the *Washington Post*, the Office of Censorship immediately contacted the syndicate that distributed *Superman* and forced them to rewrite the plot to eliminate any reference to atom smashing.

On August 14, 1945, General Leslie R. Groves, commander of the atomic bomb project, thanked the Office of Censorship for doing a splendid job in keeping the bomb secret. Having dropped the atomic bomb on Hiroshima and Nagasaki, the U.S. government could no longer deny its existence, but all technical information about the process of nuclear fission remained classified, including the most fundamental physics of heavy elements.

Most American scientists, including those who had developed the atomic bomb, recommended that wartime restrictions on nuclear information and research be removed. In late 1945, a panel of eminent scientists advised Secretary of State James Byrnes to avoid an atomic arms race by seeking international cooperation in controlling the atom. Instead, Byrnes joined President Harry Truman in arguing that America's "atomic secret" should be hidden from potential enemies. The War Department began working with Congress to draft legislation for postwar control of atomic energy. America's most prominent scientists disagreed with this approach and urged a return to the traditional openness of scientific research. Enrico Fermi warned, "Unless research is free and outside of control, the United States will lose its superiority in scientific pursuit."[2]

The first draft of an atomic energy bill reflected the scientific community's concern about federal control of science, calling for "private research and development on a truly independent basis" and free dissemination of "basic scientific information," which was defined to include, "in addition to theoretical knowledge of nuclear and other physics, chemistry, biology and therapy, all results capable of accomplishment, as distinguished from the processes or techniques of accomplishing them."[3]

The bill authorized the newly created Atomic Energy Commission (AEC) to withhold technical information on national security grounds, but only "within the meaning of the Espionage Act." In hearings and executive sessions, the bill gradually took on a more-restrictive approach to information access, contrary to what the scientific community had advocated. Indicative of this conservative political direction, the name of Section 9 of the bill was changed from "Dissemination of Information" to "Control of Information." In addition, a special category of classified information called "Restricted Data" was created to include "all data concerning the manufacture or utilization of atomic weapons, the production of fissionable material, or the use of fissionable material in the production of power."[4]

This new category of Restricted Data became the basis for the controversial concept of "born classified," the notion that certain kinds of scientific data are automatically classified from the moment they are conceived, whether by government scientists or private researchers. Two Senate staff members who played a major role in drafting the Atomic Energy Act of 1946 explained: "It does not matter whether these [restricted] data are discovered or compiled in a government laboratory or in connection with the private research of an individual scientist. . . . [I]f the Act does not restrict the liberty of scientific thought, it without question, abridges freedom of scientific communication."[5]

Despite subsequent amendments to the Atomic Energy Act, the concept of "born classified" continued to be applied under the broad range of Restricted Data.

THE OPPENHEIMER AFFAIR

The unprecedented scope and authority of the Atomic Energy Act were a political response to the early Cold War tensions and the seemingly mysterious threat of atomic weapons. Predictably, the decision to control scientific data was followed by political pressure to control the scientists themselves. What could not have been predicted was the choice of J. Robert Oppenheimer, known as "the father of America's atom bomb," as the first political scapegoat within the scientific community. As head of the prestigious Los Alamos Laboratory, Oppenheimer had led the scientific race to develop an atomic bomb before Nazi Germany could do so. Throughout his work on the Manhattan Project, Oppenheimer had the full trust and confidence of the project's director, General Leslie R. Groves. After the war, Oppenheimer became the government's most trusted adviser on atomic policy and related security, heading the General Advisory Committee (GAC) of the AEC.

Oppenheimer's political troubles began in 1949, when the GAC he chaired recommended that the United States delay a crash program to develop a thermonuclear bomb—what would become known as the hydrogen bomb or H-bomb—until an attempt had been made to reach an agreement with the Soviet Union to jointly foreswear development of the "super weapon." President Harry Truman quickly overruled the GAC recommendation, and Oppenheimer was removed as its chairman in 1952.

On February 17, 1953, Oppenheimer gave a speech at a closed meeting of the Council on Foreign Relations in which he complained that almost everything associated with nuclear weapons was classified. "I must reveal its nature without revealing anything," he said. "It is my opinion that we should all know—not precisely, but quantitatively and, above all, authoritatively—where we stand in these matters. . . . We do not operate well when they [nuclear weapons issues] are known, in secrecy and fear, only to a few men." Oppenheimer concluded that such "follies can occur only when even the men who know the facts can find no one to talk about them, when the facts are too secret for discussion, and thus for thought."[6]

Oppenheimer's adversary during the government's H-bomb debate had been fellow AEC member Lewis Strauss, who came to despise Oppenheimer for his persistent intrusion of morality and candor into public policy. President Eisenhower was initially impressed by Oppenheimer's call for candor, but Strauss, who had contributed heavily to Eisenhower's campaign, convinced the president that secrecy was essential and that Oppenheimer could not be trusted. Strauss was soon appointed as the president's atomic energy adviser and then elevated to chairman of the AEC. Almost immediately after assuming that office, Strauss asked J. Edgar Hoover to send him a copy of the FBI's latest summary report on Oppenheimer.

Armed with the FBI's surveillance data, Strauss formed an alliance with William Liscum Borden, the staff director for the Joint Committee on Atomic Energy, who shared Strauss's hostility toward Oppenheimer. Together they agreed on a plan to end Oppenheimer's influence in government. Borden was given permission to check out Oppenheimer's security file from the AEC's security vault. Using the AEC file, Borden began preparing a prosecutor's brief against Oppenheimer, which he mailed to the FBI on November 7. The major conclusion was, "[M]ore probably than not J. Robert Oppenheimer is an agent of the Soviet Union."[7]

Borden offered little evidence to support his charge, but he argued that the central issue was not whether Oppenheimer had ever been a Communist, but whether "he in fact did what a Communist in his circumstances, at Berkeley, would logically have done."[8]

J. Robert Oppenheimer lost his security clearance in 1954 as a result of a McCarthy-era political vendetta. He was photographed in his study at the Institute for Advanced Studies, December 15, 1957. (AP Photo/John Rooney)

The FBI forwarded Borden's letter to President Eisenhower, who called AEC chairman Strauss to the White House. Joseph Alsop, perhaps the most influential political columnist of that time, said in his memoirs that the Red-hunting senator Joseph McCarthy pressured Strauss to convict Oppenheimer or risk becoming a target himself. Alsop wrote that Strauss agreed "to offer Oppy, bound on the altar, as a sacrifice to appease McCarthy's wrath."[9]

Oppenheimer had never sought to hide his youthful association with leftists, and it was widely known throughout scientific and government circles. He had confided his past associations to General Leslie Groves, his boss during the Manhattan Project, and Groves saw them as no impediment to a security clearance. But now, at the height of Cold War hysteria, Oppenheimer became a target of political zealots like Strauss, Borden, and Senator Joseph McCarthy.

On December 21, 1953, Strauss summoned Oppenheimer to his office and offered him a choice: resign from the AEC or face charges by a board to be appointed by Strauss. Oppenheimer was given only a few hours to make his choice. Seeking legal advice, he went to the office of Joe Volpe, the former counsel of the AEC, where they were joined by Herbert Marks, Oppenheimer's friend and attorney. What the three men did not know was that Strauss had anticipated their meeting and bugged Volpe's office, violating the sanctity of client-attorney privilege.

Oppenheimer eventually rejected the offer to resign, stating in his letter: "Under the circumstances, this course of action would mean that I accept and concur in the view that I am not fit to serve this government, that I have served for some twelve years. This I cannot do."[10]

Upon receipt of Oppenheimer's letter, Strauss suspended Oppenheimer's security clearance and set in motion an extraordinarily personal and vindictive investigative process. Kenneth Nichols, the AEC's general manager and a Strauss ally, told the attorney drafting the charges against Oppenheimer that the physicist was "a slippery sonuvabitch, but we're going to get him this time."[11]

Senator Joseph McCarthy publicly characterized the action to suspend Oppenheimer's security clearance as "long overdue—it should have been taken years ago. . . . I think it took considerable courage to suspend the so-called untouchable scientist—Oppenheimer."[12]

The hearings would be conducted by a three-man board chaired by Gordon Gray, president of the University of North Carolina and former secretary of the army. The other two members of the board were conservative industrialist Thomas A. Morgan, former president of the Sperry Corporation, and Ward Evans, a chemistry professor at Northwestern University who had an unblemished record of denying security clearances on previous AEC boards.

The AEC appointed an aggressive, conservative prosecutor, Roger Robb, to argue the case against Oppenheimer, who chose Lloyd K. Garrison as his chief counsel. Joseph Alsop described Garrison as follows: "An eminently well-groomed New Yorker, Garrison was the epitome of high-mindedness and it is always a mistake to pay for high-mindedness when you are hiring a lawyer. In the end, Garrison allowed himself to be so hustled by Robb's well-practiced nastiness that he failed to get it squarely on the record that Strauss has seen fit to approve Oppenheimer's security clearance only a little before the case was brought on."[13]

When the hearing board first convened on April 12, 1954, Allan Ecker, one of Garrison's assistants, was shocked to see the board members seated behind a table stacked with black binders filled with classified FBI documents. "They had examined [those documents] in advance; they knew what was in there," recalls Ecker. "We did not know what was in there. We did not have a copy; we had no opportunity to challenge whatever documents were not brought forward. . . . So I thought that the proceeding was skewed from the outset."[14]

It soon became clear that there was little distinction between the prosecutor (Roger Robb) and the judge/jury (the AEC board). The AEC classified most of the documents to be used as evidence against Oppenheimer and refused to grant a security clearance to Oppenheimer's lawyer. As a result, the entire defense team was excluded from the hearing room whenever such documents were presented. To make matters worse, throughout the hearing the AEC refused even to provide the defense with unclassified summaries of classified documents used against Oppenheimer.

As the AEC security panel conducted its hearings, the FBI was feeding Strauss daily summaries of Oppenheimer's movements and conversations with his lawyers, giving Strauss the ability to anticipate and counteract any legal strategy by the defense. Oppenheimer's phones had been monitored at Los Alamos and at his Berkeley home. In addition, the FBI had recruited at least one confidential informant close to Oppenheimer. Even details on the contents of his trash at his Los Alamos home were being provided to AEC prosecutors. When an FBI agent suggested discontinuing the electronic surveillance of Oppenheimer's home "in view of the fact that it might disclose attorney-client relations," J. Edgar Hoover refused.[15]

Most scientists, including Albert Einstein, came to Oppenheimer's defense. Einstein argued that Oppenheimer "had no obligation to subject himself to the witch hunt, that he had served his country well, and that if this was the reward that she (the United States] offered he should turn his back on her."[16] As the hearings proceeded, Einstein would declare, "The trouble with Oppenheimer is that he loves a woman who doesn't love him—the United States government. . . . All Oppenheimer needed to do was go to Washington, tell the officials that they were fools, and then go home."[17]

Einstein was not the only person to offer such advice. Joe Volpe, the AEC's former general counsel, told Oppenheimer, "Robert, tell them to shove it, leave it, don't go on with it because I don't think you can win."[18]

John McCloy, chairman of the Council on Foreign Relations and a member of President Eisenhower's private "kitchen cabinet," wrote to Eisenhower: "I am very distressed, as I hope you are, over the Oppenheimer matter. I feel that it is somewhat like inquiring into the security risk of a Newton or a Galileo. Such people are themselves always 'top secret.'"[19] Eisenhower responded only by expressing hope that the board would exonerate Oppenheimer.

McCloy then decided to offer his own testimony before the board. When asked if Oppenheimer was a security risk he answered, "We are only secure if we have the best brains and the best reach of mind. If the impression is prevalent that scientists as a whole have to work under such great restrictions and perhaps great suspicion in the United States, we may lose the next step in the [nuclear] field, which I think would be very dangerous for us."[20]

When former AEC chairman David L. Lilienthal appeared at the hearing, he was shocked to see Oppenheimer's attorneys expelled from the room. "When I saw what they were doing to Oppenheimer, I was ready to throw chairs," recalled Lilienthal. "How can a lawyer defend his client's interests if he isn't even in the hearing room? There hasn't been a proceeding like this since the Spanish Inquisition."[21]

Vannever Bush, leader of the American mobilization during World War II and science adviser to the president after the war, testified at the hearing and accused the board of making a serious mistake by regarding Oppenheimer's opposition to the hydrogen bomb as a basis for removing his security clearance. "[H]ere is a man who is being pilloried because he had strong opinions and had the temerity to express them," said Bush. "When a man is pilloried for that, this country is in a severe state."[22]

Because of his scientific credentials, Edward Teller, the father of America's H-bomb, was the most anticipated witness against Oppenheimer. He was understandably outraged by Oppenheimer's opposition to the H-bomb program, but he felt the board was making a mistake by focusing on security clearances, an

Edward Teller uses a long lens camera to examine the site of the previous day's Project Gnome underground nuclear test, near Carlsbad, New Mexico, December 11, 1961. (AP Photo)

issue that was not broad enough to threaten Oppenheimer's long-term influence. Charter Heslep, an AEC public relations officer, summarized Teller's position after a lengthy interview with him. "Since the case is being heard on a security basis, Teller wonders if some way can be found to 'deepen the charges' to include a documentation of the 'consistently bad advice' that Oppenheimer has given. . . . Teller feels that this 'unfrocking' must be done or else—regardless of the outcome of the current hearing—scientists may lose their enthusiasm for the [atomic weapons] program."[23]

Even when he testified before the board, Teller could not question Oppenheimer's loyalty. "I have always assumed, and now assume, that he is loyal to the United States," he declared. "I believe this and I shall believe it until I see very conclusive proof to the opposite." But Teller quickly added, "If it is a question of wisdom and judgment, . . . then I would say one would be wiser not to grant clearance."[24]

The final witness to testify against Oppenheimer was William Liscum Borden, the man whose accusatory letter to the FBI had set the entire trial in motion. Borden did little more than read his letter aloud, making the same unsubstantiated charges. Following Borden, Oppenheimer himself was called to testify by his own counsel, who asked, "I wish you would tell us why you felt it was your function as a scientist to express your views on military strategy and tactics?"

Oppenheimer answered, "I felt, perhaps quite strongly, that having played an active part in promoting a revolution in warfare, I needed to be as responsible as I could with regard to what came of this revolution."[25]

Following Oppenheimer's testimony, Garrison presented his summation, concluding: "There is more than Dr. Oppenheimer on trial in this room. . . . The government of the United States is here on trial also. Our whole security process is on trial here, and is in your keeping, as is his life. . . . If we are to be strong, powerful, electric and vital, we must not devour the best and the most gifted of our citizens in some mechanical application of security procedures and mechanisms."[26]

As the hearing concluded, Strauss and Board Chairman Gray were confident that the handpicked board would vote unanimously to revoke Oppenheimer's security clearance, but just days before a final verdict was due, Gray was shocked to learn that Ward Evans, the lone scientist on the board, had penciled a draft dissent in favor of Oppenheimer. AEC prosecutor Robb was so concerned about the effect of Evans's defection on the other board members that he asked the FBI to have Director J. Edgar Hoover intercede directly with the board.

A recently released memo from FBI agent C. E. Henrich reveals, "Robb said that he feels it will be a tragedy if the decision of the Board goes the wrong way and that he considers this a matter of extreme urgency." Nonetheless, agent Henrich concluded, "This all boils down, it seems to me, to a situation where Strauss and Robb, who want the Board to make a finding that Oppenheimer is a security risk, are doubtful that the Board will find so at this point. . . . It is my feeling that the Director should not see the Board."[27]

Hoover decided not to intercede, but Strauss was relieved when Evans cast the lone dissent. In his testimony, Evans seemed to rebuke his fellow board members for their treatment of Oppenheimer: "To deny him clearance now for what he was cleared for in 1947, when we must know that he is less of a security risk now than he was then, seems hardly the procedure to be adopted in a free country. . . . I personally feel that our failure to clear Dr. Oppenheimer will be a black mark on the escutcheon of our country. His witnesses are a considerable segment of the scientific backbone of our Nation and they endorse him."[28]

On May 27, 1954, the Personnel Security Board submitted its verdict in a 15,000-word report. Oppenheimer was judged to be a security risk, and his clearance was revoked. The report's introduction warned that the "present peril" required some "undue restraints upon freedom of mind and action," and it's emphasis on Oppenheimer's reluctance to support the H-bomb program suggested a disturbing precedent: that American scientists must espouse appropriate political positions or risk losing their security clearances, government funding, and access to the federal laboratories essential for significant scientific research. The board's report concluded: "We find his [Oppenheimer's] conduct in the hydrogen bomb program sufficiently disturbing as to raise doubt as to whether his future participation, if characterized by the same attitudes, in a government program related to the national defense, would be clearly consistent with the best interests of security." [29]

The report explained that if Oppenheimer had "enthusiastically supported" the H-bomb project, it would have increased the possibility of earlier success. More important, the board concluded that "enthusiastic support on his part would *perhaps* have encouraged other leading scientists to work on the program."[30]

The implications of destroying the career of a great and valued scientist because of his insufficient enthusiasm for a federal program are grave. Dael Wolfle writes: "It has been pointed out by a variety of writers that adherence to such a doctrine will dampen freedom of discussion—not only in public but in secret councils. Who wants to risk such drastic punishment years after a decision was made, for having honestly opposed the decision before it was made?"[31]

The judgment of the three-man Personnel Security Board was now referred to the five-man Atomic Energy Commission, which, by a vote of four to one, affirmed that verdict. The AEC dismissed the charge that Oppenheimer was insufficiently enthusiastic about the H-bomb program, but faulted him for "fundamental defects in his character" and political associations that the AEC considered "far beyond the tolerable limits of prudence and self-restraint."[32]

Just as had been the case with the Personnel Security Board, the full commission's lone dissenting vote came from its lone scientist, Henry Smyth, who asserted that maintaining Oppenheimer's security clearance would be no threat to national security and, indeed, would "continue to strengthen the United States." He concluded, "In my opinion, the most important evidence in this record is the fact that there is no indication that Dr. Oppenheimer has ever divulged any secret information."[33]

The extraordinary trial of J. Robert Oppenheimer was over, establishing the politics of nuclear science for generations to come. Outraged by the AEC's verdict, 282 Los Alamos scientists signed a letter to Strauss defending Oppenheimer. Nationwide, more than 1,100 scientists and academics signed a petition protesting the decision.

In their 2006 Pulitzer Prize–winning biography of Oppenheimer, *American Prometheus: The Triumph and Tragedy of J. Robert Oppenheimer,* authors Kai Bird and Martin Sherwin conclude: "One scientist had been excommunicated. But all scientists were now on notice that there could be serious consequences for those who challenged state policies." Bird and Sherwin acknowledge that the personal animus of Lewis Strauss was the force behind the AEC security trial, but they blame Board Chairman Gordon Gray for tolerating the blatant illegality of the proceedings. "[A]s chairman of the board, Gordon Gray could have ensured that the hearing was conducted properly. He did not do his job. . . . [T]he Gray Board hearings were patently unfair and outrageously extrajudicial," they write. "The Gray Board was, in sum, a veritable kangaroo court in which the head judge accepted the prosecutor's lead. As AEC commissioner Henry D. Smyth would insist, any objective legal review of how the hearing was conducted would result in nullification."[34]

Bird and Sherwin decided that they would initiate just such a nullification process by organizing a movement to overturn the 1954 revocation of Oppenheimer's security clearance. In 2005, Sherwin and Bird provided evidence of government wrongdoing to a pro bono committee at Washington's WilmerHale law firm. "We thought they could overturn the ruling because there had been so many violations and laws broken during the hearing," said Sherwin. "There was a host of illegal government activities that controlled the outcome of the verdict. For example, the FBI tapped Oppenheimer's lawyer's telephone and sent transcripts of their discussions to the Atomic Energy Commission's prosecutor during the hearings. There was witness tampering. The prosecutor, Roger Robb, informed Edward Teller before his testimony, for example, what Oppenheimer said in the secret hearing. It was just blatantly illegal action."[35]

But in August 2005, WilmerHale law partner C. Boyden Gray withdrew from the project. Gray's late father, Gordon Gray, had presided as chairman of the review board that had dealt so harshly with Oppenheimer. Perhaps because of this awkward conflict of interest, WilmerHale was replaced by the law firm of Arnold & Porter. Bird still hopes to have Oppenheimer's verdict nullified and receive a formal statement from the government clearing Oppenheimer's name. "This sends a message to current officeholders that they should not break the law to tarnish the reputations of their political enemies," said Bird.[36]

MAINTAINING AN UNINFORMED CITIZENRY

The Oppenheimer trial had validated an official policy toward atomic energy that directly contradicted the definitive advice of America's greatest scientist, Albert Einstein:

Through the release of atomic energy, our generation has brought into the world the most revolutionary force since prehistoric man's discovery of fire. The basic power of the universe cannot be fitted into the outmoded concept of narrow nationalism. For there is no secret and no defense. . . . We scientists recognize our inescapable responsibility to carry to our fellow citizens an understanding of the simple facts of atomic energy and its implications for society. In this lies our only security and our only hope—we believe that an informed citizenry will opt for life and not for death.[37]

Instead, the federal government opted for a policy of enforced public ignorance of atomic science, allowing political leaders to determine America's nuclear policy unfettered by public opinion. Even before the Oppenheimer affair, the AEC had established guidelines for restraining communication by anyone associated with the government's atomic energy project. In 1950, the AEC showed its power over scientific expression by exercising the most constitutionally circumscribed form of censorship: prior restraint.

Hans Bethe, one of the pioneers of modern physics, submitted an article on thermonuclear fusion for publication in the April 1950 issue of *Scientific American*. Bethe had sent copies of his paper to several colleagues, including one who was a member of the AEC. All who read it agreed that the scientific data in Bethe's paper had already been widely published and had no national security implications. The article, titled "The Hydrogen Bomb: II," went to press on March 15, but the AEC immediately sent a telegram to the publisher demanding that the presses be stopped and the article pulled until its technical portions could be deleted. *Scientific American* capitulated to the AEC's threat of an injunction.

Publisher Gerard Piel recalled the humiliating experience: "We acceded to ritual cuts made by AEC agents on security grounds and published a mutilated article."[38] The AEC was not yet satisfied. An AEC officer went to the printing plant to supervise the destruction of the type and printing plates and the burning of 3,000 copies of the original article.

Piel believed that the AEC confused ignorance with secrecy. "In the thirty years since America lost its imagined monopoly on the atomic secret, we should have learned that there never was a secret that could keep another country from making a bomb," wrote Piel. "The power of prior restraint of publication is not invoked to protect any other military secret in peacetime. It can only stifle public discussion of the awesome questions that confront Government officials every day."[39]

Piel would later characterize the government's use of prior restraint as an attempt to acquire arbitrary power to determine the direction of America's nuclear policy. He concluded: "We consider that the Commission's action with regard to the Bethe article and the sweeping subsequent prohibition issued to the nation's atomic scientists raises the question of whether the Commission is thus suppressing information which the American people need in order to form intelligent judgments on this major problem."[40]

It would be almost 30 years before another publisher would have the temerity to challenge the government's cloak of secrecy over atomic science. By 1979, even government officials had difficulty pretending that the fundamentals of nuclear physics were "secrets," but Cold War politics required continuation of the pretense. In early July 1979, a young freelance writer named Howard Morland submitted an article titled "The H-Bomb Secret" to *The Progressive*, a popular political magazine. The article treated technical data superficially and was intended primarily to stimulate public debate and understanding of the weapons industry while demonstrating that the secrecy surrounding nuclear weapons had no scientific basis.

In introducing his article, Morland writes: "What you are about to learn is a secret. . . . I discovered it by simply reading and asking questions, without the benefit of security clearance or access to classified materials. . . . I am telling the secret to make a basic point as forcefully as I can: Secrecy itself, especially the power of a few designated 'experts' to declare some topics off limits, contributes to a political climate in which the nuclear establishment can conduct business as usual."[41]

The technical information in Morland's article was taken largely from an article by Edward Teller in the *Encyclopedia Americana*, supplemented by magazine articles, textbooks, unclassified government reports, and conversations with scientists and government officials. Years after he wrote his controversial article, Morland told me of his unlikely journey to journalistic notoriety: "I had done virtually no formal writing before the *Progressive* article. I had been an Air Force pilot in the Vietnam War. . . . I was pretty much a peace activist, advocating nuclear disarmament and non-intervention overseas, but I didn't really know very much about the bomb."[42]

I asked Morland how his political views led him to write the H-bomb article. He responded:

The dangers of our nuclear policy had been pointed out numerous times and no one had ever censored the expression of that view, but we had difficulty effectively communicating a sense of urgency to the general public. I eventually considered publishing the H-bomb secret in a way that might provoke government censorship. I was certain that if the government did take the bait, it would look foolish in the end. . . . I thought common sense and the Bill of Rights would prevail against government censors.

I had examined the Atomic Energy Act and saw that it declared *all* information related to nuclear technology to be classified unless it was specifically declassified. So the act cast its net broadly over all atomic research. I thought, this is totally absurd. The notion of classifying a whole subject area was completely out of date, absurd and ridiculous. The act's provisions are so broad and vague that you couldn't tell what was and wasn't classified.

To me it was irrelevant whether I dug this thing out of public sources or some guy slipped me a blueprint when I was walking through the plant. I thought the point was that we needed to seriously discuss the issue and pursue nuclear disarmament. We deserved to have an understanding of the fusion bomb if we were to discuss its use. The government had made an icon of this secret, a secret that clearly could be reinvented by any government that wanted to devote resources to it. Whether I got the secret by legal or illegal means didn't matter, because it was a bogus secret.[43]

Morland said that word of his impending article was leaked to the government by MIT scientist George Rathjeans, to whom he had shown his preliminary sketch of the bomb. Morland's draft of the full article ended up in the hands of Secretary of Energy James Schlesinger, who took it to Attorney General Griffin Bell. Bell would later recall, "No cabinet secretary in my tenure ever pushed us harder to move in court."[44]

On March 1, shortly before the deadline for *The Progressive's* April issue, the Department of Energy's (DOE) general counsel called the magazine and said it would take legal action to prevent publication unless Morland's article was removed. After consulting with *The Progressive's* staff, the magazine's attorney notified the DOE that, despite the threat of legal action, the April issue would be published without change.

Before the April 1979 issue could be printed, the DOE had Federal Judge Robert Warren issue a restraining order that Warren acknowledged was "the first prior restraint against a publication in this fashion in the history of this country." Nonetheless, on March 26, Warren formalized his order with an injunction barring *The Progressive* from "publishing or otherwise communicating, transmitting or disclosing in any manner any information designated by the Secretary of Energy as Restricted Data contained in the Morland article."[45]

Judge Warren admitted that his injunction "would curtail defendants' First Amendment rights in a drastic and substantial fashion" and "infringe upon our right to know and to be informed as well," but he justified his action as necessary to prevent "nuclear annihilation."[46] Warren had accepted the government's characterization of the article as a threat to national security, although he had not read it.

The *New York Times* editorialized: "What the Government really aims to protect is a system of secrecy, which it seeks now to extend to the thought and discussion of scientists and writers outside Government." *In These Times* wrote: "The Government's attempt to prohibit publication by *The Progressive* of a story on 'The H-bomb Secret' has less to do with anxiety over nuclear proliferation than over the proliferation of legitimate information about the nuclear weapons industry among the American people."[47]

During the trial, all scientific documents and testimony were censored. Even Morland's elementary physics textbook from college, one of the sources for his article, was seized by the government because some its passages had been underlined. Morland explained that the underlining had been done years earlier when he was studying for a test, but the textbook was classified "secret" until the underlining was erased.

The affidavits for the government were led by declarations from the secretaries of state, defense, and energy. In contrast, all affidavits for the defense were from physicists, who declared that the data in Morland's article was from unclassified, indeed popular, literature and represented no threat to national security.

The government's case against *The Progressive* began to unravel when an ACLU investigator found highly sophisticated technical reports on the H-bomb sitting on the open shelves of the public library at the Los Alamos Laboratory, reinforcing *The Progressive's* claim that the technical information in Morland's article was all publicly available. An embarrassed DOE seized the Los Alamos reports, classified them, and closed the public library.

To make matters worse, several physicists from the prestigious Argonne National Laboratory wrote a letter to Senator John Glenn (R-OH) confirming Morland's claim that Edward Teller's article in the *Encyclopedia Americana* contained the H-bomb "secret." Once more, an embarrassed DOE responded by seizing the letter and classifying it as "secret/restricted data," but not before a student named Charles Hansen had acquired a copy and circulated it to numerous newspapers. Hansen then infuriated DOE officials by organizing a nationwide "H-bomb Design Contest," stating that the first entry that the DOE felt obliged to classify would be declared the winner.

In addition, Hansen summarized the technical information from Morland's article and other sources and mailed it to several newspapers. The government again went to court seeking a restraining order against one of the newspapers. On September 16, Hansen's summary of Morland's article was published in a Madison, Wisconsin, newspaper.

Morland recalled the effect of Hansen's actions: "He essentially duplicated my research without access to my materials. Hansen included drawings which he produced on his kitchen table, tracing concentric circles from the jars in his cupboard. The Hansen letter got the government to throw in the sponge."[48]

The "secret" was out. The next day, the Justice Department announced that it would drop its case against *The Progressive*. Griffin Bell stated, "The printing of the Hansen letter by one publication, an action that was repeated throughout the world, made pointless any effort to restrain publication by others."[49]

Morland does not believe that the Hansen letter was the major reason for the government's decision to withdraw from the case.

[N]one of us believed that was the real reason they dropped the case. The judges were openly ridiculing the government's case in court, making fun of the government's lawyers and cracking jokes. The audience was laughing. It was humiliating for them. Everyone assumed that the three-judge appeals panel was going to rule in favor of the magazine, forcing the government to appeal to the Supreme Court. They didn't want to do that, so they used the Hansen letter as an excuse to drop the case.[50]

Just what was the legal precedent, if any, established by the *Progressive* case? Morland had intended to challenge the constitutionality of the Atomic Energy Act's sweeping secrecy provisions, but when the government dropped its case against *The Progressive*, the judgment became "moot," meaning no binding precedent could be taken from the trial.

The Progressive tried to add some significance to the outcome by asking the appeals court to rule that the Atomic Energy Act was unconstitutionally broad and that Judge Warren had acted improperly in imposing prior restraint. In that regard, *The Progressive* submitted a brief stating: "This case clearly is capable of repetition both for these defendants and others. Yet it will continue to evade review until these defendants, another magazine, newspaper, or individual again forfeits—however temporary—First Amendment rights to litigate the fundamental issues raised by the Atomic Energy Act."[51]

The Progressive's plea was to no avail. The case remained moot. The secrecy provisions of the Atomic Energy Act continue to leave the American public, along with its corporate eyes and ears, the media, ignorant of the scientific data necessary to evaluate the government's nuclear policy, including vital issues of war and peace.

SELLING A WAR, DISTORTING SCIENCE

In the aftermath of the September 11, 2001, terrorist attacks on New York's twin towers and the Pentagon, America's political leadership, Republican and Democrat, felt the need for action. There was convincing evidence that the attacks had been directed by the shadowy international terrorist organization al Qaeda, which was known to have a major presence in Afghanistan, where the fundamentalist Taliban government provided it with protection. As bipartisan support for an invasion of Afghanistan grew, "neoconservatives" within the Bush administration saw an opportunity to accomplish some unfinished business: the overthrow of Iraqi dictator Saddam Hussein.

Years earlier, under the elder Bush's presidency, the United States had invaded Iraq to expel its army from Kuwait. Having decimated Saddam Hussein's military and completed the mission of expelling him from Kuwait, the victorious American forces departed, leaving Hussein in power. Now under new president George W. Bush, neoconservatives, led by Vice President Dick Cheney, were determined to finish the job. The American intelligence community could find no evidence to link Hussein to 9/11, but Cheney seized upon the threat of weapons of mass destruction (WMDs), and nuclear weapons in particular, to make the case for war with Iraq. Given the public apprehension and ignorance of nuclear weapons, the case for preemptive war to avoid nuclear catastrophe would be an easy sell.

Just four days after 9/11, President Bush assembled his cabinet officials and close advisers to present the arguments for and against war with Iraq. The CIA said that the current evidence did not support a connection between Saddam Hussein and the 9/11 attacks, and that including Iraq as a military target would not be appropriate at that time. Colin Powell agreed with the CIA. Vice President Cheney did not. A final decision was deferred.

Cheney soon began pressing the CIA to find evidence linking Saddam Hussein and Osama bin Laden. When the agency could find no link, Cheney and Rumsfeld simply created their own intelligence network at the Pentagon, where they had total access to all levels of intelligence. The vice president began appearing regularly on the television news shows, warning of the imminent danger posed by Saddam Hussein's weapons of mass destruction.

In August 2002, after hearing Vice President Cheney declare on television that Saddam Hussein would have nuclear weapons "fairly soon," Jonathan Landay, a reporter for the Knight-Ridder news agency, began examining the technical problems involved in enriching uranium for an atomic bomb. He called a nuclear expert responsible for monitoring nonproliferation, who told Landay bluntly, "The Vice President is lying."[52]

Landay's research soon revealed that enriching uranium required a specific infrastructure, including tens of thousands of centrifuges and a large facility with huge power requirements. Given the fact that Hussein's Iraq was currently being scrutinized by a team of expert U.N. inspectors, Landay asked, "Could he really have done it with all of these eyes on his country?"[53]

One of Cheney's most effective public relations ploys involved leaking secret and unsubstantiated information on Hussein's nuclear programs to a trusted *New York Times* reporter, Judith Miller, and then citing Miller's story as proof of the allegation. In early September 2002, the vice president's chief of staff Lewis "Scooter" Libby met with Miller and gave her classified information alleging that Iraq was vigorously trying to procure uranium for an atomic bomb. On September 8, Miller's byline appeared on a front-page story in the *Times* citing anonymous government sources claiming: "In the last 14 months, Iraq has sought to buy thousands of specially designed aluminum tubes which American officials believe were intended as components of centrifuges to enrich uranium. . . . The diameter, thickness and other specifications of the aluminum tubes has persuaded American intelligence experts that they were meant for Iraq's nuclear programs, officials said, and that the latest attempt to ship the material had taken place in recent months."[54]

Miller concluded the article by stating that the Bush administration "dare not wait until analysts have found hard evidence that Mr. Hussein has acquired a nuclear weapon. The first sign of a 'smoking gun,' they argue, may be a mushroom cloud."[55]

That same morning, Vice President Cheney appeared on *Meet the Press* and referred to "a story today in the *New York Times*" that revealed Iraq's purchase of the aluminum tubes. "It's now public," Cheney said, "that he [Saddam Hussein] has been seeking to acquire the kinds of tubes that are necessary to build a centrifuge [which] is required to take low grade uranium and enhance it into highly enriched uranium, which is what you have to have in order to build a bomb"[56]

As Cheney told NBC viewers of Iraq's nuclear threat, Condoleezza Rice appeared on CNN and stated, "We do know that there are shipments going into Iraq . . . of high quality aluminum tubes that are only really suited for nuclear weapons programs, centrifuge programs. . . . We don't want the smoking gun to be a mushroom cloud."[57] Defense Secretary Donald Rumsfeld also appeared on television that morning, and like the others, he used the same words that appeared in the *Times* article, including the "smoking gun as mushroom cloud" metaphor.

Bob Simon, a veteran CBS reporter, was one of the few journalists who challenged the government's "scientific" evidence on WMDs. After the *New York Times* story and the simultaneous TV blitz by Bush administration officials, Simon said, "It was remarkable. You leak a story and then you quote the story. That's a remarkable thing to do." Simon investigated the "aluminum tubes" claims and found them highly dubious. "We were talking to scientists," he said, "to scientists and researchers, people who had been investigating Iraq for some time. I think many of them would have been available to any reporter that called."[58]

But few journalists bothered to call. They preferred political sources to technical experts. As a result, a batch of aluminum tubes, the lone physical evidence of alleged Iraqi nuclear weapons, became sufficient evidence of an imminent "mushroom cloud." The intelligence source for the aluminum tubes allegation was a man known as "Joe T.," who believed these 3-foot-by-3-inch tubes were intended for use in centrifuges for enriching uranium. This, he said, was "the smoking gun," but most scientists and engineers had strong doubts.

Nuclear experts at the Department of Defense said the tubes were the wrong size and material for use in centrifuges, but they were exactly the kind of tubes used for rocket casings. Indeed, the dimensions and alloy used were identical to tubes Iraq had acquired for rockets in the 1980s. Gregory Thielman, a State Department intelligence veteran, recalls, "We listened to the experts, and more and more evidence came in that told us, no, this can't be true."[59] One DOE analyst explained to Senate investigators that the tubes were so poorly suited for centrifuges that it would benefit the United States to "just give them the tubes."[60]

The nation's top experts on centrifuges concluded that the tubes were:

- Too narrow and too thick for centrifuges
- Manufactured with an anodized coating that could react with uranium gas, making them unsuitable for uranium enrichment
- Three times too long for use in centrifuges
- Identical to tubes the Iraqis had previously purchased for rocket casings

Dr. David Albright, a weapons expert and president of the Institute for Science and International Security, has noted, "This case serves to remind us that decision makers are not above misusing technical and scientific analysis to bolster their political goals. It bespeaks something seriously wrong that a proper technical adjudication of this matter was never conducted."[61]

Soon, Congress was feeling pressure from the Bush administration to authorize military action against Iraq, but they would not approve such action without more-solid evidence of the WMD allegations. At a closed meeting of the Senate Intelligence Committee, CIA Director Tenet was asked to prepare a National Intelligence Estimate (NIE) on Iraq's weapons of mass destruction.

Cheney and his chief of staff, Scooter Libby, began making regular visits to CIA headquarters, where they personally advised the analysts on what was needed in the NIE. Today, many CIA analysts admit they were pressured to include information supporting Cheney's claim of WMDs in Iraq.

In early October 2002, CIA Director Tenet delivered the hastily produced NIE, which was titled "Iraq's Continuing Program for Weapons of Mass Destruction." Much of the evidence was outdated data from the 1990s, but there were two new allegations. The first was, of course, the aforementioned aluminum tubes, and the second was a claim that Iraq had attempted to buy "yellowcake" uranium from the African nation of Niger.

Paul Pillar, who worked at the National Intelligence Office from 2000 to 2005, said the alleged purchase of uranium yellowcake, a lightly processed ore, was particularly dubious: "There were serious questions raised by the yellowcake, and that's why the people in the intelligence community advised the White House not to use it publicly. . . . [T]here were doubts about the credibility of the report, which turned out to be fabricated."[62]

The bogus account rested primarily on forged documents that were originally passed by a retired member of Italian military intelligence to a reporter, who turned them over to the U.S. embassy in Rome. The documents could have quickly been identified as forgeries, but analysts at the International Atomic Energy Agency (IAEA) were not given access to them until March 7, 2003, just days before the U.S. invasion of Iraq. Once in the hands of the IAEA, a simple Google search showed the documents to carry an obsolete government letterhead and incorrect names of Niger officials.

There is strong circumstantial evidence that many in the U.S. Intelligence community also recognized the Niger documents as forgeries. Early in 2002, the CIA had sent former U.S. ambassador Joseph Wilson to Niger to investigate claims about Iraq's interest in the country's uranium, and Wilson could find no evidence that Iraq sought the uranium. Wilson reported back to the CIA and the State Department that the claims were "unequivocally wrong," but his findings were overlooked or ignored by senior U.S. officials.

Wilson went so far as to publish a *New York Times* op-ed in which he admitted that the charge was groundless. The article began, "Did the Bush administration manipulate intelligence about Saddam Hussein's weapons program to justify an invasion of Iraq? Based on my experience with the administration in the months leading up to the war, I have little choice but to conclude that some of the intelligence related to Iraq's nuclear weapons program was twisted to exaggerate the Iraqi threat."[63]

Niger's two uranium mines are run by a French, Spanish, Japanese, German, and Nigerian consortium. If the government wanted to sell any uranium, it would have to notify the consortium, which in turn is strictly monitored by the International Atomic Energy Agency. Moreover, selling uranium would require the approval of Niger's minister of mines, the prime minister, and the president. "In short," concludes Wilson, "there's simply too much oversight over too small an industry for a sale to have transpired."[64]

Niger's ambassador to the United States told Wilson that she was well aware of the allegations of uranium sales to Iraq and, indeed, had already debunked them in her reports to Washington. Still, she recommended that Wilson interview anyone who might have knowledge of such a deal. After numerous interviews, Wilson concluded: "It did not take long to conclude that it was highly doubtful that any such transaction had ever taken place."[65]

Former CIA officer Vincent Cannistraro recalls, "The CIA's assessment was sheep-herded by a national intelligence officer who works very closely with the Vice President's office. It's a fatally flawed document that should never have seen the light of day."[66]

At this point, the CIA's NIE warning of Iraq's WMDs had been discredited, but the White House clung to it. Unfortunately, Congress took the flawed NIE at face value, and on October 10, 2002, passed a resolution authorizing the president to use force against Iraq if Saddam Hussein refused to give up his weapons of mass destruction. President Bush said, "Inaction is not an option, disarmament is a must."[67]

The resolution required President Bush to declare to Congress, either before or within 48 hours after beginning military action, that diplomatic efforts to enforce U.N. disarmament resolutions had failed. Because the Bush administration was on record as believing that Iraq had nuclear weapons, it seemed clear that war was unavoidable. In a desperate effort to stave off the American invasion, Iraq's deputy prime minister, Abdul Huwaish, offered to let U.S. officials inspect the sites they alleged to be WMD facilities.

"If the American administration is interested in inspecting these sites," said Huwaish, "then they're welcome to come over and have a look for themselves."[68]

The White House immediately rejected the offer and began preparing its argument for war. On December 21, 2002, President Bush was given a detailed presentation of the WMD case against Saddam Hussein. Carl W. Ford, Jr., then the State Department's director of intelligence, was in attendance and recalls: "The President said, 'Is this all you've got?' And the answer should have been, 'Yes sir, unfortunately that's all we've got.'" Instead, recalls Ford, CIA Director Tenet replied, "'Slam dunk.'"

Ford recalls that Tenet's assurance that the WMD evidence was, in basketball parlance, a "slam dunk," brought the following response: "Well George [Tenet], if this is right, then you're going to have to come up with a different way of saying this, because a normal person is going to look at it and say, 'Is this all you've got?'"[69]

Nonetheless, President Bush used the unsubstantiated information in the NIE as the basis for his State of the Union address on January 28, 2003.

It is up to Iraq to show exactly where it is hiding its banned weapons, lay those weapons out for the world to see, and destroy them as directed. . . . The British government has learned that Saddam Hussein recently sought significant quantities of uranium from Africa. Our intelligence sources tell us that he has attempted to purchase high-strength aluminum tubes suitable for nuclear weapons production.[70]

The final link in the public relations blitz over Iraqi WMDs was Secretary of State Colin Powell's notorious presentation before the United Nations. Powell, who had been a skeptic on the administration's WMD claims, was not only pressured by the White House, but force-fed the text for his speech by Scooter Libby, the vice president's chief of staff. Richard Clark, former director of counterintelligence for the National Security Council, recalls, "Powell gets a speech, written by Scooter Libby, sent to him, and he's told, 'This is the kind of speech we would like you to give at the U.N.' It's very strange."[71]

Only after Tenet assured Powell that the information he was being fed was "iron clad" did the secretary of state agree to include nuclear weapons allegations in his presentation. On February 5, Powell told the packed U.N. chamber:

We have no indication that Saddam Hussein has ever abandoned his nuclear weapons program. On the contrary, we have more than a decade of proof that he remains determined to acquire nuclear weapons. . . . Saddam Hussein is determined to get his hands on a nuclear bomb. He is so determined that he has made repeated covert attempts to acquire high-specification aluminum tubes from 11 different countries. . . . By now, just about everyone has heard of these tubes, and we all know that there are differences of opinion. . . . Most U.S. experts think they are intended to serve as rotors in centrifuges used to enrich uranium. Other experts, and the Iraqis themselves, argue that they are really to produce the rocket bodies for a conventional weapon, a multiple rocket launcher . . . I am no expert on centrifuge tubes, but just as an old army trooper, I can tell you a couple of things: First, it strikes me as quite odd that these tubes are manufactured to a tolerance that far exceeds U.S. requirements for comparable rockets. . . . Second, . . . [w]hy would they go to all that trouble for something that, if it was a rocket, would soon be blown into shrapnel when it went off?

Powell concluded:

Leaving Saddam Hussein in possession of weapons of mass destruction for a few more months or years is not an option, not in a post-September 11th world.[72]

Powell's speech won over most skeptics, at home and abroad. On March 20, 2003, an American-led invasion was initiated, and within three weeks a triumphant President Bush declared the now famous words: "mission accomplished." What

followed was a bloody, open-ended occupation, during which the presumably simple task of finding those much-publicized WMDs would fall to the CIA. The
agency hired former U.N. weapons inspector and nuclear expert David Kay to conduct the search, but soon Kay would report the bad news directly to Tenet. Kay
recalls, "From early on I said, 'Things are not panning out the way you thought
they existed here, . . . whether you're talking about the aluminum tubes or the
nuclear program in general.'"[73]

The promised WMDs were never found. The charade was over. The Bush
administration's disdain for science had encouraged fabricated evidence of
nuclear weapons. An uninformed and, for the most part, docile press had
accepted that evidence and helped to stampede the country into a war that
seems to have no end.

NOTES

1. "Superman," *Washington Post*, April 11, 1945, 7B.
2. Quoted in Richard G. Hewlett, "A Historian's View," *Bulletin of Atomic Scientists*, December 1981, 20.
3. Ibid.
4. Ibid., 21.
5. *Science, Technology, and the First Amendment: Special Report* (Washington, DC: Office of Technology Assessment, 1988), 45.
6. White House Office of Special Assistant for National Security Affairs, "Armaments and American Policy: A Report of a Panel of Consultants on Disarmament of the Department of State," Washington, DC, January 1953, NSC Series, Policy Papers Subseries, Disarmament folder, box 2, Dwight D. Eisenhower Presidential Library.
7. U.S. Atomic Energy Commission, *In the Matter of J. Robert Oppenheimer: Transcript of Hearing Before Personnel Security Board and Texts of Principal Documents and Letters* (Cambridge: MIT Press, 1971), 837–838.
8. Ibid.
9. Joseph Alsop, "Witness to the Persecution," *Washington Post Magazine*, February 2, 1992, 29.
10. Letter from J. Robert Oppenheimer to Lewis Strauss, December 22, 1953, Strauss Papers, Herbert Hoover Presidential Library.
11. Quoted in Barton J. Bernstein, "The Oppenheimer Loyalty-Security Case Reconsidered," *Stanford Law Review,* July 1990, 1449.
12. John Mason Brown, *Through These Men* (New York: Harper & Bros., 1956), 242.
13. Joseph Alsop, "Witness to the Persecution," *Washington Post Magazine*, February 2, 1992, 30.
14. Kai Bird and Martin J. Sherwin, *American Prometheus: The Triumph and Tragedy of J. Robert Oppenheimer* (New York: Knopf, 2005), 499.
15. FBI cable, March 17, 1954, sect. 24, doc. 1024, J. Robert Oppenheimer FBI file.
16. Quoted in Verna Hobson, review of *In the Matter of J. Robert Oppenheimer*, a play by Heiner Kipphardt, *Princeton History*, no. 1 (1971): 95–97.
17. Quoted in Abraham Pais, *A Tale of Two Continents: A Physicist's Life in a Turbulent World* (Princeton, N.J.: Princeton University Press, 1997), 326.

18. Philip M. Stern, *The Oppenheimer Case: Security on Trial* (New York: Harper & Row, 1969), 244.

19. Kai Bird, *The Chairman: John J. McCloy and the Making of the American Establishment* (New York: Simon & Schuster, 1992), 423.

20. Ibid., 424–425.

21. U.S. Atomic Energy Commission, *In the Matter of J. Robert Oppenheimer: Transcript of Hearing Before Personnel Security Board and Texts of Principal Documents and Letters* (Cambridge: MIT Press, 1971), 415.

22. Ibid., 567.

23. Memo from Charter Heslep to Lewis Strauss, May 3, 1954, Teller folder, AEC Series, box 111, Strauss Papers, Herbert Hoover Presidential Library.

24. U.S. Atomic Energy Commission, *In the Matter of J. Robert Oppenheimer: Transcript of Hearing Before Personnel Security Board and Texts of Principal Documents and Letters* (Cambridge: MIT Press, 1971), 710, 726.

25. Ibid., 759.

26. Ibid., 990.

27. FBI memo from C. E. Hennrich to A. H. Belmont, May 20, 1954, doc. 1690, J. Robert Oppenheimer FBI file.

28. U.S. Atomic Energy Commission, *In the Matter of J. Robert Oppenheimer: Transcript of Hearing Before Personnel Security Board and Texts of Principal Documents and Letters* (Cambridge: MIT Press, 1971), 1020.

29. Ibid., 1, 1019.

30. Quoted in Philip M. Stern, *The Oppenheimer Case: Security on Trial* (New York: Harper & Row, 1969), 371. [Emphasis mine.]

31. Dael Wolfle, "The Trial of a Security System," *Science*, June 18, 1954, 7A.

32. "Science and the Citizen: Verdict," *Scientific American*, August 1954, 36.

33. Ibid.

34. Kai Bird and Martin J. Sherwin, *American Prometheus: The Triumph and Tragedy of J. Robert Oppenheimer* (New York: Knopf, 2005), 537.

35. Kai Bird and Martin Sherwin, interview on *NewsHour with Jim Lehrer*, PBS, April 27, 2006.

36. Amy Argesting and Roxanne Roberts, "Clearing Oppenheimer's Name," *Washington Post*, March 2, 2006, C3.

37. Quoted in Howard Morland, "The H-Bomb Secret," *The Progressive*, November 1979, 17.

38. Irwin Knoll, "Born Secret," *The Progressive*, May 1979, 17.

39. Gerard Piel, "Idi Amin and the H-Bomb," *The Progressive*, May 1979, 17.

40. Gerard Piel, "Concerning H-Bomb Reactions," *Scientific American*, May 1950, 26.

41. Howard Morland, "The H-Bomb Secret: To Know How Is to Ask Why?" *The Progressive*, November 1979, 3.

42. Howard Morland, interview by Herbert N. Foerstel, April 10, 1997, *Banned in the Media: A Reference Guide to Censorship in the Press, Motion Pictures, Broadcasting, and the Internet* (Westport, CT: Greenwood Press, 1998).

43. Ibid.

44. Ellen Alderman and Caroline Kennedy, *In Our Defense* (New York: Morrow, 1991), 48.

45. Erwin Knoll, "Born Secret," *The Progressive*, May 1979, 12, 18.

46. Ibid., 18–19.

47. Quoted in "The Way the Press Saw It," *The Progressive*, May 1979, 44–46.

48. Howard Morland, interview by Herbert N. Foerstel, April 10, 1997, *Banned in the Media: A Reference Guide to Censorship in the Press, Motion Pictures, Broadcasting, and the Internet* (Westport, CT: Greenwood Press, 1998).

49. Quoted in Ellen Alderman and Caroline Kennedy, *In Our Defense* (New York: Morrow, 1991), 53.

50. Howard Morland, interview by Herbert N. Foerstel, April 10, 1997, *Banned in the Media: A Reference Guide to Censorship in the Press, Motion Pictures, Broadcasting, and the Internet* (Westport, CT: Greenwood Press, 1998).

51. Erwin Knoll, "Wrestling with Leviathon," *The Progressive*, November 1979, 27.

52. "Buying the War," *Bill Moyers Journal*, PBS, April 25, 2007.

53. Ibid.

54. Michael R. Gordon and Judith Miller, "U.S. Says Hussein Intensifies Quest for A-Bomb Parts," *New York Times*, September 8, 2002, A1.

55. Ibid.

56. Vice President Richard Cheney, interview on *Meet the Press*, NBC, September 8, 2002.

57. CNN, "Late Edition, with Wolf Blitzer," September 8, 2002. CNN.com/Transcripts. http: transcripts.cnn.com/TRANSCRIPTS/0209/08/le.00.html

58. "Buying the War," *Bill Moyers Journal*, PBS, April 25, 2007.

59. "Dead Wrong: Inside an Intelligence Meltdown," *CNN Presents*, CNN, October 28, 2005.

60. David Barstow, "The Nuclear Card: The Aluminum Tube Story," *New York Times*, October 3, 2004.

61. Seth Shulman, *Undermining Science: Suppression and Distortion in the Bush Administration* (Berkeley: University of California Press, 2006), 80, 110.

62. "The Dark Side," *Frontline*, PBS, June 20, 2006. www.pbs.org/wgbh/pages/frontline/darkside/

63. Joseph C. Wilson, "What I Didn't Find in Africa," *New York Times*, July 6, 2003, www.nytimes.com/2003/07/06/opinion/06WILS.html.

64. Ibid.

65. Ibid.

66. Ibid.

67. "Senate Approves Iraq War Resolution," CNN.com, October 11, 2002, http://archives .cnn.com/2002.

68. Ibid.

69. "The Dark Side," *Frontline*, PBS, June 20, 2006. www.pbs.org/wgbh/pages/frontline/darkside.

70. The White House, "President Delivers State of the Union," January 28, 2003, www.whitehouse.gov/releases/2003/01/20030128-19.html.

71. "The Dark Side," *Frontline*, PBS, June 20, 2006. www.pbs.org/wgbh/pages/frontline/darkside.

72. The White House, "Iraq: Denial and Deception," February 5, 2003, www.whitehouse .gov/news/releases/2003/02/20030205-1.html.

73. "The Dark Side," *Frontline*, PBS, June 20, 2006. www.pbs.org/wgbh/frontline/darkside.

2

The Politics of Space Science

Apollo 11 astronaut Edwin E. "Buzz" Aldrin, Jr., takes a "moonwalk" near the lunar module, July 20, 1969. (AP Photo)

THE SPACE RACE

The American space program, which began in the 1950s, was a unique combination of science and politics. It could not have been otherwise, given the Cold War anxieties and the media's representation of the "space race" as an international contest between two adversaries and their conflicting ideologies.

The popular history of this period presents a picture of a doddering, old American president, Dwight D. Eisenhower, ignorant of the potential of space technology and caught asleep at the switch when the Soviet Union launched the world's first space satellite, Sputnik. Only then did a humiliated Eisenhower, facing domestic outrage and international derision, make a political decision to begin a crash program to restore America's prestige by establishing its leadership in space.

The recent release of previously secret documents on the early American space program has shown this popular account to be largely false. Eisenhower did, in fact, have an informed grasp of the power of space flight and a clear vision of its exploitation, but his was not a romantic vision of exploration and space travel. His eye was on spy satellites, with which he hoped to establish continuous surveillance of the Soviet Union and thus ward off the possibility of a surprise attack on the United States.

In the early 1950s, Eisenhower had already begun spy flights over the Soviet Union using high-altitude B-2 bombers, but these flights were risky. Because the B-2 could not fly above the range of Russian antiaircraft missiles, there was inherent danger in this form of reconnaissance. Indeed, in May 1954, an American B-2 was intercepted and attacked by Soviet fighters. The severely damaged bomber limped back to its base, but Eisenhower's program of spy flights was in jeopardy. He needed to find a safer, more-effective way to conduct surveillance.

Eisenhower immediately appointed a secret committee, headed by MIT president James Killian. The top-secret Killian Report, issued in early 1955, concluded that science could provide an alternative to the risky B-2 flights: spy satellites. Until the United States could produce a spy satellite, the Killian Report recommended an acceleration of the ballistic missile program. At this time, America's most experienced ballistic missile team was working for the U.S. Army in Huntsville, Alabama. It was made up primarily of German scientists and engineers who surrendered to U.S. forces when Nazi Germany was defeated.

The head of the army's team was Werner von Braun, who had developed Hitler's terror weapon, the V-2 rocket, which rained bombs on Britain. The German factories producing the V-2s used slave labor from the concentration camps. Working conditions were horrendous, and Michael Neufeld, von Braun's biographer, explains, "Dozens of people were dying every day, from starvation, from beatings, from executions, . . . and von Braun was confronted very directly with the horrifying and murderous conditions of the concentration camp workers."[1]

Little of von Braun's Nazi past was known to the American public, and his highly publicized work on intercontinental ballistic missiles (ICBMs) soon made him a national celebrity, appearing on the cover of *Time* and *Life* magazines. Von Braun's team was perfecting the Redstone rocket, a powerful ICBM that would later be modified to put America's first satellite into orbit. But in early 1955, President Eisenhower was struggling with a legal obstacle to launching a satellite: the limits of sovereign "air space." At this time, national boundaries were considered to extend into the atmosphere, and no doctrine of "freedom of space" had been formulated by international convention. How, then, could the United States launch a satellite that would fly over the Soviet Union without violating its air space, something that could be regarded as a provocation to war?

The Eisenhower administration decided to aggressively argue for international recognition of "freedom of space" while simultaneously pursuing a satellite launch as an application of that legal doctrine. If no nation protested the satellite's overflight, an international precedent would be established. Toward that end, Eisenhower decided to exploit the International Geophysical Year (IGY), scheduled to run from 1957 through 1958, as scientific cover for his planned satellite launch. In July 1955, Eisenhower publicly declared that the United States would launch a "scientific" satellite as part of the IGY. Within days, the Soviet Union announced that it too would launch a scientific satellite during IGY.

On September 26, 1956, Werner von Braun's team intensified its ICBM tests, launching a Redstone rocket modified with extra booster stages. This modified rocket, named Jupiter C, achieved orbital velocity, which meant that if it had carried a satellite head, it would have been the first ever placed in orbit. Lee Webster, a physicist on von Braun's team, recalls, "When we fired that, we knew we could put a vehicle in orbit, because we had the velocity it required. If we had been given the go-ahead, we could have beaten Sputnik by a year."[2]

But Eisenhower's plan to use a civilian satellite to establish precedent for a spy satellite made it inappropriate to use von Braun's Jupiter C, a military ICBM, for America's first satellite launch. Instead, he assigned a parallel program to produce a brand-new orbital rocket called Vanguard. The delays involved in producing a specialized rocket for launching a satellite led CIA Director Allan Dulles to warn Eisenhower that the Soviets were probably capable of launching a satellite very soon. Indeed, on October 4, 1957, Sputnik, the world's first satellite, reached orbit.

The American public was shocked, but Eisenhower, having been warned by the CIA, was neither surprised nor alarmed. He met with his advisers and was assured by the Defense Department representative, "The Soviets have in fact done us a good turn."[3]

Roger Launius of the Smithsonian Institution explains that Sputnik "established a precedent for overflight, exactly what Eisenhower had wanted to do initially."[4] The Soviets had done it for him.

Four weeks later, the Soviets successfully orbited another satellite, Sputnik II, carrying a live dog. The response of the American press and public was so strong that Eisenhower felt obliged to give the von Braun team permission to launch its satellite, called Explorer. On January 4, 1958, four months after Sputnik, America's first satellite was lifted into orbit by the same Jupiter C rocket previously used for an ICBM. Whereas Sputnik had carried little more than a beeper whose signal could be tracked by amateur radio operators around the world, Explorer was outfitted with sophisticated equipment that would assemble more scientific data than Sputnik I and II combined. More important, Explorer had affirmed Sputnik's precedent for "freedom of space," opening the way for America's more-important business of state: spy satellites.

Eisenhower's continuing focus on the national security use of space made him skeptical of romantic notions like manned space flight, but public clamor led him to create a new civilian agency, the National Aeronautics and Space Administration (NASA), which would run the nation's scientific space program. Spy satellites would be launched separately and secretly by intelligence agencies like the National Reconnaissance Organization (NRO).

NASA's POLITICAL DISASTER

Despite NASA's nominally civilian character, it has been buffeted by politics from its inception, sometimes with tragic consequences. Under new president John F. Kennedy, NASA would enter its glory days, including the successful Apollo program and the spectacular "moon walk." But America's space program would falter under President Richard Nixon, who imposed severe budget cuts on NASA and ordered it to restrict all space missions to low Earth orbit. Indeed, for the next twenty years, astronauts would do little more than rocket into low orbit, perform a few experiments, and fly back.

In the 1980s, the Budget Office told NASA that the shuttle program had to be more cost-effective, something that would require more launches and therefore more customers. NASA sought to market the shuttle, but the only available customers were the Department of Defense and the intelligence agencies. As a result, NASA began carrying more military satellites and payloads, and the number of shuttle missions increased from four in 1983 to five in 1984 and a record nine in 1985.

NASA engineer Don Nelson recalls, "We kept saying safety was the number one consideration, but launch schedule was right up there with it. . . . So it was extremely important that we meet these schedules and keep the operating costs for the vehicle down."[5]

John Logsdon, director of the Space Policy Institute at George Washington University, explains, "The engineers down close to the vehicle knew how risky this was, but the upper management chose to ignore the messages of problems."[6] Howard McCurdy, NASA scholar and professor at American

The space shuttle *Challenger* explodes little more than a minute after takeoff, January 28, 1986. (AP Photo/Bruce Weaver)

University, says the subsequent shuttle disaster was, in effect, "planned from the moment of conception."[7]

At 11:38 a.m. on January 28, 1986, amid massive press and television coverage and frenzied political manipulation, the space shuttle *Challenger* lifted off its Cape Canaveral launch pad. Just one minute and thirteen seconds into its journey, it exploded into an inferno before millions of horrified television viewers. The disaster was internationally mourned, particularly because *Challenger* carried a public school teacher, Christa McAuliffe, the first teacher in space. Plagued by technical problems, the *Challenger* launch experienced several delays but stubbornly maintained a launch schedule that would coincide with President Ronald Reagan's State of the Union address.

It was common knowledge that NASA had submitted a flowery, public relations text to the White House for inclusion in Reagan's State of the Union address to the nation. Reagan was to refer to *his* Teacher-in-Space program and also honor a high school student for his studies on space flight. The proposed text for Reagan's speech began: "Tonight, while I am speaking to you, a young secondary school teacher from Concord, New Hampshire, is taking us all on the ultimate field trip, as she orbits the earth."

After describing the "rich return of scientific, technical, and economic benefits" of the *Challenger* flight, President Reagan was to conclude, "Mrs. McAuliffe's week in space is just one of the achievements in space which we have planned for the coming year."[8] After the destruction of

Challenger during launch, all mention of the highly publicized flight was excised from the State of the Union address.

The *Challenger* flight was originally scheduled several days before the president's address, but a series of mysterious delays, the last of them an unprecedented cancellation on a warm and sunny day, carried the final launch date right up to January 28, State of the Union day. That day turned out to be unseasonably cold in Florida, with freezing temperatures that threatened the proper function of the shuttle's critical "O-rings," a technical term that would soon become a household word.

It was reported in the press, and denied by the White House, that Donald Regan, the president's chief of staff, gave orders for the Challenger to be launched, saying, "Tell them to get that thing up."[9]

Richard Cook, a manager in NASA's shuttle resources analysis branch, was responsible for analyzing technical hardware problems and their effects on the shuttle's solid-fuel booster rockets. On July 23, 1985, Cook had circulated an internal memo at NASA warning that the safety seals, called O-rings, on the shuttle's booster rockets were dangerously vulnerable to leaks, especially at cold temperatures. Cook warned that flight safety was being compromised by potential erosion of the seals and that a catastrophe could result.

Cook's memo was based on warnings he had received from propulsion engineers. He recalls, "They began to tell me that some of these things [O-rings] were being eaten away, and rather innocently I asked what does that mean? They said to me, almost in a whisper in my ear, that the thing could blow up." Cook says that the moment that he came to NASA, the propulsion engineers whispered their fears about the O-rings and "held their breath each time a shuttle was launched." Still, after the *Challenger* disaster, Cook's colleagues and superiors were so fearful of repercussions that they asked him to bury a memo, written three days after the explosion, that said that the shuttle had been flying "in an unsafe condition" for more than a year and that the accident "was probably preventable."[10]

Cook explains, "There was no indication to me that this memorandum had been passed up the line, or that anyone else had looked at it, or that any weight was given to it." He therefore concluded, "You aren't going to find an engineer with 20 years experience and a livelihood to protect stand up and say, 'Excuse me, but we might have an explosion on the next shuttle flight because the O-rings might break. . . .' There is always the nagging thought in the engineers' minds that, 'Gee, we may be wrong. Maybe nothing will happen.'"[11]

Still, the unease within NASA became common knowledge and led to the creation of a presidential commission to investigate the accident. Chaired by William P. Rogers, the commission seemed more concerned about the leaked warnings within NASA than it was about improving safety. Indeed, Cook's role as a whistle-blower was hostilely criticized, and Rogers himself attacked Cook's motives, leading John Pike of the Federation of American Scientists to conclude that the commission was trying to minimize safety problems by discrediting Cook.

Witnesses before the Rogers Commission were carefully selected and often coached in their testimony. Larry Mulloy, NASA's Solid Rocket Booster Project director, told the commission that NASA's managers considered the unusually cold weather the night before the launch, but concluded that there was no more risk in flying *Challenger* the next morning than there had been since the second flight of the shuttle, when the erosion of an O-ring was first observed.

This specious argument was best refuted by physicist Richard Feynman, a member of the Rogers Commission, who characterized such an approach as " a kind of Russian roulette." Feynman explained that because the shuttle had previously flown with O-ring erosion and survived, "it is suggested, therefore, that the risk is no longer so high for the next flights. . . .You got away with it, but it shouldn't be done over and over again like that."[12]

The final report of the Rogers Commission concluded that, although the decision to launch *Challenger* may have been flawed, NASA had no direct responsibility for the disaster. The report failed to explain why *Challenger* was launched despite the protests of the contractor in charge of the booster rockets, Morton Thiokol, whose engineers feared that the cold weather would further weaken the O-rings. Even James Beggs, NASA's former administrator, wondered why the commission didn't question the manipulation of the launch date: "The commission ignored or did not wish to address why did they launch [Tuesday] and why didn't they launch when the weather was good?"[13]

The person most competent to explain NASA's compulsion to launch on January 28 was William Graham, then action administrator of NASA, but the commission chose not to interview him. Cook says, "[I]f there was political pressure from the White House, it probably came through Graham. . . . In fact, the most striking aspect of the Rogers Commission's investigation of the possibility of White House pressure is that they never interviewed anyone from the White House."[14]

Like NASA, Morton Thiokol, the Utah engineering firm contracted by NASA to supply its booster rockets, struggled with the political pressure to meet the launch schedule. Roger Boisjoly, a Thiokol structural engineer who designed seals and joints on the booster rockets, argued frequently with upper management about the O-rings. Boisjoly and other Thiokol engineers were particularly concerned about the effects of the cold weather on the seals, and they recommended postponing the launch.

Boisjoly says he pleaded in vain with his superiors at Thiokol and NASA the night before the launch, telling them that it would be like Russian roulette. "I can't characterize it [the Challenger disaster] as an accident," he said. "It was a horrible, terrible disaster. But not an accident. Because we could have stopped it. We had initially stopped it."[15]

On July 22, 1985, Boisjoly had sent a memo to his supervisors warning of a "horrifying flight failure" if a solution to the O-ring problem was not found.[16] Just nine days later, Boisjoly would send a frantic follow-up:

"This letter is written to insure that management is fully aware of the seriousness of the current O-ring erosion problem. . . . The mistakenly accepted position on the joint problem was to fly without fear of failure. . . . The result would be a catastrophe of the highest order—loss of human life. . . . It is my honest and very real fear that if we do not take immediate action to dedicate a team to solve the problem with the field joint having the number one priority, then we stand in jeopardy of losing a flight along with all the launch pad facilities."[17]

Thiokol's managers responded by arranging a private consultation on the advisability of launch. At this off-line caucus, Boisjoly showed photographs of previously damaged O-rings to demonstrate what was likely to occur if the launch went ahead. " I was literally screaming at the managers to look at the photos, but they wouldn't look at them."[18]

That meeting, attended by Thiokol engineers who also had managerial responsibility, was the turning point in the run-up to the tragic *Challenger* launch. A later investigative report describes the meeting as follows:

"Thiokol was recommending an unheard of delay on the eve of a launch, with schedule ramifications and NASA-contractor relationship repercussions. In the Thiokol off-line caucus, a senior vice president who seldom participated in these engineering discussions championed the . . . rationale for flight. When he told the managers present to 'take off your engineering hat and put on your management hat,' they reversed the position their own engineers had taken. . . . Not willing to be responsible for a delay . . . the contractor did not act in the best interest of safety."[19] Boisjoly says the pressure to "change hats" was directed at a single manager who refused to agree to the launch. "He changed his hat and changed his vote," said Boisjoly.[20]

Thus, despite the strong recommendations of Boisjoly and the other engineers, Thiokol's managers decided to go ahead with the launch. Boisjoly recalls, "I went home, opened the door and didn't say a word to my wife. She asked me what was wrong and I told her, 'We just had a meeting to go launch tomorrow and kill the astronauts, but outside of that it was a great day.'"[21]

After a sleepless night, a dejected Boisjoly returned to work the next morning, still hoping that the launch would be scrapped. At the last minute, Boisjoly and a fellow engineer, Bob Ebling, decided to go to a conference room and watch the launch on television. Boisjoly recalls, "When Challenger's SRBs (solid rocket boosters) ignited and the vehicle cleared the launch tower, I whispered to Bob that we had just dodged a bullet, as it was my expectation—and that of my colleagues—that it would blow up right on the pad."[22] Within seconds, *Challenger* exploded before the shocked engineers, who sat in stunned silence.

Nearly a month later, Boisjoly would testify before the Rogers Commission, which treated him like a messenger of unwanted news. Things were even worse back on the job at Thiokol, where officials believed his testimony had jeopardized the company's billion-dollar contract with NASA. His candor was regarded as against Thiokol, and he was soon shunned by fellow workers. The strain was more than he could handle, and doctors diagnosed him with traumatic stress disorder. In January 1987, he went on disability leave, and Thiokol quickly fired him.

Despite the shabby treatment that whistle-blowers like Boisjoly received, scientists and engineers at Thiokol and NASA have continued to agonize over the disaster to this day. Recently, Asa Gordon, a retired astrophysicist from NASA's Goddard Space Flight Center, recalled his misgivings about the *Challenger* launch and the soul-searching that followed the disaster.

I was coming to work at Goddard on the day of the launch, and I remember it was very cold. I stopped to buy some gas for the car, and when I finished I tried to close the car door. It wouldn't close, because the rubber seals around the door had hardened from the cold. They weren't pliable enough to allow the door to close. I almost had to drive with the door open, and I put on the heater to warm up the car. As I was driving in I said to myself, I'm sure they're not going to launch today. I had heard that it was as cold down in Florida as it was in Washington, and I knew there would be trouble with the rubber seals in the booster rocket.

When I arrived at Goddard I saw the monitors they had there showing the launch site preparations. I asked, "You mean they're going to launch that thing?" and I was told that the launch would proceed as scheduled. And, of course, the disaster occurred just seconds after the launch.

Now, months later a commission was appointed to study the causes of the disaster, and one of the commissioners, physicist Richard Feynman, conducted a dramatic experiment for the commission, dropping a rubber O-ring into a glass of cold water and showing how it was pliable before and rigid afterward. That was a graphic demonstration of what the launch problem was.

Sometime after the transcript of the commission's deliberations was released, I attended a meeting at Goddard at which I represented the union in a negotiation with management. Before we started the negotiations, we were talking informally about the *Challenger* disaster. As we discussed the transcript's account of the pre-launch debate between management and engineering, it became clear that there was still a difference of opinion between managers and scientists over the cause of the disaster. The managers were critical of the Rogers report, and Richard Feynman in particular, for suggesting that the problem with the O-rings should have caused a delay of the launch. I took the position that we shouldn't have launched.

The transcript showed an engineer from Thiokol describing the technical problems facing the launch as the management representative from Goddard presented the arguments for proceeding as scheduled. The Thiokol representative, who was the liaison between NASA and the contractor, was a manager, but he was also a scientist. He wasn't one of those MBAs who has no scientific background and believes that if you are a manager you can manage anything.

He said his engineers were telling him not to launch because the weather was too cold and the seals were too rigid. But the manager from Goddard, which controls the contract, told the engineers to go back and confer with their staff and convince them of the need to launch.

The Thiokol representative did what was asked, but he soon returned and said that his engineers were still advising against the launch. The transcript revealed that the two sides went back and forth, during which time the decision to launch was delayed. As we reviewed that part of the transcript at our Goddard meeting, I said, "They're safe."

At this point in the transcript, the management representative warned the engineering representative that the time for the "hook-up" with President Reagan was approaching, and this would be the last window of opportunity for this significant public relations event. Remember, the President was scheduled to hold a much-publicized conversation with the teacher-astronaut once the rocket reached orbit. The engineer went back once more to confer with his people, but soon came back with the recommendation, "Don't launch."

At our Goddard meeting, I once more declared, "Safe."

But now, the transcript revealed the crucial action taken by the management representative, who urged the engineer to take off his "engineer's hat" and put on his "management hat." In this way, the engineer was told that he could see the big picture. At this point, the Thiokol engineer backed down and agreed to launch.

When we came to that part of the transcript, I said, "They're dead." Once the engineers put on their managers hats, those astronauts were dead. They were safe during the entire process, so long as they were listening to the scientists and engineers. It was the "management culture" that killed them, a culture that always insists that, no matter how disastrous the outcome, a manager would make the same decision, given the same circumstances.

In the *Challenger* case, the manager who said, "Take off your engineer's hat and put on your management hat," he was promoted. The engineer who exposed the flawed decision-making process leading to the disaster, he was fired. It comes out of our Darwinian philosophy that presumes that if you rise to a managerial position, you must be a superior individual with unfailing judgment. If you admit that the superior individual failed, you admit that the Darwinian view is not applicable. To maintain the idea that our decision-makers reach their status through natural selection, we must protect the idea that they cannot fail.[23]

NASA's MANAGEMENT CULTURE PERSISTS

The painful soul-searching that followed the *Challenger* disaster identified a number of problems in NASA's space program, including undue political pressure, arbitrary deadlines, and a management culture that ignored the safety concerns of engineers. Unfortunately, the recommendations of the Rogers

Commission, the investigative body convened after the *Challenger* disaster, fell on deaf ears within NASA and its contractors.

After the *Challenger* disaster, NASA decided to turn over much of the shuttle operations to a private contractor. In 2002, President Bush appointed Sean O'Keefe, then deputy director of the White House Office of Management and Budget, as NASA's new administrator. O'Keefe's assignment was to cut costs. NASA's engineers were concerned about this approach. Author and NASA historian Howard McCurdy says, "Private industry can go in with its cost-cutting models that are used in grocery stores and parts dealerships that allow you to squeeze increasingly large numbers of people and money out of a program and run it as close to the margin as you possibly can. But when you push the shuttle to the margin, that's very dangerous."[24]

But over time, as the shuttle continued to launch and land safely, management concluded that there was no flight risk. Foam fragments continued to break loose during shuttle flights, and just three months before the scheduled launch of *Columbia*, the shuttle *Atlantis* suffered a small crater in one of its booster rockets due to foam fragments that missed a key electronics box by inches. NASA ordered an investigation of the safety implications of the *Atlantis* incident, but it was decided that *Columbia*'s launch should not be delayed, because its mission had to be completed to expedite construction of the International Space Station.

On January 16, 2003, the *Columbia* space shuttle blasted off from the Kennedy Space Center without incident, and the flight proceeded uneventfully. But on the second day of the flight, engineers reviewing film noticed that a large piece of foam had broken off the main tank just 81 seconds after liftoff, hitting the left wing of the orbiter. The engineers reported their concern, but mission managers concluded that the foam impact did not represent a flight risk.

On the eighth day of the mission, the *Columbia* crew was notified of the foam-strike incident in a perfunctory communication from ground control, which said, "this item is not even worth mentioning other than wanting to make sure that you're not surprised by it in a question from a reporter. There is absolutely no concern for entry."[25]

On February 1, 2003, NASA personnel, families, and reporters gathered at Kennedy Space Center to welcome home the *Columbia* astronauts, but as the descending shuttle passed over the California coast, communications with *Columbia* ceased. Amateur shuttle enthusiasts watching the sky in Texas saw the shuttle explode into pieces. Once again, seven astronauts had died. Once again, an investigation board would seek to isolate the cause of the accident.

The *Columbia* Accident Investigation Board (CAIB), established within the first 24 hours after the disaster, was headed by retired Navy admiral Hal Gainen. Scott Hubbell, head of NASA's Ames Research Center, was NASA's designated representative on the board. The board's first task was retrieving the debris from *Columbia*, which was scattered over a 200-mile stretch of land from Los Angeles to Dallas. Next came the study of film footage of the foam impact on the shuttle during liftoff. The foam had broken loose from the same area that had endangered the shuttle *Atlantis* three months earlier, but the nature of the damage could not be determined from the *Columbia* debris.

The board listened to the tapes of a NASA mission managers team (MMT) meeting on January 21, the fifth day of the *Columbia* mission. Don McCormack, who oversees in-flight engineering operations, says, "As everyone knows, we took a hit on the, somewhere on the left wing leading edge."[26]

Team manager Linda Ham responds, "I'm not sure that the area is exactly the same area where the foam came from but the carrier properties and density of the foam wouldn't do any damage. . . . And really, I don't think there is much we can do, so, you know it's not really a factor during the flight, because there is not much we can do about it."[27]

On January 24, the ninth day of the mission, McCormack again addressed the foam-strike issue, saying, "We do not see any kind of safety of flight issue here yet in anything that we've looked at." Chairman Linda Ham summarizes the issue; "No safety of flight, no issue for this mission. Nothing that we're going to do different."[28]

The managers clearly had no concern about the foam. But after the accident, the CAIB took a harder look at the problem. From their limited video footage they were able to determine the transit time for the dislodged piece of foam, allowing them to calculate the impact force of this very light piece of foam. It turned out to be an astounding 3,000 pounds of force!

The board then constructed a facsimile of the shuttle wing and fired pieces of foam at the leading edge, the place where film had shown the impact had occurred. The test produced a gaping hole in the wing, a hole that would have allowed superheated gas to enter the shuttle upon reentry, destroying it from within.

Retired astronaut Story Musgrave complained, "After the accident people said, 'Well, during the launch a problem happened and it was all over for the crew then.' It was not all over." Musgrave said the astronauts could simply have done a space walk to determine the extent of damage. "Just do a walk," Musgrave repeated.[29]

NASA engineers agreed with Musgrave. They said a space walk would probably have revealed a hole in the wing, after which the engineers could have come up with sound proposals on how to save the astronauts.

The CAIB's final report, released in 2003, said, "Mission Management team decision-making operated outside the rules even as it held its engineers in a stifling protocol. Management was not able to recognize that in unprecedented conditions, when lives are on the line, flexibility and democratic process should take priority over bureaucratic response."[30] The report said that during *Columbia's* flight, NASA's managers allowed deadline pressures to squelch the aggressive pursuit of information about the possible damage to the wing and its consequences.

In examining the causes of the accident, the CAIB faulted national politics as well as NASA's management culture, saying, "The past decisions of national leaders—the White House, Congress, and NASA Headquarters—set the *Columbia* accident in motion by creating resource and schedule strains that compromised the principles of a high-risk technology organization. The measure of NASA's success became how much costs were reduced and how efficiently the schedule was met. . . . We cannot explore space on a fixed cost basis."[31]

The CAIB concluded, "NASA remained a politicized and vulnerable agency, dependent on key political players who accepted NASA's ambitious proposals and then imposed strict budget limits."[32]

The CAIB noted that "the causal roots of the accident" could be traced to the demise of the Soviet Union as a competitor in the space race, making it more difficult for NASA to obtain funding. Noting NASA's failure to adjust to the new political and fiscal realities, the report stated, "The end of the Cold War in the late 1980s meant that the most important political underpinning of NASA's human space flight program . . . was lost."[33]

The report said, "In the Board's view, NASA's organizational culture had as much to do with this accident as the External Tank foam. . . . The organizational causes of the accident are rooted in the space shuttle program's history and culture, including the original compromises that were required to gain approval for the shuttle, subsequent years of resource constraints, fluctuating priorities, schedule pressures, mischaracterization of the shuttle as operational rather than developmental, and lack of agreed national vision for human space flight."[34]

The CAIB suggested that management's arrogance may have cost the lives of the astronauts: "In highly uncertain circumstances, when lives were immediately at risk, management failed to defer to its engineers and failed to recognize that different data standards—qualitative, subjective, and intuitive—and different processes—democratic rather than protocol and chain of command—were more appropriate. . . . As a result, many signals of danger were missed. Relevant information that could have altered the course of events was available but was not presented."[35]

Time and time again, the CAIB investigators were struck by the similarities and parallels between the *Challenger* and *Columbia* disasters. Referring to "the echoes of *Challenger* in *Columbia*," the report said, "These repeating patterns mean that flawed practices embedded in NASA's organizational system continued for 20 years and made substantial contributions to both accidents. . . . In perhaps the ultimate example of engineering concerns not making their way upstream, *Challenger* astronauts were told that the cold temperature was not a problem, and *Columbia* astronauts were told that the foam strike was not a problem."[36]

Given two preventable shuttle disasters, what can we expect for the future of America's manned space program? The CAIB had a sobering forecast: "Based on NASA's history of ignoring external recommendations, or making improvements that atrophy with time, the Board has no confidence that the shuttle can be safely operated for more than a few years based solely on renewed post-accident vigilance."[37]

Perhaps as a result of the *Columbia* disaster and the CAIB report, President Bush announced a new space policy, the *Vision for Space Exploration.* The February 2004 policy statement directed NASA to retire the shuttle by 2010 and build a new spacecraft to go beyond low Earth orbit. The new fleet of space vehicles, called *Constellation*, would introduce major safety improvements over the shuttle. First, the capsule would be on top of the rocket rather than on the side, preventing the capsule from being hit by the kind of debris that destroyed *Columbia*. *Constellation* would also contain a crew evacuation system, something that might have saved the *Columbia* astronauts.

In the spring of 2005, just two months before the new shuttle *Discovery* was to be launched, the journal *Space Daily* wrote: "More than two years after the shuttle *Columbia* accident . . . it does not appear that elected officials have made much effort to reform their own behavior when dealing with NASA. . . . [W]ill NASA's bad habits be overlooked by a Congress that seems less interested in establishing a vibrant American space program and more committed to giving presents to its local constituents? Based on past performance, the possibility of more *Columbia*-type tragedies—this time with an entirely new spacecraft— remains an unfortunate probability."[38]

As it turned out, the July 2005 *Discovery* flight was successfully completed, but not without another scare from breakaway foam insulation. The continuing concern about the foam grounded *Discovery* for almost a year, during which tests and technical modifications were made. Even after *Discovery* was cleared for a July 2006 flight, NASA officials acknowledged that they had failed to produce a new design that would stop the foam insulation loss from the external fuel tank. Still, they decided to proceed with the launch.

The July 4, 2006, *Discovery* launch was only the second shuttle flight after the *Columbia* disaster. About two-and-a-half minutes into the flight, three or four pieces of foam came off the external fuel tank. Two more foam pieces came loose about two minutes later. Nonetheless, the shuttle completed its mission as scheduled.

There were two shuttle flights in 2007, and a third was twice scrapped because of malfunctioning sensors. Intense political pressure was mounting on NASA to increase the number of space-shuttle flights in 2008, in advance of the shuttle's scheduled retirement in 2010, in an effort to speed up the final assembly of the International Space Station. Once more, fears were expressed that NASA might ignore safety considerations in an effort to rush more shuttle flights.

"This pressure feels so familiar," said Alex Rowland, a former NASA historian. "It was the same before the *Challenger* and *Columbia* disasters; this push to do more with a spaceship that is inherently unpredictable because it is so complex."[39]

John Logsdon, an earlier member of the *Columbia* Accident Investigation Board, argued for grounding the space shuttle as soon as possible, warning, "Every time we launch a shuttle, we risk the future of the human space flight program. The sooner we stop flying this risky vehicle, the better it is for the program."[40]

Logsdon has warned that another shuttle accident could delay or even end the U.S. program of human space flight. Noting that NASA has estimated the odds of losing the crew on any single shuttle mission as 1 in 80, Logsdon writes, "The chances for disaster if 10 additional shuttle flights are scheduled between 2011 and 2015 are simply too high." He concludes, "The prudent choice here is to get on with current plans, which call for a U.S.-led international effort to return to the moon and then prepare for voyages to Mars. This is a smarter and more forward-looking decision than continuing to operate a costly, flawed system."[41]

But members of Congress wanted more, not fewer, shuttle flights. In December 2007, 32 members of the Texas congressional delegation, citing concerns for NASA workers who could lose their jobs when the shuttle program ends, sent a letter to President Bush asking for additional shuttle flights beyond the 2010 shutdown date. Representative Dave Weldon, a Republican from Florida, introduced a bill that would require the shuttle to continue flying to the space station until 2013.

The politics of Russian-American relations then intruded on the future of America's space program. The Iran–North Korea–Syria Nonproliferation Act (INKSNA), signed in 2000, prevents "entities" in the United States from doing business with Russia if Russia is believed to be helping the development of nuclear technology in Iran, North Korea, or Syria. Despite the fact that Russia has assisted Iran with its civilian nuclear program, NASA has been able to work with Russia's space program because of a congressional waiver that extends through 2010. But unless Congress agreed to extend the waiver, NASA would essentially be denied access to space after the shuttle was retired in 2011.

On September 22, 2008, Senator Barack Obama, the Democratic nominee for president, sent a letter to House Speaker Nancy Pelosi and Senate Majority Leader Harry Reid urging Congress to fund one additional shuttle flight and demanding that NASA take no action precluding shuttle flights beyond 2010. At issue was the INKSNA legislation banning payments to Russia for the use of its *Progress* spacecraft to transport U.S. astronauts to the International Space Station (ISS).

On September 27, 2008, Congress passed the NASA Reauthorization Act, which left the decision on whether to continue the shuttle program beyond 2010 to the next administration. The final bill included a provision that reflected Senator Obama's letter to Congressional leaders, prohibiting NASA from taking any steps that would preclude flying the shuttle past 2010.

In October 2008, Congress came through with a waiver extension allowing the United States to use the Russian spacecraft, but NASA surprised everyone by declaring that, despite the waiver, it would seek U.S.-based commercial launch options rather than the Russian vehicle. NASA spokesman David Steitz said, "NASA will rely on U.S. commercial cargo services to resupply ISS following retirement of the shuttle, and does not intend to purchase *Progress* cargo services after 2011."[42]

STAR WARS: THE POLITICS OF MISSILE DEFENSE

In a March 1983 speech, President Ronald Reagan announced a grand plan to militarize space in the name of peace. What came to be known as the "Star Wars" speech introduced a space-based missile defense system capable of destroying not only incoming ICBMs, but satellites as well. Reagan described the new Star Wars system, officially dubbed the Strategic Defense Initiative (SDI), in dramatic terms, promising that it would render nuclear weapons "impotent and obsolete."

Reagan's proposal followed the advice of Edward Teller, the "father of the H-bomb," who passed on an overly optimistic vision of X-ray lasers that could shoot down hundreds of Soviet ballistic missiles simultaneously. Congress, urged on by defense contractors, voted to spend $1 billion on SDI research. The Defense Department warned that it would require at least $400 billion for deployment alone.

Scientists at government laboratories around the country were recruited to make Star Wars a reality, but many of them quickly realized that it was politics, not science, that drove the project. One such scientist was Roy Woodruff, a research physicist at the prestigious Lawrence Livermore National Laboratory (LLNL), where he worked on nuclear explosive design, computational physics, and strategic and tactical nuclear weapons. In 1980,

President Ronald Reagan speaks with the astronauts of the space shuttle *Challenger* shortly after they used a robotic arm to recover the satellite Solar Max, April 10, 1984. A model of the shuttle stands on the president's desk. (AP Photo/Barry Thumma)

Woodruff became associate director at LLNL, in charge of all nuclear design programs.

After Reagan's Star Wars speech, SDI became a major focus at LLNL, in part because Edward Teller, who had originally conceived Star Wars, was the lab's most prominent resident physicist. Teller proposed a "space shield" of X-ray lasers generated by nuclear explosions. Called "Excalibur," this theoretical weapon would consist of an atomic bomb packed in a batch of metal rods that would focus the X-rays produced by the nuclear explosion. Teller linked his advocacy of Excalibur to his opposition to current international arms control negotiations. This political linkage bothered Woodruff, who, though a strong advocate of SDI, felt an obligation to scrupulously examine the scientific basis for Excalibur.

On December 22, 1983, Teller communicated confidentially with then–White House science adviser George Keyworth, claiming that Excalibur had successfully passed through diagnostics and was now "entering engineering phase." The claim was absurd, but it was just what the White House wanted. When Woodruff learned of the letter and its baseless claim, he confronted Teller. "I have never called Teller a liar," Woodruff later recalled, "but the statement was nonsense— we were not in engineering phase then and we are not today."[43]

Even the most ardent supporters of SDI were beginning to realize that, because Excalibur generated only one laser beam per nuclear explosion, it could never be effective against an array of missiles and decoys. Teller himself came to recognize this and responded by proposing "Super Excalibur," a theoretical weapon that could produce many laser beams from a single nuclear blast. Once more, Teller ignored LLNL's chain of command, sending exuberant offline reports to Paul Nitze, Reagan's arms negotiator, and Robert McFarlane, head of the National Security Council. Teller described Super Excalibur as a "silver bullet" that could protect America from any Soviet attack and advised Nitze to oppose any Soviet proposals at the Geneva arms negotiations.

Woodruff recalls, "[T]o say that you had Super Excalibur just around the corner and that you ought to go to Geneva and base your policy on that . . . was nonsense, utter nonsense. Yet that was what was said in the letter to McFarlane."[44]

Woodruff was particularly concerned about the political deals being struck with the White House and Pentagon. On September 6, 1985, Lieutenant General James Abrahamson, head of the SDI Organization (SDIO), convened a meeting of government agencies and laboratories to divide up $100 million of Pentagon funding for SDI research. Woodruff was in attendance. Midway through the meeting, Teller strode into the room and declared that President Reagan had promised all the money to him for Super Excalibur research. Abrahamson promptly assigned all of the $100 million to Teller.

Using the new funding, Teller formed a research team at LLNL that included his protégé, Lowell Wood. Claims of success were soon reported to the White House and Congress and leaked to the press. When Teller continued providing secret briefings to political and military officials, Woodruff resigned his associate directorship at LLNL in protest of the lab's toleration of Teller's political representations of progress on SDI. In his letter of resignation he wrote, "It was simply unacceptable to allow the continued selling of the X-ray laser program" by Teller and Wood, allowing them "to potentially mislead the highest levels of leadership in this country."[45]

In response to Teller's groundless claims of success in X-ray lasers, Woodruff expressed exasperation at "seeing someone like Teller use his prestige and reputation to gain access to people and make statements like that, to a non-technical person in particular. . . . It was clear that at least one person—the President—believed in SDI as a reality."[46]

Woodruff's resignation did not deter Teller and Wood in their sales campaign for SDI. In testimony before Congress, Wood said that X-ray lasers could be used to destroy any type of platforms in space, including defensive platforms. He concluded that the "counterdefensive role" was the most likely use for X-ray lasers.[47]

The irony of Wood's forceful claim was that it once and for all removed the pretense that SDI was a defensive weapon. Now, it was revealed as a "counter-defensive" weapon, which would presumably spell the *end* of missile defense. "It was an anti-SDI weapon," Woodruff explained. "It had very little potential for *defending* against ballistic missile attack."[48]

George Miller, Woodruff's successor as associate director at LLNL, quickly wrote to the House Armed Services Committee's panel on SDI to refute Wood's testimony, but the cat was out of the bag. Hugh DeWitt, another prominent Livermore physicist who was concerned about the selling of SDI, wrote to the *New York Times*, stating: "After five presumed tests in Nevada in six years, the nuclear pumped X-ray laser program . . . is still in its infancy. Weapon design experts at Los Alamos estimate that developing [it] might require 100 to 1200 more nuclear tests and could easily require ten to twenty more years. And if the device is ever perfected as a space weapon, its primary use will be in an offensive mode for attacking Soviet satellites."[49]

DeWitt and a Livermore colleague, Ray Kidder, wrote to Senator Edward Kennedy and Representative Joseph Markey complaining that Livermore appeared to be opposing a nuclear test ban treaty solely because it might decrease funding for their X-ray laser program. California Representative George Brown, Jr., publicly criticized Livermore for leaving Teller's politically motivated claims unchallenged. "The President thinks he is speaking with revealed wisdom," said Brown.[50]

Brown requested that the General Accounting Office (GAO) begin an investigation of the entire process at Livermore. In December 1987, the GAO determined that Teller and Wood had bypassed Woodruff and other Livermore staff, conveying unverified versions of the X-ray laser program to the White House.

By this time, other Livermore scientists were complaining about the lab's politicized image due to Teller's manipulation of scientific data. "Your technical credibility is the only thing that you ever have to offer anyone," said John Harvey, Livermore's project manager for advanced strategic systems. "When I go to Washington now, people jokingly ask me what's the next lie that's going to come out of here."[51] Physicist W. Lowell Morgan, who had worked on Excalibur at Livermore, admitted that the "few scientific results we had were being grossly misrepresented."[52]

The demise of the Warsaw Pact and the dissolution of the Soviet Union between 1989 and 1991 undercut the original justification for Star Wars, but the new administration of George H. W. Bush nonetheless provided $3 billion to $4 billion per year for missile defense. More disturbing was the continued politicization of the SDI research and the harassment of scientists who criticized the program. One such target was Aldric Saucier, a leading researcher in the SDI program and a top physicist in integrated systems for national defense and space exploration. He had been a team leader in the *Saturn/Apollo* project that brought us to the moon, but he was now caught in the political battle over Star Wars.

Since 1979, Saucier had worked as a civilian scientist at the U.S. Army's Strategic Defense Command, where he helped to design America's missile defenses. His work was highly praised until Star Wars came under his careful scrutiny. Indeed, his 1984 evaluation praised "his unselfish contributions to the furtherance of strategic defense," and his 1988 evaluation called him "a skillful, innovative, highly qualified individual."[53] Suddenly, he became the target of FBI surveillance and break-ins, had his security clearance arbitrarily revoked, and was threatened with dismissal.

The last straw came in January 1992, when Saucier was fired because his superiors rejected as "unacceptable" his study proposing a modified Patriot missile defense system to track and respond to incoming enemy missiles.

In April 1991, Saucier submitted an affidavit to lawyers for the Government Accountability Project (GAP), a whistle-blower support organization, charging that he was being targeted as retaliation for his criticism of SDI. In his affidavit, he recounted his "unblemished record until I started challenging 'Star Wars' abuses." Saucier said, "Star Wars has been a high risk, space age, national security pork barrel for contractors and top government managers."[54]

Among Saucier's complaints about the SDI program were:

1. The program had made no significant scientific progress, and the scientific method had been grossly distorted by politics.
2. There had been over $10 billion spent on duplicative, often fraudulent, and consistently wasted research and development in the SDI program.

Among the specific examples of fraud documented in Saucier's affidavit were:

1. Officials from Livermore led the government to believe falsely that the X-ray laser had proven itself, when they knew that genuine data did not exist. Saucier's verbal warnings were ignored and written critiques destroyed.
2. When an inexpensive, ground-based laser system proved itself successful in laboratory tests, it was suppressed, and funding for a more-expensive system, which has never worked, was increased.

3. The cost estimates from missile defense studies underestimated the cost of the programs in an effort to justify Star Wars budget requests. The performance projections were also inaccurate, promising at least twice as effective a shield as the data supported.
4. Pentagon officials publicized the cost of "Brilliant Pebbles," a theoretical new version of Super Excalibur, at $40 billion to $60 billion, when the real price tag was $60 billion to $90 billion. In addition, Brilliant Pebbles can only remain in orbit for a limited number of days, rather than the ten years that is claimed.

On February 14, 1992, Saucier was served with a two-page notice of dismissal by Colonel James Roberts, chief of staff for the army's Strategic Defense Command. "He was fired because he was telling the truth," said Jeff Ruch, one of GAP's lawyers. "If he had gone along with all the things he was complaining about, he not only would not have been fired but would have been given merit-pay increases and probably promoted."[55]

Representative John Conyers, Jr., chairman of the House Government Operations Committee, which had been investigating the SDI program, said Saucier's firing "gives every appearance of retaliation." In fact, said Conyers, the firing occurred "at the precise moment he [Saucier] was meeting with my staff . . . concerning technical problems [with SDI]."[56]

Less than a year later, Bill Clinton took office as president and approved $3 billion to $4 billion per year for missile defense research, despite the fact that Defense Secretary Les Aspin had proclaimed Star Wars dead. Political pressure to continue funding Star Wars had been brought to bear through Representative Newt Gingrich's "Contract with America," which contained a section "requiring the Defense Department to deploy antiballistic missile systems." Clinton was able to forestall an immediate commitment by offering the "3 + 3" plan: three years of research and testing followed by a three-year crash program to deploy a system, *if* the president decided it was necessary, feasible, and affordable. This compromise allowed Clinton to delay a decision until after he left office, leaving Al Gore holding the bag as the Democratic presidential nominee in 2000.

As John Pike of the Federation of American Scientists put it, "This is a political decision driven by the need to defend Al Gore from Republicans rather than defend America against missiles."[57]

As it turned out, Al Gore won the popular vote in the 2000 presidential election, but George W. Bush became president, leaving a decision on Star Wars in his hands. From the start of his presidency, Bush made missile defense a top priority, revoking the 1972 Anti-Ballistic Missile Treaty in order to clear the way for space-based missile systems. He tripled the missile defense budget, which reached $10.7 billion in 2004 and is projected to reach $55 billion by 2011.

Even as Bush displayed unqualified optimism about SDI, his science advisers expressed doubt. Philip Coyle, who served as the Pentagon's top weapons tester during the 1990s, told a House committee in 2009, "Currently U.S. missile defenses have not demonstrated effectiveness to defend Europe or the U.S. under realistic operational conditions."[58]

Thomas Christie, Coyle's successor at the Pentagon's testing and evaluation office, wrote in his fiscal year 2004 annual report that the components of the SDI system "remain immature," making it impossible to "estimate the current mission capability" of the system.[59] In response to such published doubts, the Bush administration removed Christie's annual reports from the Pentagon Web site.

Lieutenant Colonel Gregory Bowen, the commander at Fort Greely, Alaska—where SDI has been fielded—told a reporter, "Does the capability exist this minute to shoot if we see something? The answer to that is no. . . . And if I contradict anything the generals have said, they're right."[60]

Bush's full system envisioned three defensive layers. A "boost-phase" intercept would be a satellite-based weapon orbiting over suspected nuclear sites, ready to shoot down enemy missiles shortly after they are launched. The "midcourse intercept" would consist of missiles or lasers based on ships, planes, or land that would shoot down missiles in their trajectory in outer space. Finally, the "terminal intercept" would shoot down enemy warheads as they plunge toward their targets in the United States.

The advanced weapons in this three-prong system are years away from being developed, much less built and deployed. Only the third prong, "terminal intercept," has been subject to testing, and that has been so limited and controlled that it has generally been considered rigged.

Nonetheless, in 2007, the Bush administration announced a plan to expand its ballistic missile defense to Europe, in order to counter any possible threat from Iran. The plan would place 10 interceptor missile silos in Poland and a linked radar station in the Czech Republic. The plan was protested by Russia, already surrounded by current and prospective NATO members, and it found little public support from Poles and Czechs. How could Europe have confidence in an American missile defense system that had not been proven in the United States?

Then, on February 20, 2008, came what seemed to be a spectacular success for America's missile defense system. Using an Aegis Standard Missile-3 (SM-3), a relatively simple interceptor fired from a U.S. cruiser in the Pacific, the U.S. military shot down one of its own spy satellites that was in a decaying orbit and about to enter the atmosphere. The Aegis missile system aboard the cruiser was developed primarily for intermediate missile defense against low-altitude, incoming warheads, and it had already been successfully tested against warhead targets. Why was a defensive system used offensively to shoot down a satellite?

The State Department said there was concern that an unused fuel tank on the satellite might pass through the atmosphere without burning up, spraying toxic fuel on a populated area. Michael Krepon of the Henry L. Stimson Center observed, "There has to be another reason behind this. In the history of the space age, there has not been a single human being who has been harmed by man-made objects falling from space."[61]

Theresa Hitchens, director of the Center for Defense Information, doubted the State Department's claim that the falling satellite represented a threat to human life. "I think they were using the threat as cover to do something they have wanted to do for a long time," said Hitchens. "It shows that our missile defense programs are not just missile defense programs, they're also anti-satellite programs."[62]

David Wright of the Union of Concerned Scientists said, "There's a real concern among people here and in other nations that the U.S. is trying to develop space weapons in the guise of other systems."[63]

In December 2008, the Missile Defense Agency conducted a successful test, shooting down a simulated long-range ballistic missile. The target missile was launched from Alaska and intercepted 3,000 kilometers away, over the Pacific Ocean. "The kill vehicle was sent to a very accurate spot in space," said Lieutenant General Patrick O'Reilly, chief of the Missile Defense Agency, adding that the result "does give us great confidence." The bad news, said O'Reilly, was that the target missile failed to deploy its programmed countermeasure, such as decoys or chaff. As a result, the successful shoot down once more seemed rigged. "Countermeasures are very difficult to deploy," explained O'Reilly.[64]

As the United States approached the change of administrations in 2009, the future of Star Wars was as murky as ever. Twenty-five years after President Reagan's promise of an impenetrable space shield to defend against enemy ICBMs, the Pentagon continues to spend more than $12 billion annually on unproven missile defense system. What the Pentagon has demonstrated is a willingness to use a rudimentary *offensive* system to destroy space satellites. This is not the promise of the Strategic Defense Initiative. It is the nightmare of Star Wars.

NOTES

1. "Sputnik: Declassified," *NOVA*, PBS, November 6, 2007, www.pbs.org/wgbh/nova/transcripts/3415_sputnik.html.
2. Ibid.
3. Ibid.
4. Ibid.
5. "Space Shuttle Disaster," *NOVA*, PBS, October 14, 2008, www.pbs.org/wgbh/nova/transcripts/3512_columbia.html.
6. Ibid.
7. Ibid.
8. Richard Cook, "The Rogers Commission Failed," *The Washington Monthly*, November 1986, 20.
9. Ibid.
10. "Analyst Who Gave Shuttle Warning Faults 'Gung Ho, Can-Do' Attitude," *New York Times*, February 14, 1986, B4.
11. Ibid.
12. Presidential Commission on the Space Shuttle Challenger Accident (Rogers Commission). Report of the Presidential Commission on the Space Shuttle Challenger Accident, Washington, D.C.: U.S. Government Printing Office, 1986, p. 148.
13. Richard Cook, "The Rogers Commission Failed," *The Washington Monthly*, November 1986, 21.
14. Ibid.

15. Patricia Werhane, *Moral Indignation & Management Decision-Making,* New York: Oxford University Press, 1999, p. 68.

16. Robert E. Allinson, *Saving Human Lives: Lessons in Management Ethics*, New York: Springer, 2005, p. 178.

17. Memo from Roger Boisjoly to R. K. Lund, Vice President, Engineering, Morton Thiokol, Inc. on O-Ring Erosion, July 31, 1985. Online Ethics Center for Engineering, August 29, 2006. www.onlineethics.org/CMS/profpractice/exempindex/RB-intro/Erosion.aspx.

18. "Remembering the Mistakes of Challenger," NASA Spaceflight.com, January 28, 2007, p. 3. www.nasaspaceflight.com/2007/01/remembering-the-mistakes-of -challenger/.

19. *Columbia* Accident Investigation Board Report, vol. 8, sec. 5, August 2003, www.nasa .gov/columbia/home/CAIB.html.

20. "Remembering the Mistakes of Challenger," NSA Spaceflight.com, January 28, 2007, p. 3. www.nasaspaceflight.com/2007/01/remembering-the-mistakes-of -challenger/.

21. Ibid.

22. Ibid.

23. Asa Gordon, retired Goddard Space Science physicist, interview by Herbert N. Foerstel, January 3, 2008.

24. "Space Shuttle Disaster," *NOVA*, PBS, October 14, 2008, www.pbs.org/wgbh/nova/ transcripts/3512_columbia.html.

25. William Harwood, "Foam Strike Email to Shuttle Commander Released," *Space-flight Now*, June 30, 2003, www.spaceflightnow.com/shuttle/sts107/030630emails/.

26. "Columbia Accident Investigation Board: Decision-Making During the Flight," Spaceflight Now, 2009. www.spaceflightnow.com/columbia/report/inflight.html.

27. Ibid.

28. Ibid.

29. "Space Shuttle Disaster," *NOVA*, PBS, October 14, 2008, www.pbs.org/wgbh/nova/ transcripts/3512_columbia.html.

30. *Columbia* Accident Investigation Board Report, vol. 8, sec. 6, August 2003, www.nasa .gov/columbia/home/CAIB.html.

31. *Columbia* Accident Investigation Board Report, vol. 8, sec. 6, August 2003, www.nasa .gov/columbia/home/CAIB.html.

32. *Columbia* Accident Investigation Board Report, vol. 8, sec. 3, August 2003, www.nasa .gov/columbia/home/CAIB.html.

33. *Columbia* Accident Investigation Board Report, Introduction to vol. 5, August 2003, www.nasa.gov/columbia/home/CAIB.html.

34. *Columbia* Accident Investigation Board Report, Introduction to vol. 7, August 2003, www.nasa.gov/columbia/home/CAIB.html.

35. *Columbia* Accident Investigation Board Report, vol. 8, sec. 5, August 2003, www.nasa .gov/columbia/home/CAIB.html.

36. *Columbia* Accident Investigation Board Report, vol. 8, sec. 5 and 6, August 2003, www.nasa.gov/columbia/home/CAIB_Vol1.html.

37. NASA, "Excerpts from the CAIB Report," August 2003, http://history.nasa .gov/columbia/Troxell/Columbia%20Web%20Site/Documents/Congress/House/SEP.

38. Robert Zimmerman, "Space Watch: How Politics Drives NASA," *Space Daily*, April 7, 2005, 1, www.spacedaily.com/news/nasa-05f.html.

39. Marc Kaufman, "Crowded Shuttle Schedule Sparks Worries," *Washington Post*, January 6, 2008, A4.
40. Ibid.
41. John M. Logsdon, "It's Time to Retire the Shuttle," *Washington Post*, October 16, 2008, A19.
42. "NASA Will Not Use Russian *Progress* Vehicle Despite Waiver," *Universe Today*, October 7, 2008, www.universetoday.com/2008/10/07/nasa-will-not-use-russian -progress-vehicle-despite-waiver/.
43. Robert Sheer, "The Man Who Blew the Whistle on 'Star Wars,'" *Los Angeles Times Magazine*, July 17, 1998, 10.
44. Ibid., 29.
45. Deborah Blum, "Weird Science: Livermore's X-Ray Laser Flap," *Bulletin of the Atomic Scientists*, July/August 1988, 12.
46. Robert Sheer, "The Man Who Blew the Whistle on 'Star Wars,'" *Los Angeles Times Magazine*, July 17, 1998, 30.
47. "Red Flag at a Weapons Lab," *Time*, January 18, 1988, 52.
48. Robert Sheer, "The Man Who Blew the Whistle on 'Star Wars,'" *Los Angeles Times Magazine*, July 17, 1998, 11.
49. "Scientist of Conscience," *Progressive*, December 1986, 4.
50. "Red Flag at a Weapons Lab," *Time*, January 18, 1988, 52.
51. Ibid.
52. "Twice Burned," *Scientific American*, January 1988, 16.
53. "Scientist Says Army Seeks to Fire Him for Criticizing SDI," *Washington Post*, January 10, 1992, A17.
54. Ibid.
55. "Defense Scientist Who Complained About SDI Is Dismissed," *Washington Post*, February 15, 1992, A11.
56. "Conyers Assails Firing of Pentagon Scientist," *Washington Post*, February 19, 1992, A20.
57. William D. Hartung, "Star Wars II: Here We Go Again," *The Nation*, June 19, 2000, 4, www.thenation.com/doc/20000619/hartung.
58. Philip E. Coyle, Prepared Remarks before the House Committee on Armed Services, Subcommittee on Strategic Forces, February 25, 2009, Center for Defense Information, February 26, 2009. www.cdi.org/pdfs/CoyleHASCfull2_25_091.pdf.
59. U.S. Department of Defense, *Director of Operational Test and Evaluation Report, FY2004*, February 2005, www.cdi.org/PDFs/DOTE_FY04.pdf.
60. Alex Fryer, "Unproven Missile Defense Program Continues to Stir Controversy," *Seattle Times*, July 21, 2005.
61. "Bush Orders Attempt to Shoot Down Satellite," *Washington Post*, February 15, 2008, A18.
62. "Spy Satellite's Downing Shows a New U.S. Weapon Capability," *Washington Post*, February 20, 2008, A3.
63. "Effort to Shoot Down Satellite Could Inform Military Strategy," *Washington Post*, February 20, A3.
64. "U.S. Shoots Down Missile in Simulation of Long-Range Attack," *Washington Post*, December 6, 2008, A2.

3

The Politics of Sexual Reproduction

"Abstinence-only" sex education was promoted by many conservatives in the administration of President George W. Bush despite evidence of its lack of effectiveness. (Jimmy Margulies/The Record/PoliticalCartoons.com)

ABSTINENCE-ONLY

High school biology class was supposed to teach us everything we needed to know about the *science* of human reproduction, but there was a separate course to tell us about "sex." What's the difference? What does a sex education course

teach us that a biology course cannot? Does sex education even belong in a
school curriculum, or is it better left to parents and the church? This has become
a rousing political debate over the last two generations, putting science, religion, and politics at each other's throats. More recently, as politics and religion
formed a powerful and effective alliance, science has taken a beating in health
education.

Biology textbooks tell us that, throughout the animal kingdom, sexual inter-
course has the sole purpose of propagating the species. Ironically, most religions teach the same precept, but they add the moral judgment that premarital
sexual gratification without a reproductive purpose is contrary to the laws of
God and nature. The Catholic Church extends this logical argument to conclude
that the use of birth control perverts natural and religious law and encourages
promiscuity.

The growing problem of sexually transmitted diseases (STDs) has complicated and intensified the debate over what constitutes healthy and appropriate
human sexual behavior. The medical profession strongly advocates the use of
condoms to protect against STDs. With the rising threat of AIDS in the last
20 years, medical science has led the way in an international campaign of education and action to stop the spread of AIDS through "safe sex." Conservative
religious leaders have argued that the only truly safe sex is no sex at all, and
political programs encouraging and often mandating abstinence until marriage
have been endorsed and heavily subsidized by recent American presidents.

The legislative origins of abstinence-only education date to the Reagan era,
when Congress passed the 1981 Adolescent Family Life Act (AFLA), known as
the "chastity law," which funded education programs to promote "self-discipline"
or "chastity education." The ACLU brought suit against AFLA, charging that it
was imposing religious education—particularly opposition to abortion—on
school children at public expense. Years later, the Supreme Court would hold that
federally funded programs must delete direct references to religion, but abstinence-only programs continued to be funded in the name of public health.

In 1996, Congress once more endorsed abstinence education, attaching a
provision to welfare legislation that would fund abstinence-until-marriage programs exclusively. According to the statute, a qualifying program must teach:

(a) As its exclusive purpose, the social, psychological, and health gains to be real-
     ized by abstaining from sexual activity
(b) Abstinence from sexual activity outside marriage as the expected standard for
     all school-age children
(c) That abstinence from sexual activity is the only certain way to avoid out-of-
     wedlock pregnancy, sexually transmitted diseases, and other associated health
     problems
(d) That a mutually faithful, monogamous relationship in context of marriage is the
     expected standard of human sexual activity
(e) That sexual activity outside of the context of marriage is likely to have harmful
     psychological and physical effects

(f)   That bearing children out of wedlock is likely to have harmful consequences for the child, the child's parents, and society

(g)   Young people how to reject sexual advances and how alcohol and drug use increases vulnerability to sexual advances

(h)   The importance of attaining self-sufficiency before engaging in sexual activity[1]

When George W. Bush became president in January 2001, he continued a policy that began during his years as governor of Texas, promoting "abstinence-only-until-marriage" programs in the public schools. These programs withheld or removed from the curriculum any information about contraception, safe sex, and AIDS, because it was considered inconsistent with an abstinence-only message. The Bush administration's Community-Based Abstinence Education (CBAE) program requires that grantees adhere to the rigid definition of "abstinence education" established in Clinton's 1996 welfare bill. The CBAE statute requires that grantees not provide any other sex education in the same setting, preventing youth in these programs from learning any methods for prevention of disease or unwanted pregnancy other than abstinence.

In 2005, a group of education and public-health organizations, including the National Education Association, the American Civil Liberties Union, and the Association of Reproductive Health Professionals, issued a "Joint Statement" on abstinence-only education. The endorsing organizations said they were "deeply concerned about publicly-funded sexuality education programs that restrict students' access to information and limit learning to one 'approved' message about human sexuality. . . . The result of this focus on abstinence-until-marriage has been widespread censorship of sexual information. Material on contraception, sexually transmitted disease, and sexual orientation has been razored out of textbooks. Articles about sexuality have been censored in the student press. Teachers have been warned about talking about certain topics, and cannot answer students' questions fully or candidly.

The statement concluded: "The evidence shows that providing students uncensored access to comprehensive sex education does not promote sexual activity. . . . Moreover, students who receive uncensored comprehensive sex education, which includes but is not limited to information about abstinence, are more likely than students who do not receive this education to practice safer sex more consistently if they do become sexually active."[2]

Representative Henry Waxman, ranking minority member on the House Committee on Government Reform, protested the new guidelines in a letter to the secretary of Health and Human Services (HHS). His letter concluded, "The new funding announcement for abstinence-only-until-marriage programs places ideology ahead of teen health and well-being. The new guidelines omit public health purposes, insert definitions that track not health concerns but narrow moral views, contain no review for scientific accuracy, and measure attendance and attitudes instead of actual health outcomes. This is a program driven by fealty to a political constituency, not public health or scientific evidence. I ask that the entire funding announcement be retracted."[3]

The guidelines were retained, and in fiscal year 2006, the CBAE received $113 million in federal funding.

The narrowly tailored message of abstinence-only was enforced outside the classroom setting, even intruding on ostensibly objective scientific gatherings. In the spring of 2006, the Centers for Disease Control and Prevention held a national conference on the prevention of STDs. A scheduled panel titled "Are Abstinence-Only-Until-Marriage Programs a Threat to Public Health?" was replaced at the last minute with a panel titled "Public Health Strategies of Abstinence Programs for Youth." The speakers were changed, and a critic of abstinence-only education was replaced with two proponents, one of whom said his goal was to "serve the Lord through medical missions and the preaching of the Gospel."[4]

The program change reportedly occurred as the result of pressure from U.S. Representative Mark Sonder (R-IN), an outspoken opponent of contraception and comprehensive sex education. When this became known, Representative Henry Waxman, the ranking minority member on the House Government Reform Committee, wrote to Michael Leavitt, secretary of the Department of Health and Human Services, asking for an explanation. The letter said, "In effect, it appears that presentations at a public health conference were censored because they criticized abstinence-only education. This attempt at thought control should have no place in our government. . . . This is not the first example of this Administration distorting scientific process related to reproductive health for ideological reasons. CDC has censored information about condom effectiveness; the Food and Drug Administration is indefinitely postponing a decision on emergency contraception; and scientists at the National Institutes of Health have been pressured not to do research on 'controversial' subjects in human sexuality. The list of these cases is long and growing."[5]

The letter concluded, "Finally, I ask for an assurance that in the future, decisions about the content of public health and medical conferences be left to the CDC's scientists and their expert colleagues and not subjected to political litmus tests."[6]

The requested assurance was never forthcoming, as HHS claimed that they were simply seeking "balance" in the conference.

Despite growing controversy over the president's abstinence-only program, it was publicized as a significant success. At a 2003 press briefing, White House spokesperson Ari Fleischer asserted that "abstinence is more than sound science, it's a sound practice. . . . [A]bstinence has a proven track record of working."[7]

In 2006, the White House announced new funding guidelines for the CBAE program that eliminated the use of health-based goals and standards. The new guidelines also required grantees to teach abstinence from any "sexual stimulation," a term so broad it would include kissing. It soon became clear that there was no verifiable evidence of success, and, indeed, no scientific standards by which success could be measured. During the Clinton administration, Health and Human Services had developed meaningful scientific measures to assess

Rep. Henry Waxman (D-California), ranking Democrat on the House Government Reform Committee, presents a report on former lobbyist Jack Abramoff's ties to the White House, September 20, 2006. (AP Photo/Lauren Victoria Burke)

whether abstinence education achieved its purposes, including rates of sexual activity and pregnancy for female participants in the program. But the Bush administration had dropped those measures and replaced them with a set of standards that had no measurable outcomes.

Nonetheless, the Bush administration's confident expressions of hope and progress were sufficiently convincing to bring increased congressional funding for abstinence-only programs. From 1998 to 2002, about $500 million in federal and state matching funds were spent on abstinence-only education. Because of the requirement that states match federal funds for such programs, state money previously used for comprehensive sex education was diverted to abstinence-only programs.

By 2007, Congress was allocating $176 million in annual funding for abstinence-only programs. State governments were authorized to apply for portions of a $50 million fund that could be used to promote abstinence programs through schools, community groups, state and local health departments, and media campaigns. But by 2008, a number of states began rejecting such funding, foregoing more than $15 million of the $50 million fund.

Individual state governors began to express discomfort with the Bush program. A spokesman for Virginia governor Timothy Kaine said, "The governor has often stated that abstinence-only education does not show any results. It doesn't work. He's a firm believer in more comprehensive sex education." Even some conservative governors said the Bush programs were too restrictive and ideologically driven. A spokesman for Ohio governor Ted Strickland said, "The governor supports abstinence education. What he does not support is abstinence-*only* education."[8]

"The wave of states rejecting the money is a bellwether," said William Smith of the Sexuality Information and Education Council of the United States. "We hope that it sends a message to the politicians in Washington that this program needs to change, and states need to be able to craft a program that is the best fit for their young people and that is not dictated by Washington ideologues."[9]

Cecile Richards of Planned Parenthood agreed, saying, "This abstinence-only program is just not getting the job done. This is an ideologically based program that doesn't have any support in science."[10]

In January 2009, a new study seemed to end the debate on the effectiveness of abstinence-only programs, showing that teenagers who pledge sexual abstinence until marriage are just as likely to have premarital sex as those who do not make the pledge. The study, by Janet Rosenbaum of the Johns Hopkins Bloomberg School of public Health, was published in the January 2009 issue of the journal *Pediatrics*; Rosenbaum: "Taking a pledge doesn't seem to make any difference at all in any sexual behavior. But it does seem to make a difference in condom use and other forms of birth control that is quite striking. . . . It seems that pledgers aren't really internalizing the pledge. Participating in a program doesn't appear to be motivating them to change their behavior."[11]

BIRTH CONTROL AND CONTRACEPTION

The political and religious campaign in support of abstinence has inevitably led to public policies opposing birth control. In particular, condom use is being discouraged and disparaged as ineffective in preventing STDs, an approach that the National Institutes of Health (NIH) says "places policy in direct conflict with science because it ignores overwhelming evidence."[12]

Among the more-effective lobbyists for abstinence and against "safe sex" is Dr. Joe McIlhaney, the conservative Christian founder and president of the Medical Institute for Sexual Health, which strongly challenges the ability of condoms to prevent most STDs. Under the Bush administration, McIlhaney has served on the advisory committee to the director of the Centers for Disease Control and Prevention and the President's Advisory Council on HIV and AIDS. McIlhaney has ridiculed the effectiveness of condom use, declaring, "It's just this simple sort of little latex device, and we're talking about the futures of young people."[13]

In fact, the medical evidence of condom effectiveness is compelling. A 2001 review by the NIH said condoms have been positively proven effective in preventing HIV, gonorrhea, and unwanted pregnancy, and the study noted that condoms have been shown to block "particles of similar size to those of the smallest STD viruses."[14]

In spite of the evidence, McIlhaney and congressional allies like Senator Tom Coburn (R-OK) have waged an unrelenting war on condom use. Coburn, who claims to have shown "the 'safe' sex myth for the lie that it is," even called for the resignation of CDC director Jeffrey Koplan, claiming that he withheld "the truth of condom ineffectiveness."[15]

McIlhaney's claims have had considerable influence on the Bush administration, which pressed the CDC and the State Department's Agency for International Development (USAID) to alter their informational materials to downplay the effectiveness of condoms. In October 2002, the CDC replaced a comprehensive fact sheet about condoms with one lacking information about condom use and efficacy. The original sheet, titled "Condoms and Their Use in Preventing HIV Infection and other STDs," included sections on the proper use of condoms and their effectiveness. It also noted that "a World Health Organization (WHO) review . . . found no evidence that sex education leads to earlier or increased sexual activity in young people."[16]

In contrast, the revised fact sheet begins by emphasizing condom failure rates and the effectiveness of abstinence, deleting specific information on condom effectiveness and evidence that sex education does not lead to increased sexual activity.

Like the CDC, USAID censored its Web site to remove information on the effectiveness of condoms. Through early 2003, the site had included a document titled "The Effectiveness of Condoms in Preventing Sexually Transmitted Infections," which stated, "Latex condoms are highly effective in preventing HIV/AIDS" and "Public and government support for latex condoms is essential for disease prevention."[17]

A second document on the USAID Web site had stated that condoms are "highly effective for preventing HIV infection" and called condom distribution "a cornerstone of USAIDS's HIV prevention strategy."[18]

Later in 2003, the first of these documents was removed from the Web site, and the second was edited to say only that condoms can reduce the risk of HIV and some other STDs.

Because condoms are used for both contraception and disease prevention, conservative politicians have found it useful to couch their religious objections in scientific jargon. But what about the wide variety of purely contraceptive devices available with and without prescription? Their suppression requires a more devious bureaucratic approach. Consider the campaign against the "morning after" pill, marketed under the name Plan B. The pill uses a higher dose of the drug available in standard birth-control pills, dramatically reducing the risk of pregnancy if taken within 72 hours after unprotected sex. Plan B prevents ovulation, fertilization, or implantation of the egg in the uterus, and it has no effect on women who are already pregnant. It had been used safely and effectively for several years as a prescription drug, but in 2003, when its manufacturer applied to the FDA's Reproductive Health Drugs Advisory Committee for approval to sell as an over-the-counter drug, there were political repercussions.

In December 2003, the FDA's advisory committee met with a number of over-the-counter drug experts and could find no medical problems with Plan B. Indeed, one of the doctors at the meeting characterized Plan B as "the safest product that we have seen brought before us."[19] The advisory committee quickly voted 23-4 to approve Plan B for over-the-counter sales.

Despite this strong recommendation from its scientific advisors, the FDA in May 2004 rejected Plan B's application, citing an unusual reason: inadequate data on how younger adolescents might use the drug. In its rejection letter, the FDA said that "some members" of its advisory committee had raised questions about "inadequate sampling of younger age groups."[20]

Such data had never been required for previous contraceptive approvals, and, in fact, had never been required for any drug approval. It turned out that, after the advisory committee's 23-4 vote of approval, one member of the committee, an obstetrician and gynecologist named W. David Hager, sent a "minority report" to the FDA commissioner. Before Hager's appointment to the advisory committee in 2002, he had earned the admiration of the Bush administration by lobbying the FDA to reverse its approval for RU-486, the so-called abortion pill (more on this later), claiming that its use would promote promiscuity.

With his wife, Hager had also coauthored a book—*Stress and the Woman's Body*—that offers the reader a "spiritual perspective" on women's health and promises to "direct you toward a personal relationship with Jesus Christ."[21] Another of his books, *As Jesus Cared for Women*, endorses concepts like "demonic possession" and "miraculous healing."[22]

How did the minority report of such a man influence the FDA to overrule its science advisers? Hager explains, "The opinion I wrote was not from an evangelical Christian perspective. . . . I argued it from a scientific perspective, and God took that information, and he used it through this minority report to influence the decision. You don't have to wave your Bible to have an effect as a Christian in the public arena. We serve the greatest Scientist. We serve the Creator of all life."[23]

Having been convinced by Hager to withhold approval for over-the-counter sales of Plan B, the FDA ignored all subsequent applications by the manufacturer, including a proposal that attempted to accommodate Hager's objection by restricting sales to those over sixteen years of age. In January 2005, after the FDA missed a deadline to respond to a new application by Plan B, the Center for Reproductive Rights filed a lawsuit charging the FDA with arbitrarily rejecting a safe and effective drug. When the FDA failed to respond, Susan Wood, director of the FDA's own Office of Women's Health, resigned, explaining that the FDA's actions were "contrary to my core commitment to improving and advancing women's health."[24]

Dr. Frank Davidoff, a member of the FDA's Nonprescription Drug Advisory Committee, also resigned from the agency in protest. "I can no longer associate myself with an organization that is capable of making such an important decision so flagrantly on the basis of political influence rather than the scientific and clinical evidence," explained Davidoff.[25]

In her resignation letter, Wood charged that FDA commissioner Lester Crawford overruled his own scientists' recommendation for Plan B, and concluded, "I can no longer serve as staff when scientific and clinical evidence, fully evaluated and recommended by the professional staff here, has been overruled."[26]

Women's organizations applauded Wood's action as women in Congress criticized the FDA's inaction. Hillary Rodham Clinton (D-NY) and Patty Murray (D-WA) issued a statement that concluded, "Science has taken a back seat to politics in the FDA's decision-making process."[27]

Clinton added, "Day by day, the public's confidence in the FDA's ability to make decisions based on scientific evidence of safety and efficacy is eroding."[28]

Eventually, the growing public criticism led the FDA to approve Plan B as an over-the-counter drug, but a number of state governments imposed local restraints on its sale. In 2008, a district judge in the state of Washington ruled that pharmacists could refuse to sell Plan B if they had religious objections. That same year, the Missouri state legislature introduced a bill that would classify Plan B as an abortion-inducing medication, contrary to the FDA's definition of such drugs. Under this arbitrary definition, Missouri could impose the same restrictions on the sale of Plan B that it imposed on abortions.

ABORTION

On January 23, 1973, the *New York Times* headline blared, "High Court Rules Abortion Legal the First Three Months," announcing the Supreme Court's landmark ruling in *Roe v. Wade*. The court held that a Texas statute criminalizing abortion violated a woman's privacy right under the Fourteenth Amendment, seemingly resolving the legal debate over abortion. But the political battle was just beginning.

The 1980 elections revealed the power of anti-abortion politics as a new conservative movement brought Ronald Reagan to the White House, added 45 new congressional seats, 4 governorships, and 220 state legislative seats. The conservative Moral Majority claimed to have registered 4 million voters and brought an additional 10 million to the polls. The conservative political revolution was victorious, and its "pro-life" agenda was ascendant. Still, this undeniable political reality was in conflict with public attitudes, as reflected in national polls.

One poll showed that even among Reagan voters, only 3 percent considered abortion the most important issue in the campaign. Another poll found that 57 percent of Reagan supporters opposed a ban on abortion. The influential pro-life group Life Amendment Political Action Committee (LAPAC) explained, "It really doesn't matter what the polls say. Whoever can deliver politically is the group that's going to get its way."[29] Indeed, pro-life politics was delivering the goods.

In Congress, a newly formed anti-abortion caucus claimed 200 to 250 votes in the House and 41 in the Senate. The caucus targeted not only abortion rights but also family planning, sex education, and the nation's leading family planning organization, Planned Parenthood. Donald Devine, Reagan's head of the Office of Personnel Management (OPM), used his authority over the Combined Federal Campaign (CFC), which listed officially approved charities to which military and civilian employees could donate, to remove Planned Parenthood from the approved list.

Planned Parenthood brought suit and won. Judge Joyce Hens Greer ordered Devine to reinstate the organization to CFC's approved list, citing Devine's "differential treatment" and "admitted bias."[30]

Conservative groups were undaunted, and by the time of the 1984 GOP convention, they had succeeded in adding a new plank to the party's platform: to "eliminate funding for organizations which advocate or support abortion." Jerry Falwell performed the benediction on the evening that Reagan was nominated for a second term. At a prayer breakfast, Reagan himself declared that "religion and politics are necessarily related. We need religion as a guide."[31]

Abortion was a central theme in the fall presidential campaign, and pro-life groups hounded Democratic running mates Walter Mondale and Geraldine Ferraro, carrying tombstone signs accusing them of being a death squad. Such aggressive and emotional campaigning helped carry the elections for Reagan.

During the late 1980s, Reagan's director of family planning services, Jo Ann Gasper, attempted to defund Planned Parenthood, whose clinics received roughly $34 million in Title X funds each year to serve low-income women and teenagers. These private clinics, whose costs per patient were 22 percent lower than city and county health departments, were nonetheless unacceptable to pro-lifers. On the January 1987 anniversary of the *Roe v. Wade* decision, Gasper ordered the Title X regional offices to refuse funding for Planned Parenthood, claiming that because the organization had advocated public funding for abortion, it had a higher than usual risk that grant funds would be misused. Yet intensive audits of Planned Parenthood had found no evidence that Title X funds had been used to pay for abortion or to advise clients to have abortions.[32]

Gasper's order had been made without consulting either her superiors at Health and Human Services or the general counsel, and the department was soon forced to rescind the order under a hail of criticism. Despite continuing arbitrary behavior that would eventually result in her firing, Gasper never lost the support of the president, who took action on his own to restrict the influence of groups like Planned Parenthood. In an address to a pro-life group in July 1987, Reagan promised to prohibit any mention of abortion in a federally funded clinic or any sharing of staff or space with a clinic that provides abortions. Called the "gag rule" by the press, the new guidelines dramatically changed federal policies on family planning.

Several Planned Parenthood affiliates and the National Family Planning and Reproductive Health Association filed suits that ended up in three different appeals courts. Two of the three courts ruled that the gag orders were unconstitutional. Nonetheless, a week before the 1988 GOP convention, HHS announced that it would enforce the gag on any clinics not covered by court injunctions. Congress tried several times to reverse the gag order while it was still being considered by the courts but was unsuccessful, and when newly elected President George H. W. Bush took office, he stood solidly by the ban on counseling or referring for abortion. Indeed, when the Supreme Court ruled in May 1991 that the gag rule did not violate the Constitution, the Bush administration was free to impose it with increased vigor.

Despite the use of the president's bully pulpit to support the gag rule, neither the medical profession nor the general public was convinced. Twenty-one medical groups, including the American Medical Association (AMA), said the gag rule was a clear violation of medical ethics. AMA board member Nancy Dickey asked, "Do patients really want judges and politicians on the examining table with them? I want the right to tell my patients what the options are."[33]

The American public was even more decisive in rejecting the gag rule. A 1988 Gallup poll showed 66 percent were opposed to the gag rule, compared to 27 percent in favor, and, surprisingly, 57 percent of evangelical Christians opposed it, compared to 34 percent in favor.[34] Nonetheless, conservative politics maintained its sway over abortion policy, and the gag order remained in force until 1993, when President Bill Clinton reversed it during his first year in office. Eight years later, newly elected President George W. Bush reinstated the gag rule on his third *day* in office, which coincided with the 28th anniversary of the *Roe v. Wade* decision.

The domestic "gag rule" on abortion has an international version as well. Known as the "global gag rule," it bans U.S. funding for international health groups that perform abortions, promote legalizing abortions, or provide counseling for terminating pregnancies. Like its domestic counterpart, the "global gag rule" was originated by President Reagan, reversed by President Clinton, and reinstated by President Bush in 2001.

A more recent anti-abortion regulation, whose draft version was titled "The Problem," is the responsibility of President George W. Bush alone. Formally introduced just 30 days before the end of the Bush administration, the regulation would deny federal funding to any hospital, clinic, health plan, or other entity that doesn't allow its employees to withhold care that runs counter to their personal or religious convictions, including providing birth control pills, IUDs, and, of course, abortions.

The online *Huffington Post* wrote, "Under this new rule, doctors and health care workers of all kinds can deny patients vital health care information and service, without the patient even knowing. No patient is exempt from the reach of this rule. Sexual assault victims could be denied information about emergency contraception that could prevent unintended pregnancy, moms hoping to time their pregnancies can be denied contraception at their local pharmacy, young adults hoping to be tested for sexually transmitted infections could be denied treatment by health care employees who oppose premarital sex."[35]

Seven states and two organizations responded to the new regulation with suits to block its implementation. In January 2009, Connecticut Attorney General

Richard Blumenthal filed a lawsuit on behalf of California, Illinois, Massachusetts, New Jersey, Oregon, and Rhode Island, declaring, "On its way out, the Bush administration has left a ticking legal time bomb set to explode literally the day of the inauguration and blow apart vital constitutional rights and women's health care. Women's health may be endangered—needlessly and unlawfully—if this rule is allowed to stand."[36]

The Planned Parenthood Federation of America and the ACLU, acting on behalf of the National Family Planning and Reproductive Health Association, also filed separate suits. Planned Parenthood issued a statement saying, "For any health provider to intentionally withhold information about widely embraced treatment options from a patient—for any health condition—is absolutely unconscionable under any circumstances. It's outrageous that President Bush used his last days in office to implement a rule that would limit the rights of patients to receive complete and accurate reproductive health information. A woman's ability to manage her own health care is at risk of being compromised by politics and ideology."[37]

HEALTH CONSEQUENCES OF ABORTION

The religious and legal arguments against abortion resonated with conservative political leaders during the 1980s, but in the absence of strong medical evidence, the public remained unconvinced. Recognizing this, pro-life organizations and conservative politicians opened a new front against abortion, claiming evidence of a broad range of post-abortion illnesses, both physiological and psychological. The origins of this new strategy can be found in a 1987 memo by White House policy analyst Dinesh D'Souza, in which he called on the surgeon general to prepare a report on the health consequences of abortion comparable to reports by previous surgeons general on the dangers of smoking. The memo suggested a shift away from legal analysis and toward a health-oriented approach. President Reagan liked the idea and called on Surgeon General C. Everett Koop to produce such a report. Despite his personal opposition to abortion, Koop shocked conservatives by declining to create such a report, telling Reagan that "the scientific studies do not provide conclusive data about the health effects of abortion on women."[38]

The political right was understandably angered at Koop's intransigence. Conservative Caucus chair Howard Phillips called Koop's action "contemptible," but Koop explained, "[T]he very worst thing I could have done for the people who have been angry at me is to do what they wanted me to do. If I had put out the kind of report that was not scientific, that did not recognize the lack of physical evidence of what they wanted to know, it would have been attacked and destroyed by scientists and statisticians."[39]

Angry conservatives rejected Koop's argument and vowed to document the health risks of abortion without his help. First came a claimed link between abortion and breast cancer, publicized by the Breast Cancer Prevention Institute, a conservative think tank that first proposed the "ABC (abortion/breast cancer)" link. The institute was founded by Joel Brind, an evangelical Christian and professor of human biology, who has advised pro-life members of Congress such as Representative Dave Weldon (R-FL). At Brind's urging, conservative members of Congress have introduced legislation requiring doctors to provide counseling about the alleged risk to all women seeking abortions, and several states have already passed laws requiring women to learn about breast cancer risks before having an abortion.

Until the summer of 2002, the National Cancer Institute (NCI) had provided an analysis on its Web site concluding that the current body of scientific evidence did not support the claim that abortions increase a woman's risk of developing breast cancer. The Web site explained that the issue had been resolved by several medical studies, the largest of which had been published in the *New England Journal of Medicine*,[40] finding no link between abortion and breast cancer.

In November 2002, the Bush administration removed the analysis from the NCI Web site, replacing it with a fact sheet that stated:

Some studies have reported statistically significant evidence of an increased risk of breast cancer in women who have had abortions, while others have merely suggested and increased risk. Other studies have found no increase in risk among women who have had an interrupted pregnancy.[41]

The medical profession responded promptly to the revised "fact sheet," characterizing it as a distortion of the medical evidence. The medical director of epidemiology research for the American Cancer Society declared bluntly, "This issue has been resolved scientifically. . . . This is essentially a political debate."[42]

Embarrassed by the resulting public confusion, the NCI convened a three-day conference of experts on abortion and breast cancer. Participants reviewed all existing population-based, clinical, and animal data available and concluded that it was "well-established" that "[i]nduced abortion is not associated with an increase in breast cancer risk."[43]

On March 21, 2003, a chastened NCI corrected its Web site to reflect the medical consensus, but the Bush administration never renounced the "ABC" strategy. During 2006, it was discovered that federally funded pregnancy resource centers were telling women that abortion causes increased risk of breast cancer, infertility, and deep psychological trauma. A congressional report said that 20 of 23 federally funded centers were told false or misleading information about the risks of abortion. The report concluded that the misinformation "denies the teenagers and women vital health information, prevents them from making an informed decision, and is not accepted public health practice."[44]

Some in the pro-life movement have concluded that it is too difficult to prove a medical link between abortion and physiological illness. The existing medical studies showing no link are too widely accepted, and overturning them would be a daunting task. But what about mental and emotional illness? Surely the scientific evidence concerning that issue is less settled, and the rigor required to refute that evidence would presumably be less. Leading such a campaign was a conservative Christian named David Reardon, who had made a name for himself with his book *Aborted Women: Silent No More*. In a 2002 essay in the conservative journal *Ethics and Medicine*, Reardon advocated the "neglected rhetorical strategy" of opposing abortion because it hurts women, rather than simply rejecting it on moral grounds. He explained that "because abortion is evil, we can expect, and even know, that it will harm those who participate in it. Nothing good comes from evil."[45]

In an effort to propound the theory that abortion causes mental illness, Reardon founded the Elliot Institute for Social Sciences Research. The first sign of success for the Elliot Institute came in 2004, when Representative Joe Pitts (R-PA) sponsored a bill to provide $15 million in federal funding for research on post-abortion depression. But once more, the medical profession had trouble with the "science" of groups like the Elliot Institute.

A 2003 Reardon study published in the *Canadian Medical Association Journal* had reported that women who undergo abortions are admitted for psychiatric care more frequently than those who do not. Critics pointed out that Reardon's group failed to include a statistical control for the life circumstances of the subjects studied. For example, women who choose abortion are less likely to be married or in a serious relationship, factors which are themselves linked to increased mental-health problems. In this regard, Arizona State University psychologist Nancy Felipe Russo notes that "in well-designed studies that control for variables Reardon fails to take into account, legal abortion is not found to be associated with degradation in mental health."[46]

In short, the medical consensus continues to reject a causal link between abortion and negative health consequences, whether physiological or psychological.

NOTES

1. *Personal Responsibility and Work Opportunity Reconciliation Act of August 22, 1996,* (110 Statutes-at-Large 2105) Public Law 104–193 (1996).

2. National Coalition Against Censorship, "Abstinence Only: A Joint Statement," 2005, www.ncac.org/sex/statement.cfm.

3. Letter from Representative Henry Waxman, House Committee on Government Reform, to Secretary Michael O. Leavitt, Department of Health and Human Services, February 16, 2006. http://oversight.house.gov/documents/20060216121250 - 30800.pdf

4. National Coalition Against Censorship, "When Eyes Remain Wide Shut on Abstinence," *Atlanta Journal-Constitution*, May 19, 2006, 1, http://ncac.org/science/ajc.

5. Letter from Representative Henry Waxman, House Committee on Government Reform, to Secretary Michael O. Leavitt, Department of Health and Human Services, May 9, 2006, http://oversight.house.gov/documents/20060509105051-30240.pdf.

6. Ibid.
7. Ari Fleischer, White House press briefing, January 27, 2003, www.whitehouse.gov/news/releases/2003/01/20030127-2.html.
8. "Abstinence Programs Face Rejection," *Washington Post*, December 16, 2007, A3.
9. Ibid.
10. Ibid.
11. "Premarital Abstinence Pledges Ineffective, Study Finds," *Washington Post*, December 29, 2008, A2.
12. National Institutes of Health, *Interventions to Prevent HIV Risk Behaviors*, NIH Consensus Statement, vol. 15, no. 2, February 11–13, 1997, 15–16.
13. Medical Institute for Sexual Health, "Do Condoms Make Sex Safe Enough?" www.medinstitute.org/products/index.html.
14. National Institute of Allergies and Infectious Diseases, *Workshop Summary: Scientific Evidence on Condom Effectiveness for Sexually Transmitted Disease (STD) Prevention*, July 21, 2001, 11.
15. Representative Tom Coburn, "Safe Sex Myth Exposed by Scientific Report; Condoms Do Not Prevent Most STDs," press release, July 19, 2001.
16. CDC, "Condoms and Their Use in Preventing HIV Infection and other STDs," September 1999, www.house.gov/reform/min/pdfs/pdf_inves/pdf_admin_hhs_info _condoms_fact-sheet-orig.pdf.
17. USAID, "The Effectiveness of Condoms in Preventing Sexually Transmitted Infections," 2003, www.usaid.gov/pop_health/aids/TechAreas/condoms/condom_effect .html.
18. USAID, "USAID: HIV/AIDS and Condoms," 2003, www.usaid.gov/pop_health/TechAreas/condoms/condomfactsheet.html.
19. FDA, meeting transcript of Nonprescription Drugs Advisory Committee in joint - session with the Advisory Committee for Reproductive Health Drugs, December 16, 2003, 263, www.fda.gov/ohrms/dockets/ac/03/transcripts/4015T1.pdf.
20. Ibid, 137.
21. W. David Hager and Linda Hager, *Stress and the Woman's Body* (Grand Rapids: Fleming H. Revell, 1996), 64.
22. W. David Hager, *As Jesus Cared for Women* (Grand Rapids: Fleming H. Revell, 1998), 30, 57.
23. W. David Hager, "Standing in the Gap," *Standing in the Gap.* compact disc, Asbury College Tape Ministry, October 29, 2004.
24. "FDA Official Quits Over Plan B Pill Delay," *USA TODAY*, August 31, 2005, www.usatoday.com/news/washington/2005-08-31-fda-official-quits_x.html.
25. Nick Turse, "The Fallen Legion: Casualties of the Bush Administration," CommonDreams.org, October 14, 2005, www.commondreams.org/views05/1014 -24.html.
26. Ibid.
27. Rita Rubin, "FDA Official Quits over Plan B Pill Delay," USAToday.com, August 31, 2005, www.usatoday.com/news/washington/2005-08-31-fda-official-quits_x.html.
28. Ibid.
29. Michele McKeegan, *Abortion Politics: Mutiny in the Ranks of the Right* (New York: The Free Press, 1992), 38.
30. Ibid, 52.

31. Elizabeth Drew, "A Political Journal," *New Yorker*, September 10, 1984, 128.
32. Comptroller General, *Restrictions on Abortion and Lobbying Activities in Family Planning Programs Need Clarification* (Gaithersburg, MD: GPO, 1982), 32.
33. "The AMA Vote," *San Francisco Chronicle*, June 27, 1991.
34. George Gallup, Jr., *The People's Religion: American Faith in the 1990's* (New York: Macmillan, 1989, 175.
35. "Bush's Parting Shot Undermines Health Care," Huffington Post, January 25, 2009, www.huffingtonpost.com/cecile-richards/bushs-parting-shot.
36. "Lawsuits Filed Over Bush Health-Care Workers Regulation," CNNPolitics.com, January 16, 2009, http://politicalticker.blogs.cnn.com/2001/01/16/lawsuit.
37. Planned Parenthood, "Planned Parenthood Sues Over Disastrous Midnight Regulation," December 18, 2008, www.plannedparenthood.org/issues-action/birth-control/title-x-family-planning-funding.
38. Chris Mooney, *The Republican War on Science,* New York: Basic Books, 2005, 47
39. Ibid.
40. M. Melbye et al., "Induced Abortion and the Risk of Breast Cancer," *New England Journal of Medicine*, January 9, 1997: 81–85.
41. National Cancer Institute, "Early Reproductive Events and Breast Cancer," November 25, 2002, www.house.gov/reform/min/pdfs/pdf_inves/pdf_admin_hhs_info_abc_fact_sheet_revis.pdf.
42. "Abortion Foes Seize on Reports of Cancer Link in Ad Campaign," *Los Angeles Times*, March 24, 2002.
43. National Cancer Institute, *Summary Report: Early Reproductive Events and Breast Cancer*, March 4, 2003, www.cancer.gov/cancerinfo/ere-workshop-report.
44. Marc Kaufman, "Pregnancy Centers Found to Give False Information on Abortion," *Washington Post*, July 18, 2006, A8.
45. Chris Mooney, *The Republican War on Science,* New York: Basic Books, 2005, 211.
46. Ibid, 210.

4

The Politics of Stem Cells

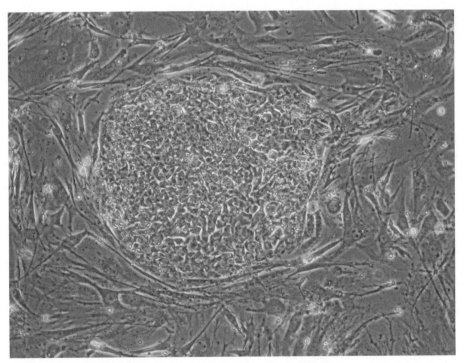

Stem cell. (Courtesy of the National Institute of Health.)

In the November 6, 1998, issue of *Science*, the prestigious journal of the American Association for the Advancement of Science, James Thomson, a University of Wisconsin professor and researcher, published a three-page paper describing how he grew the first viable human embryonic stem cells (hEMC) in his laboratory.[1]

A MEDICAL REVOLUTION

Thomson had obtained human embryos from a local *in vitro* fertilization (IVF) clinic. Each embryo contained eight cells surrounded by a thin membrane. Thomson placed them into culture dishes and after four or five days, they grew into blastocysts, hollow spheres consisting of about 100 cells and measuring about twice the diameter of a human hair. Thomson removed a mound of inner cells called the inner cell mass (ICM) from the blastocyst and placed it in another culture dish. Today, the term *embryonic stem cells* is used to describe the laboratory cultures of cells made from the ICM of blastocysts.

After considerable trial and error, Thomson found a growth nutrient that caused the ICM to grow. As described in Thomson's paper, the cells remained robust and multiplied for eight months. Laboratory technicians then removed the human cells from the culture dishes and injected them into mice, where they formed tumor-like structures made up of all the major human tissue types, including skin, muscle, and bone. Thomson had grown stem cells: cells that could become any tissue type in the human body.

Just a month later, Nobel Prize winner Harold Varmus, former director of the National Institutes of Health (NIH), told a government panel: "The development of cell lines that may produce almost every tissue of the human body is an unprecedented scientific breakthrough. It is not too unrealistic to say that the research has the potential to revolutionize the practice of medicine and improve the quality and length of life."[2]

There are two characteristics that distinguish stem cells from all the other types of cells in the human body. First is what is called *potency*, the ability of the stem cell to differentiate into various cell types. Second is the *asymmetric* cell division of stem cells, which replenishes the population of stem cells even as it generates the usual cell copy with specialized function and restricted developmental capacity. In this unique form of cell division, one cell retains its "stemness," becoming a part of the new generation of stem cells, whereas the other cell travels along the path to specialization.

As we shall see later in this chapter, politicians and religious leaders have made much of the difference between *embryonic stem cells* and *adult stem cells*. Embryonic stem cells are derived from the ICM of the early human embryo, the blastocyst. They have the greatest medical potential because of their ability to become any cell or tissue in the body. Adult stem cells, on the other hand, are found in small numbers in the fully developed animal, usually residing in the organs or tissue specified by their germ layer heritage. Every adult stem cell traces its origin back to the embryonic stem cells of the blastocyst.

A few examples of "regenerative medicine," the broad term currently used for stem-cell therapy, may give a hint of the medical potential of embryonic stem cells. Stem cells are now being used to treat cancer patients who formerly relied on bone-marrow transplants. For example, rather than extracting bone marrow through a needle inserted in the hip, donor cells are transplanted and travel through the blood to a cavity created in the marrow, where they colonize and produce red cells, immune cells, and platelets.

Stem cells are also used to regenerate diseased or damaged human parts, but Anthony Atala, a surgeon and researcher at Wake Forest University, warns against the science-fiction image of ready-made organs hanging in refrigerators waiting for patients. Instead, he says stem cells are better used to repair, rather than replace, organs. "If a heart has an infarct [damage], engineering new tissue from embryonic stem cells is best, because trying to biopsy a bit of the heart in order to isolate cells for tissue engineering endangers the patient."[3]

Perhaps the best-known image of successful stem-cell therapy is the video clip seen on TV programs like *60 Minutes*; the clip shows a rat with a damaged spinal cord, dragging its paralyzed hindquarters across its cage. The next video segment shows the same rat after an injection made from a line of embryonic stem cells. The rat raises itself on its hind legs and then takes a lap around the cage. This spectacular recovery was the result of a process used by University of California neurologist Hans Kierstead, who takes embryonic stem cells, differentiates them into colonies of neural cells, and injects them into rats within seven days of a spinal cord injury. Within two months of the treatment, the rats are able to walk properly.[4]

James Thomson, whose research paper initiated the stem-cell revolution, believes that stem cells will be more important as a research tool than as a method for transplanting engineered cells and tissues. Australian stem-cell biologist Alan Trounson agrees, saying, "We need to develop embryonic stem cell lines from patients who've got muscular dystrophy, Alzheimer's disease, and cystic fibrosis. That way we can develop drugs that actually block the disease from occurring."[5]

THE POLITICAL WAR ON STEM-CELL RESEARCH

The religious and political controversy surrounding stem-cell research is reminiscent of the struggle over abortion, described in the previous chapter. In both cases, the problem revolves around the connection between conception and the beginning of human life. Some religious conservatives regard the embryo as a person, regardless of whether it began naturally—through normal conception—or artificially—through *in vitro* fertilization or "nuclear transfer," the laboratory procedure used to create stem cells.

The essentially political nature of the battle over stem-cell research can be seen in the contrast between the inflexible rhetoric of conservative political leaders and the open-minded attitudes of constituencies that they claim to represent. A Harris poll conducted in 2004 found that 73 percent of Catholics supported stem-cell research, whereas only 11 percent opposed it. Among Protestants, the margin in favor of stem-cell research was eight to one. Even among evangelical Christians, the presumed base for opposition to stem-cell research, only one in five opposed it.[6]

Despite such broad public acceptance, the political baggage from the early anti-abortion movement has obscured the science and poisoned the debate on stem-cell research. In the wake of the 1973 *Roe v. Wade* decision, Congress halted federally funded embryo research pending the establishment of precise guidelines. The 1974 moratorium has been maintained to this day, keeping important medical issues like infertility, reproductive medicine, prenatal diagnosis, and embryonic stem-cell research beyond the reach of most American clinicians and scientists.

There have been fitful attempts to relax some of these restrictions on research. In 1979, the ethics advisory board of the Department of Health, Education, and Welfare (today named Health and Human Services) declared that "the human embryo is entitled to profound respect, but this respect does not necessarily encompass the full legal and moral rights attributed to humans," and recommended that the National Institutes of Health (NIH) fund research on extra-corporeal embryos up to 14 days of age.[7]

The recommendations were rejected by the full department, but seven years later a team of NIH researchers applied for funds to transplant fetal cells from elective abortions into patients with Parkinson's disease. Again, the Department of Health and Human Services (HHS) rejected the request and said it would reject all funding requests for fetal-cell tissue research. After a number of European countries conducted promising research in the field, NIH voted to fund both embryo and fetal research, but HHS secretary Louis Sullivan—a George H. W. Bush appointee—overruled the vote. In fact, Sullivan extended the moratorium indefinitely, claiming such research would increase the number of abortions.

In 1990, Congress voted to override the ban, but an outgoing President Bush vetoed the action. In 1993, President Bill Clinton issued an executive order instructing HHS secretary Donna Shalala to lift the 1974 ban. In recommending that embryo and fetal research be initiated, the NIH's Human Embryo Research Panel stated, "The promise of human benefit from [embryo] research is significant, carrying great potential benefit to infertile couples, families with genetic conditions, and individuals and families in need of effective therapies for a variety of diseases."[8]

Also in 1993, Congress passed the National Institutes of Health Revitalization Act (NIHRA), creating a system for vetting research about which ethical concerns have been voiced. The NIHRA stated that "if research has been recommended for approval . . . the Secretary may not withhold funds for the research because of ethical considerations" unless such withholding is first recommended by an advisory board convened to study the research and its implications.[9]

In compliance with the NIHRA, the Clinton administration convened such an advisory board to consider human embryonic stem-cell (hESC) research, and in 1994, the board concluded that hESC research was ethically permissible in many circumstances. Under pressure from pro-life advocates, Congress responded in 1996 by adopting the Dickey-Wicker Amendment, which prohibited funding by

HHS for research in which a human embryo is "created" or "destroyed."[10] The amendment forbade funding only for the *derivation* of the hESC, the process that destroys the source embryo. Thus, the amendment did not prohibit research on hESCs *after* their derivation, so long as no federal funds were used in the derivation process.

HHS Secretary Shalala interpreted this to mean that no embryos could be destroyed with government dollars, but that NIH funds could be used for research on embryonic stem-cell lines that had been established with private dollars. The NIH followed with a set of draft guidelines permitting research on embryos that remained after fertility treatments, provided that they were donated with informed consent and that no profit was received. Final guidelines were issued and approved by President Clinton on August 25, 2000, and the NIH began soliciting applications for research grants.

The optimism over stem-cell research dimmed during the 2000 presidential campaigns when the Republican candidate, then-Governor George Bush, promised that, if elected, he would reverse Clinton's policy. Upon taking office, newly elected President Bush called for a new HHS review of stem-cell policy, and the NIH ceased accepting grant applications for stem-cell research.

President Bush chose to ignore the NIHRA stipulation that funding may be withheld for ethical reasons only upon the recommendation of an ethics advisory board. Instead, on August 9, 2001, in his first televised address since his inauguration, Bush declared his unilateral policy: "I have given this issue a great deal of thought, prayer, and considerable reflection. . . . My position on these issues is shaped by deeply held beliefs. . . . I believe human life is a sacred gift from our Creator. I worry about a culture that devalues life, and believe as your President I have an important obligation to foster and encourage respect for life in America and throughout the world. And while we're all hopeful about the potential of this research, no one can be certain that the science will live up to the hope that it has generated."[11]

Bush said the new policy would allow federally funded research only "where the life and death decision has already been made," and in this context Bush assured his listeners that "more than sixty genetically diverse" embryonic stem-cell lines were already available for scientific research.[12]

In this highly personal and informal announcement, President Bush abandoned legal procedure, ignoring the Administrative Procedure Act's (APA) regulation-creating process and the NIHRA's mandated ethics review board. Indeed, the administration never issued an official executive order on the decision, and Congress never acted to endorse or override it. Bush's televised speech was never published in the Federal Register. Neither the speech nor the accompanying fact sheet bore the signature of the president, nor did they carry conventional titles such as "executive order" or "memorandum" that would classify them as presidential directives. Bush's informal words simply became the operative rule.

The NIH Final Guidelines, which had been promulgated through the APA process,were discarded, as announced in the Federal Register: "The President has determined the criteria that allow Federal funding for research using existing embryonic stem cell lines. . . . Thus the NIH Guidelines as they relate to human pluripotent stem cells derived from human embryos are no longer needed."[13]

In its scholarly report, "Censoring Science: A Stem Cell Story," the National Coalition Against Censorship (NCAC) concluded, "Despite the clear value of public debate on this issue, President Bush neither issued a proposed hESC policy nor collected public comment on the subject. He abandoned federal regulatory procedure and his Administration violated federal statutory law, effectively choking off federal funding for robust but regulated hESC research. President Bush restricted the marketplace of ideas and openly based his decision to do so only on his ethical and religious beliefs."[14]

Under the administration's new guidelines, federal funding would only be permitted for research on already existing stem-cell lines, and the embryos from which those lines were derived must have been created for and no longer needed for reproductive purposes, and they must have been obtained with informed consent and without financial inducement.

President Bush's decision to allow limited funding for stem-cell research helped him maintain the support of moderate Republicans, but scientists quickly pointed out that the new policy would only contribute to medical research if the number of available stem-cell lines was of sufficient size and contained quality specimens. Indeed, a senior administration official told *Time* magazine that the president's claim of "more than sixty" available lines "made this decision possible."[15]

The NIH subsequently released a list of the ten worldwide organizations that held the 64 cell lines—later revised upward to 78—that would now be eligible for federal funding. Where did this number of allegedly available lines come from? It came not from published, peer-reviewed scientific literature, but from a telephone survey conducted by the NIH. It soon became clear that the NIH figure did not refer to stem-cell *lines* but to *derivations*, the result of the process by which scientists remove the inner cell-mass of a blastocyst. But such attempts often do not succeed, because the cells fail to grow and divide sufficiently to produce a stem-cell *line*.

The president had confused *derivations* with *lines*. Paul Berg, Stanford professor of medicine and a Nobel laureate, explains that a derivation results when somebody takes a blastocyst from an IV clinic, cracks it open, pours it into a test tube, and stores it in a liquid-nitrogen tank. At that point, no one knows if it will become a line. With respect to the alleged sixty stem-cell lines Bush made available, Berg notes that "most of them died, and that's why there are so few now."[16]

Indeed, scientists soon discovered that, at best, only 22 lines were available for federal funding, and most of them were considered almost useless. In May 2003,

NIH director Doctor Elias Zerhouni told Congress that only 11 stem-cell lines were widely available to researchers, and even those few lines were potentially contaminated by viruses as a result of being developed with mouse feeder cells. Thus, what was originally claimed to be between 60 and 80 available lines was rapidly approaching 0. Chris Mooney, a journalist and author who specializes in science and environmental writing, has characterized Bush's statement on available stem-cell lines as "one of the most flagrant purely scientific deceptions ever perpetrated by a U.S. president on an unsuspecting audience. . . . Rather than seriously analyzing the number of stem cell lines in existence and assessing their viability for research, the White House cherry-picked a questionable number to justify a desired result. It used science as window dressing."[17]

THE SPECTER OF CLONING

The word *cloning* has many meanings. It can conjure up science-fiction images of vacant-eyed automatons, but it can also be as simple as ordinary cell division, where daughter cells are clones of their predecessors. Most cloning occurs naturally.

It was unfortunate that just one year before James Thomson's groundbreaking work on human stem cells, Ian Wilmut, a Scottish animal researcher, cloned a sheep named Dolly. The donor cell used to create Dolly was a somatic cell taken from the udder of a sheep. Until Dolly, animal cloning required taking nuclei directly from an embryo. Wilmut grew sheep-udder cells in a culture, then removed the nucleus from another sheep's unfertilized egg and fused the udder cell to the empty egg with a pulse of electricity. The protein in the egg's cytoplasm began to reprogram the genes in the donor nucleus, resulting in the development of blastocysts (early embryos), which were then implanted into surrogate mothers. The only successful pregnancy was Dolly. Wilmut's technique was dubbed somatic cell nuclear transfer (SCNT).

A year later, when Thomson proved that the ICM of a human embryo could be used to make a line of embryonic stem cells, scientists anticipated experiments combining the work of Wilmut and Thomson. SCNT could be used to grow a human blastocyst and then the ICM could be removed to make a line of embryonic stem cells. This is often referred to as *therapeutic cloning*, because the blastocyst is made for therapeutic purposes. It can never be implanted in a mother because it is destroyed when the ICM is removed. The belief that therapeutic cloning means making humans is a common misunderstanding. A human embryonic stem-cell line (hESC) makes cells for potential medical use and nothing more.

Nonetheless, in 2001, the U.S. House of Representatives followed the lead of the Bush administration and, by a wide majority, banned cloning of humans and voted to criminalize therapeutic cloning, the laboratory method used to generate embryonic stem cells. The penalty for conducting therapeutic cloning was set at a $1 million fine and up to 10 years in jail. In January 2002, the Senate introduced a bill that mirrored the House bill, but it never came to a vote.

Leon Kass, chairman of the President's Council on Bioethics (PCOB), reflects President Bush's view that somatic cell nuclear transfer (SCNT) could result in a human embryo, and a PCOB report declared, "We find it disturbing, even somewhat ignoble, to treat what are in fact the seeds of the next generation as mere raw materials for satisfying the needs of our own."[18]

In July 2002, Kass's PCOB recommended a four-year moratorium on all research involving SCNT if the intent is to produce human embryonic stem cells. Seven of the scientists on the Kass council voted against the moratorium, but all of the ethicists voted for it.

In May 2005, Senator Sam Brownback (R-KA) introduced the Human Cloning Prohibition Act, which makes the use of patient-matched, cloned,

National Institutes of Heath director Harold E. Varmus (with Dr. Caird E. Rexwood, Jr., right) testifies on the ethics of cloning before a House science and technology subcommittee, March 1997. In December 2008, Varmus, who shared the 1989 Nobel Prize in Physiology or Medicine with his research partner, J. Michael Bishop, was appointed co-chair of the President's Council of Advisors on Science and Technology. (AP Photo/Doug Mills)

embryonic stem cells a felony. Patients receiving therapy that had been developed through therapeutic cloning would be felons subject to the same fines and prison terms as the doctors and nurses treating them. Even American citizens who receive such treatment overseas would be subject to arrest when they return home.

Senator Brownback held a heavily publicized press conference for his bill, at which supporters spoke about the dangers of therapeutic cloning. It was claimed that there was no difference between reproductive cloning and therapeutic cloning. One speaker said, "Since it has no hope of curing patients, we have to question the motivation of scientists who want to do this cloning." Another said, "Cloning entails deliberately creating human beings in order to use their body parts."[19]

As bizarre as the claims for this bill were, they could not compare to the paranoia surrounding Brownback's "anti-chimera" bill. The word *chimera* comes from Greek mythology, referring to a freakish creature with a lion's head, a goat's body, and a serpent's tail. In science, the term can be used simply to describe an organism that has more than one set of genes. The pro-life community introduced the specter of the chimera in its campaign against therapeutic cloning.

Author Eve Herold recalls a meeting with an aide to Virginia senator George Allen, who was strongly supporting Senator Brownback's "anti-chimera" bill. The aide asked Herold, "What do you call those creatures on the evolutionary chart that aren't human—they're still apes, but they've just started to stand and walk upright?"

Herold asked if the aide was referring to *homo erectus*, and the aide answered, "Right, well we don't want any of those."[20]

Not all Republicans endorse President Bush's policy on stem cells and cloning. Former Republican senator John Danforth, an Episcopal priest and abortion opponent, says, "I find nothing in the Bible that tells me that cells in a lab dish are people. What I do find in the Gospels is an emphasis on healing—relieving people of their suffering."[21]

Senator Orrin Hatch (R-UT), a conservative icon in the party, has no moral objection to SCNT. He argues that life begins in the womb and cautions fellow conservatives: "Even those who believe that life begins at conception, even if the unison of sperm and egg takes place in the lab, need to consider carefully whether the joinder of an enucleated egg with a somatic cell nucleus, accompanied by chemical or electrical stimulation, should fairly be thought of as the same process as conception."[22]

In January 2008, scientists at a California company, Stemagen, reported that they had created the first mature cloned human embryo from skin cells, using a procedure similar to that described by Senator Hatch. The scientists had taken skin cells and fused them to eggs donated to help infertile women. Five of the resulting clones developed into blastocysts. The company hopes to harvest stem cells from the blastocysts and grow them into tissue that, when implanted into patients, would not be rejected, because the immune system would see them as a natural part of the body.

Stemagen's chief executive, Samuel Wood, emphasized that he has no interest in cloning people. "It's unethical and it's illegal," he said. "All of our efforts are being directed toward personalized medicine and diseases."[23]

Less than two weeks after Stemagen's announcement of its therapeutic cloning breakthrough, President Bush declared in his State of the Union address: "I call on Congress to pass legislation that bans unethical practices such as the buying, selling, patenting, or cloning of human life."[24]

A POLITICAL SUBSTITUTE FOR
EMBRYONIC STEM CELLS

As we saw earlier in this chapter, one does not need to target an embryo in order to find stem cells. There are specialized stem cells—called *adult stem cells*—that are located in many places throughout the human body. As these cells mature, they gradually lose their ability to change, and they eventually assume a specialized function as, say, a skin cell or a neuron. Some research laboratories have obtained experimental results suggesting the potential of adult stem cells to become virtually any cell or tissue in the body. Many political conservatives have seized upon this potential to justify the denial of federal funding for embryonic stem-cell research. After all, why intrude on the embryo if usable stem cells are available elsewhere?

The scientific community has its doubts. In 2005, acclaimed stem-cell researcher Irving Weissman said, "Several opponents [of embryonic stem-cell research] previously have claimed that any adult stem cell could turn into any other tissue, and so neither embryonic stem cell research nor nuclear transfer stem cell research would be necessary. Although this notion has been thoroughly disproven by several independent groups, the advocates persist in their claims. While we can hope that such disinformation is not accepted by the public, I fear that these claims are now being viewed through the lenses of politics and the media, and not on the basis of medical or scientific evidence."[25]

Not only is the research on adult stems inconclusive, but few scientists believe that adult stem cells can ever be the sole answer for curing disease and physical dysfunction. Instead, they say, our medical progress will require the open investigation of both types of cells. In any case, biologists are unanimous in concluding that even the most potent adult stem cells cannot approach the therapeutic power of embryonic stem cells.

Despite the scientific consensus, politics has framed the issue in "either/or" terms. Even the scientific journals have commented on this disturbing trend. The very first issue of the journal *Stem Cell Reviews* comments: "The opponents of embryonic stem cell research argue that anything that can be done with embryonic stem cells can be accomplished with adult stem cells. Proponents of embryonic stem cell research have used the negative data (that adult stem cells are not plastic) to argue that adult stem cells can never do what can be done with ESCs."[26]

The belief that adult stem cells are an *alternative* to embryonic stem cells is an article of faith among pro-life conservatives, but if that argument is to prevail it must be couched in scientific terms. Some adult stem-cell proponents, such as bioethics writer Wesley Smith, make no attempt to deny their religious agenda. But the most prominent scientist espousing the adult-stem-cell-only argument is David Prentice, former professor at Indiana State University and current fellow at the Family Research Council, a Christian conservative organization.

In a recent interview, Prentice described himself as a Christian and "definitely conservative," but claimed, "I'm arguing from the science."[27] He believes that adult stem cells may have greater biological potential than embryonic stem cells and therefore argues that we may no longer need to confront the moral issues surrounding the human embryo.

Prentice has served as an adviser to conservative Republican senator Sam Brownback of Kansas, who convened a June 2004 congressional hearing devoted to adult stem cells, at which Brownback declared that "today's hearing is about miracles" and promised the audience that "today you will see some answers to prayers."[28] Brownback held yet another hearing in September 2004, this time featuring Prentice, his scientific adviser. Prentice declared that "adult stem cells have been shown by the published evidence to be a more promising alternative for patient treatments, with a vast biomedical potential."[29]

Adult stem cells quickly became a flash point in another political venue, the President's Council on Bioethics. On February 27, 2004, Elizabeth Blackburn, a renowned researcher at the University of California and former president of the American Society for Cell Biology, was dismissed from the PCOB because of her inadequate support for adult stem-cell research. Blackburn had criticized the commission's report, *Monitoring Stem Cell Research*, for its one-sided espousal of adult stem cells, concluding, "The capabilities of embryonic versus adult stem cells, and their relative promise for medicine, were obfuscated." She would later explain that the key issue in her dismissal was her concern that the PCOB was giving great credence to what she considered to be "pretty iffy" science with respect to adult stem cells.[30]

In late 2007, research papers in the journals *Science* and *Cell* described a new method for tricking skin cells into acting like embryonic stem cells. In December 2007, James Thomson, the first scientist to create human embryonic stem cells, coauthored an op-ed article in the *Washington Post* warning that scientists were still uncertain whether "souped-up skin cells hold the same promise as their embryonic cousins do." Thomson explained that the U.S. and Japanese teams that reprogrammed the skin cells depended entirely on previous embryonic stem-cell research, and thus the promise of skin cells did not justify the current federal policy of withholding funds for embryonic stem-cell research.

Thomson concluded: "We hope Congress will override the president's veto of the Stem Cell Research Enhancement Act. Further delays in pursuing the clearly viable option of embryonic stem cells will result in an irretrievable loss of time, especially if the new approach fails to prove itself."[31]

Congress failed to override the president's veto, because many members now wondered whether embryonic stem cells were really essential to the stem-cell revolution. The research papers published in late 2007 certainly raised hopes that the controversy of embryonic stem-cell research could be bypassed, but conspiracy theorists seized upon the timing of such politically sensitive reports. Was it just coincidence that they appeared just as Congress was preparing to vote on stem-cell bills? In fact, the same thing had occurred in June 2007 and in January as well.

On January 8, 2007, after months of intense lobbying, Congress prepared to vote on a bill that would loosen President Bush's restrictions of stem-cell research. That very morning, newspapers touted exciting new research published in a British journal suggesting that viable stem cells could be made from placenta cells without the need for an embryo. The bill passed, but by an insufficient margin to override a presidential veto.

Just five months later, the House was ready to vote on a similar bill to reduce restrictions on stem-cell research. National polls indicating public support for such research buoyed Democratic hopes that the bill would pass by a sizable margin. Again, on that very morning, the lead story in almost every daily newspaper blared the news of research indicating that stem cells could be made from ordinary skin cells.

On the House floor, Democratic Caucus chairman Rahm Emanuel (IL) expressed his frustration: "It is ironic that every time we vote on this legislation, all of a sudden there is a major scientific discovery that basically says, 'You don't have to do stem cell research.'"[32]

Even those opposing the stem-cell bill couldn't resist a good-humored interpretation of events. Richard Doerflinger of the U.S. Conference of Catholic Bishops quipped, "I said to one of the congressional staffers of my general persuasion, 'Doesn't God have a sense of humor?' There is somebody looking out for us! God is telling us he is there."[33]

More-serious observers pointed out that papers on stem cells are published so regularly that the odds are high that some of them will come out when Congress is voting on the issue. The senior press officer for *Nature*, one of the journals that published stem-cell papers as Congress considered related legislation, said, "*Nature* has no hidden agenda in publishing these papers."[34]

THE STATE RESPONSE TO FEDERAL STEM-CELL POLICY

From the moment that James Thomson brought the promise of stem cells before the public, polls have indicated strong popular support for research to bring the scientific promise to fruition. We have seen how national politics has effectively blocked federal funding for that research, but state politicians in both parties have been much more independent in their approach to stem cells.

Seven large states are leading the political push for stem-cell funding. Since 2006, California, Connecticut, Illinois, Maryland, New Jersey, New York, and Wisconsin have awarded $230 million in grants, more than three times what the federal government spent on embryonic stem-cell research during that time. When all seven states' commitments are totaled, it comes to nearly $5 billion over the next 10 years. Three other states, Iowa, Massachusetts, and Missouri, have affirmed the legality of such research.

The most spectacular state response to federal restrictions came in November 2004, when the citizens of California voted to pass Proposition 71, a state ballot initiative that established an end run around federal funding.

California had already declared itself a "restriction-free" zone in late 2002, when then-Governor Gray Davis signed a law that allowed nuclear transfer and embryo research. Because no funding accompanied the legislation, an alliance was formed between state legislator Deborah Ortiz, Juvenile Diabetes Research Foundation CEO Peter Van Etten, and real-estate developer Robert Klein, who became the dynamo behind Proposition 71.

The voter initiative would raise bonds to finance a new California Institute for Regenerative Medicine (CIRM), presided over by a 29-member board and three advisory committees composed of stem-cell scientists, health advocacy representatives, and real-estate experts. Three billion dollars would be raised and spent over 15 years, primarily in nonprofit research institutions. Stanford scientists Paul Berg and Irving Weissman and University of California neuroscientist Hans Kirstead were quickly signed on to the project. Even Governor Schwarzenegger threw his weight behind Proposition 71, which passed by a comfortable margin of 59 percent in favor to 41 percent against.

A number of conservative and religious organizations brought suit to prevent CIRM from undertaking its research. Because its long-term funding was tied up in litigation, CIRM was unable to award research grants. When President Bush vetoed a federal bill to increase the number of available stem-cell lines, Governor Schwarzenegger responded by issuing a loan of $150 million from the state budget to support the stem-cell initiative. His action allowed the first CIRM grants to be awarded, leading CIRM's president Zach Hall to remark that Bush's veto had "brought us to life."[35]

CIRM quickly issued requests for proposals for seed grants, with funding of up to $200,000 per year for two years, and up to $400,000 per year for four years for comprehensive grants. CIRM also announced plans to fund 15 California facilities that will provide laboratory space and technical support for culturing embryonic stem cells, permitting researchers to work on non-approved stem-cell lines.

In April 2006, CIRM won a legal victory when a Superior Court judge rejected lawsuits challenging the institute's legality. The decision was appealed, but stem-cell advocates were optimistic. Finally, on May 16, 2007, the California Supreme Court denied a petition to review the constitutionality of Proposition 71, ending the litigation and freeing CIRM to distribute funds to researchers.

State Controller John Chiang released the following statement in response to the ruling: "I am pleased that the Supreme Court has reaffirmed the voters' will and ended the litigation that tied up the funding for California's investment in stem cell research. California can now issue the $3 billion in bonds to fund and accelerate stem cell research, offering hope of potential life-saving medical discoveries. Today's ruling will also help the State move quickly to foster opportunities in medical science and new technologies."[36]

The importance of Governor Schwarzenegger's loan initiative in providing early grant money during the litigation delays could be seen on April 8, 2008, when the first clinical trials began on a stem-cell therapy that had been funded by a seed grant from CIRM. Robert Klein, chair of the CIRM Independent Citizens Oversight Committee, said, "Our grants review committee was able to award this grant in February 2007, while our bond authority was delayed by litigation, because of the assurance of funding provided by Governor Schwarzenegger authorizing up to $150 million in loans to CIRM the previous August. The more than 100,000 Americans with these blood disorders, which are severely debilitating and can lead to leukemia, thank the Governor for advancing the CIRM model designed to accelerate the quest for cures."[37]

Even as such clinical trials were publicized, the receipt of 54 new applications for the second round of faculty grants was announced on April 8, 2008. The applications came from 30 academic and nonprofit California institutions and included 19 applications for a Physician-Scientist Award and 35 for a Scientist Award. CIRM said the awards would "strengthen the ranks of a new generation of stem cell scientists as the rapidly evolving field works to achieve a critical mass of investigators focused on stem cell research."[38]

The impressive size of CIRM may allow it to replace NIH as a stem-cell funder and even compete with foreign nations that support stem-cell research. California has become a magnet for prominent stem-cell scientists, and recent additions to CIRM have come from Harvard, Johns Hopkins, Washington University, the University of Michigan, and the Hospital for Sick Children in Toronto.

The combination of President Bush's intransigence and California's successful institute for regenerative medicine has energized state politics on stem-cell issues, because many states fear the flight of their own scientists to the California research magnet. New Jersey was actually the first state to underwrite stem-cell research, appropriating $10 million in January 2004. In 2006, Governor Jon Corzine signed a bill providing $270 million to build state research facilities, with $150 million earmarked for the Stem Cell Institute of New Jersey, for which ground was broken in late 2007.

This Democratic, pro-choice state seemed poised to lead the way in locally funded stem-cell research, but conservative opposition, led by New Jersey Right to Life and the Catholic church, continued to stymie major funding bills. Finally, in November 2007, New Jersey voters overwhelmingly turned down a bond issue that would have allowed the state to borrow $450 million over a 10-year period to support stem-cell research. Michael Werner, a biotechnology industry consultant, says, "I think the New Jersey vote demonstrates how difficult it is for individual states to make a substantial financial commitment to stem cell research. . . . [I]t is particularly true because stem cells are so controversial."[39]

Even California, the pacesetter in state support for stem cells, expressed disappointment at the New Jersey vote. Richard Murphy, president of the California Institute for Regenerative Medicine, said, "We want every state to be able to put their best minds to this [stem cell] field. Unfortunately, New Jersey, which has some great scientists, is not going to have the ability to participate in the stem cell revolution as robustly as they might have if this money was provided. And that hurts everybody."[40]

Missouri, a conservative state on most issues, has been an interesting example of conflict and compromise on stem-cell politics. Former Republican senator John Danforth cited the New Testament in support of an amendment to the Missouri Constitution establishing the legality of stem-cell research. Danforth made a moral distinction between abortion and embryonic stem-cell research, noting that the blastocysts from which stem cells are derived "have not been implanted in a uterus. They cannot become walking, talking, breathing human beings."[41]

The Missouri ballot initiative was a response to efforts by state legislators to ban somatic cell nuclear transfer (SCNT), the process by which an enucleated egg produces a blastocyst from which stem cells can be obtained. Opponents to the amendment, including the Catholic Archbishop of St. Louis and the Missouri Right to Life group, consider SCNT to be human cloning.

Donn Rubin, chairman of the Missouri Coalition for Lifesaving Cures, which led the push for the constitutional amendment, said its effect would be to ensure that any research allowed under federal law would be permitted in Missouri as well. Rubin said the quality of science, medical care, and the biotechnology industry would be at risk if the amendment fails. He concluded, "If our state were to pass laws that threaten to jail scientists merely for . . . seeking cures, it would have a devastating effect on our ability to continue to attract the best and the brightest."[42]

Supporters of the amendment included patient groups, medical organizations, academic institutions, and business groups. The campaign for the amendment was financed by Jim Stowars, founder of the Stowars Institute for Medical Research in Kansas City, which hopes to become a major center for stem-cell research. The Stowars Institute had been a prominent supporter of the state's nonprofit science research, and Stowars threatened to withdraw $250 million of its funding for a new Kansas City campus until Missouri law allowed embryonic stem-cell research. Stowars put an exclamation point on his threat by sending $6 million out of state to fund Harvard stem-cell scientist Kevin Eggan.

Eggan had considered working for Stowars but cited Missouri politics in declining an offer. "I couldn't rationalize the risk of waking up some morning to find that I was a felon because of an action taken by the state Legislature," he said.[43]

In 2006, Missouri voters narrowly approved the constitutional amendment, but conservative lawmakers introduced a bill to repeal the amendment. That initiative failed, but they succeeded in blocking bioscience funding for the University of Missouri, claiming that the money might be spent on embryonic studies. In response to the unstable Missouri politics, Stowars moved $800 million of its $2 billion private research trust to a separate, out-of-state funding organization.

Clearly, state politics on stem cells continues to be volatile, but the uncertainty of federal funding makes state money essential for the growth of the research. James Fossett, a bioethicist with the Rockefeller Institute of Government, says, "With a budget deficit and the war in Iraq, the odds of a major bump in federal stem-cell funding are slim no matter who is elected president. The economic opportunities presented by the research make it unlikely states will diminish their funding efforts."[44]

As the states compete for stem-cell research dollars, researchers welcome the infusion of state funding, but they express concern over the patchwork of laws that support it. There is a fear that without a coherent federal policy toward stem-cell research, the hit-and-miss passage of state legislation may result in an unreliable and Balkanized legal framework.

NOTES

1. James Thomson, "Embryonic Stem Cell Lines Derived from Human Blastocysts," *Science,* November 6, 1998.
2. Statement of Harold Varmus, Director, National Institutes of Health, before the Senate Appropriations Subcommittee on Labor, Health and Human Services, Education and Related Agencies, December 2, 1998. http://stemcells.nih.gov/policy/statements/120298.asp.
3. Christopher Thomas Scott, *Stem Cell Now: A Brief Introduction to the Coming Medical Revolution* (London: Plume, 2006), 113–114.
4. Daniel Schorn, "Scientist Hopes for Stem Cell Success," CBS News, February 26, 2006. www.cbsnews.com/stories/2006/02/23/60minutes/main1341635/shtml.
5. Ibid., 117.
6. Harris Poll no. 58, August 18, 2004, www.harrisinteractive.com/harris_poll/index.asp?.
7. Albert Jonson, *The Birth of Bioethics* (New York: Oxford University Press, 1988), 311.
8. National Institutes of Health Embryo Research Panel Report, vol. 1, September 1994, www.bioethics.gov/reports/past_commissions/index.html.
9. *National Institutes of Health Revitalization Act of 1993*, Public Law 103–43, sec. 113 (June 10, 1993). http://grants.nih.gov/grants/olaw/pl103-43.pdf.
10. *The Balanced Budget Downpayment Act I*, Public Law 104-99, sec. 128(2), *U.S. Statutes at Large* 110 (1996): 26, 34.
11. President George W. Bush, "President Discusses Stem Cell Research," August 9, 2001, www.whitehouse.gov/news/releases/2001/08/print/20010809-2.html.

12. Ibid.
13. Federal Register: November 13, 2001 (Volume 6, Number 220). National Institutes of Health Guidelines for Research Using Puripotent Stem Cells. Notice: Withdrawal of NIH Guidelines for Research Using Pluripotent Stem Cells Derived from Human Embryos. http://stemcells.nih.gov/staticresources/news/newsArchives/fr14no01-95.asp.
14. National Coalition Against Censorship, "Censoring Science: A Stem Cell Story," Winter 2008, www.ncac.org/images/ncacimages/Censoring_Science-NCAC.pdf.
15. Richard Lacayo, "How Bush Got There," *Time*, August 20, 2001.
16. Chris Mooney, *The Republican War on Science* (New York: Basic Books, 2005), 4.
17. Ibid., 2, 4.
18. Genome News Network, "The Politics of Stem Cells," February 21, 2003, www.genomenewsnetwork.org/articles/02_03/stem.shtml.
19. Eve Herold, *Stem Cell Wars* (New York: Palgrave Macmillan, 2006), 106.
20. Ibid., 108.
21. Susan Okie, "Stem-Cell Politics," *New England Journal of Medicine* 355, no. 16, (2006): 1633.
22. Genome News Network, "The Politics of Stem Cells," February 21, 2003, www.genomenewsnetwork.org/articles/02_03/stem.shtml.
23. "Mature Human Embryos Created from Adult Stem Cells," *Washington Post*, January 8, 2008, A1.
24. "Full Text of President Bush's 2008 State of the Union Address," January 29, 2008, Voice of America.com. www.voanews.com/english/archive/2008-01/2008-01-29 -voa6.cfm?CFID.
25. Stanford School of Medicine, Office of Communication and Public Affairs, "Stanford Q & A," December 2005, http://mednews.stanford.edu/releases/2005/december/stemcell5ques.html.
26. Stewart Sell, "Adult Stem Cell Plasticity," *Stem Cell Reviews* 1 (2005): 1–5.
27. Chris Mooney, *The Republican War on Science* (New York: Basic Books, 2005), 195.
28. Ibid, pp. 197–198.
29. Ibid.
30. Elizabeth Blackburn, "A 'Full Range' of Bioethical Views Just Got Narrower," *Washington Post*, March 7, 2004.
31. Alan I. Leshner and James A. Thomson, "Standing in the Way of Stem Cell Research," *Washington Post*, December 3, 2007, A17.
32. Rick Weiss, "Darn Cells, Dividing Yet Again!" *Washington Post*, June 10, 2001, D5.
33. Ibid.
34. Ibid.
35. Susan Okie, "Stem-Cell Politics," *New England Journal of Medicine* 355, no. 16 (October 19, 2006): 1633.
36. "Litigation to Stop California Stem Cell Funding Finally Over," *Wired Science*, May 16, 2007, http://blog.wired.com/wiredscience/2007/05/litigation_to_s.html.
37. CIRM, "First Clinical Trial Begins for a Therapy Enabled by CIRM Funding," April 8, 2008, www.cirm.ca.gov.
38. CIRM, "CIRM Receive 54 Applications for Second Round of New Faculty Grants," April 8, 2008, www.cirm.ca.gov.

39. Terri Somers, "Defeat in New Jersey of Stem Cell Initiative Raises Alarm,"
    SignOnSanDiego.com, November 11, 2007, 2, www.signonsandiego.com/news/
    business/20071111-9999-1b11njstems.html.

40. Ibid., 4.

41. Susan Okie, "Stem-Cell Politics," *New England Journal of Medicine* 355, no. 16
    (October 19, 2006): 1633.

42. Ibid., 1636.

43. "States Vie for Stem-Cell Scientists," Stateline.org, January 15, 2008, 3, www
    .stateline.org/live/details/story?contentId=270951.

44. Ibid., 5.

5

The Heated Politics of Global Warming

Former Vice President Al Gore testifies on global climate change before the Senate Foreign Relations Committee, January 28, 2009. (AP Photo/ Susan Walsh)

PROPHETS OF CLIMATE CHANGE

Al Gore is popularly accepted as the Paul Revere of global warming, but scientists have been aware of the "greenhouse effect," the cause of global warming, for over a century. Late in the 19th century, Swedish scientist Svante Arrhenius described the role of industrial emissions in raising carbon-dioxide levels in the atmosphere, trapping radiated heat that would otherwise escape. Arrhenius calculated that increases in these greenhouse gases could result in dramatic warming of the Earth. Although the data was indisputable, most scientists were unconcerned, believing that the oceans could absorb enough of the carbon dioxide to prevent the accumulation of greenhouse gases in the atmosphere.

Not until the 1950s did climate research show that the oceans could not absorb enough carbon dioxide to offset growing auto and industrial emissions. At the same time, researchers examining the carbon content of ancient air samples embedded in artic ice discovered that carbon-dioxide levels and temperature correlated closely throughout the Earth's history. By the 1980s, global warming was an acknowledged fact among most climate scientists, and the decade set an all-time record for recorded temperatures.

On June 23, 1988, Senator Timothy Wirth (D-CO), one of the few politicians who had expressed concern about global warming, convened a hearing on the issue before his Senate Energy Committee. Wirth made good political use of the sweltering summer heat, calling the weather bureau to help select the hottest day of the year for the hearing. Wirth recalls, "We scheduled the hearing that day, and, bingo, it was the hottest day in Washington."[1]

Wirth may have thought he needed to stage-manage the hearing, but over the next decade climate research would reveal that:

1. Seventeen of the eighteen hottest days on record would occur after 1980.
2. The decade of the 1990s would be the hottest in the last millennium.
3. The year 1998 would be the hottest year in recorded human history.
4. The Earth is heating at a rate faster than at any time in the last 10,000 years.

Clearly, Wirth did not need to dramatize the heat to make the case for global warming. The weather would speak for itself, but Wirth's star witness, NASA climatologist James Hansen, could help explain it. Hansen testified, "Number one, the earth is warmer in 1988 than at any time in the history of instrumental measurements. Number two, global warming is now large enough that we can ascribe, with a high degree of confidence, a cause and effect relationship to the greenhouse effect."[2]

Hansen's testimony was dramatic but measured. Of all his words, the phrase that was most frequently cited by the press was "99 percent confidence," his characterization of the likelihood that the Earth was warming due to human-made greenhouse gases. Hansen himself acknowledges, "I think it was that 99 percent probability statement which got a lot of attention."[3]

The scientific debate was intensifying worldwide. Within a week of Hansen's testimony, more than 300 leaders in science, politics, law, and environmental studies gathered in Toronto to address problems related to climate change and global warming. A year later, Senator Al Gore (D-TN) invited Hansen to testify once more before his Committee on Commerce, Science, and Transportation, but President George H. W. Bush required Hansen to revise his prepared text, deleting his assertion that the greenhouse effect was warming the planet. This blatant attempt at scientific censorship, described in detail later in this chapter, could not silence the indomitable Hansen, whose research and writing had won him scientific allies around the world.

Climate change became an issue in the 1992 presidential campaign when Democratic candidate Bill Clinton challenged President Bush to attend the upcoming Earth Summit in Rio de Janeiro and commit the United States to a global warming treaty. Bush's EPA administrator, William Reilly, himself a strong advocate for action on climate change, recalls that many of the president's advisers urged him not to attend, saying it would be an "environmental jamboree" and that "we would be the punching bag down there."[4]

Bush eventually decided to attend the Earth Summit, which turned out to be the largest gathering of world leaders in history. He signed an important treaty on climate change, committing the United States to reducing its emissions by the year 2000 to the level they had been in 1990—a relatively easy target. But the signature came with a catch, because Bush insisted that the targets be voluntary. EPA Administrator Reilly had recommended that the president commit to a mandatory program to control carbon-dioxide emissions, but he was a lonely proponent of that position.

In 1993, when Bill Clinton and Al Gore took over the White House, environmentalists were optimistic. Early on, Clinton introduced a "BTU tax," a tax on energy consumption designed to reduce carbon emissions. The issue was quickly politicized when Republicans charged that a BTU tax would hurt middle-class families. Clinton's own party joined Republicans in opposition, as Democrats from western states rich in oil and coal rejected it before it even came to a vote.

Philip Clapp, president of the National Environmental Trust, said, "They got the policy right, but they got the politics entirely wrong." Eileen Claussen, a member of Clinton's State Department, said, "Either they did not know how to do the politics, or they were not serious about really getting it done."[5]

Meanwhile, the evidence presented on global warming became more ominous. In 1995, Hansen wrote, "The continued increase of fossil-fuel use would lead to about 2.5 degrees C [4.5 degrees F] global warming by the end of the twenty-first century, making the earth warmer than it has been in millions of years—in fact, approaching the warmth of the Mesozoic, the age of the dinosaurs."[6]

That same year, the Intergovernmental Panel on Climate Change (IPCC) concluded, "The balance of evidence suggests that there is a discernible influence on global climate" due to greenhouse gas emissions.[7]

By 1997, worldwide pressure to address global warming led President Clinton to send Vice President Gore to the Kyoto, Japan, negotiations on an international climate treaty. In Kyoto, Gore set out the administration's position, a mandatory cap on carbon emissions, and committed the United States to the Kyoto climate treaty. When he returned to Washington, it was clear that the votes for ratification of the Kyoto treaty were not there, and Clinton decided not to bring it to the Senate at all. Indeed, the administration never bothered to fight for it. Eileen Claussen, the administration's State Department representative, resigned her post, in part because of the way the Clinton administration handled the Kyoto treaty.

"I thought it was dishonest to negotiate a treaty that you had no hope of getting ratified," said Claussen.[8]

Despite its inability to achieve ratification of the Kyoto Protocol, the Clinton administration remained engaged with the ongoing international negotiations and maintained its commitment to Kyoto's major goal: to reduce aggregate carbon emissions in the industrialized world by 5.2 percent below 1990 levels.

In January 2001, the Intergovernmental Panel on Climate Change (IPCC) brought together more than 2,000 scientists from 100 countries to form the largest peer-reviewed scientific collaboration in history. They concluded that droughts, floods, and violent storms across the planet would intensify as emissions from coal and oil drove up temperatures.

In covering the IPCC's findings, *The Washington Post* reported, "The most comprehensive study on the subject [showed] that Earth's average temperature could rise by as much as 10.4 degrees over the next 100 years—the most rapid change in 10 millennia and more than 60 percent higher than the same group predicted less than six years ago."[9]

The work of the IPCC was a major irritant to the new administration of President George W. Bush, whose position on global warming was in conflict with the IPCC. When Bush took office, ExxonMobil lobbyist Randy Randol sent a memo to the White House Council on Environmental Quality denouncing IPCC chairman Robert Watson—a leading atmospheric scientist—and claiming that he had been "handpicked by Al Gore" in order to "get media coverage for his views." The memo asked, "Can Watson be replaced at the request of the U.S.?" It then identified several other climate experts and asked about their being "removed from their positions of influence."[10]

A year later, the Bush administration successfully campaigned against Watson's reelection as IPCC chairman, and Watson was replaced by a State Department–supported candidate.

Next, the Bush administration tried to rebut the IPCC findings by requesting a review by the U.S. National Academy of Sciences (NAS). To the consternation of conservatives, the 2001 NAS review agreed with the IPCC conclusions, stating that "greenhouse gases are accumulating in Earth's atmosphere as the result of human activities, causing surface air temperatures and subsurface ocean temperatures to rise." As if that were not explicit enough, the NAS report clearly states, "The IPCC's conclusion that most of the warming of the last 50 years is likely to have been due to the increase in greenhouse gas concentrations accurately reflects the current thinking of the scientific community on this issue."[11]

Despite such a forceful confirmation of the IPCC findings, the Bush administration claimed that the NAS report was still not unequivocal on the issue of global warming. A Bush campaign spokesman told *Science* magazine that "the nation's most respected scientific body found that key uncertainties remain concerning the underlying causes and nature of climate change."[12]

President Bush's chaotic and controversial climate policies were signaled during the first few months of his presidency, when he appointed Christine Todd Whitman as EPA administrator and then renounced her authority. During his 2000 campaign, Bush had surprised and angered conservatives by promising mandatory cuts in greenhouse gas emissions. The campaign pledge was widely regarded as a political ploy to "outgreen" his environmentalist opponent, Al Gore, but his appointment of Whitman, who had a strong environmental record, raised more eyebrows.

Whitman's first major assignment was attendance at the ongoing climate treaty talks in Trieste, Italy. Whitman sent a memo to the president warning that a failure to commit the United States to cutting greenhouse gases would undermine the nation's standing among its allies. She wrote, "Mr. President, this is a credibility issue for the U.S. in the international community. It is also an issue that is resonating here at home. We need to appear engaged."[13]

Given Bush's public promise to cap greenhouse gas emissions, Whitman had no reason to believe that the president would object to her repeating the same pledge in Trieste, but, just to be sure, she ran it by Bush's chief of staff Andrew Card, his national security adviser Condoleezza Rice, and others in the administration whom she thought would be interested. No one saw any problem with her message, and just before her trip she appeared on CNN, where she reminded her interviewer of Bush's campaign pledge and added, "He has also been very clear that the science is good on global warming."[14]

Whitman had no way of knowing that as soon as she left for Italy, Vice President Cheney would secretly convene an energy task force at which representatives of the oil, gas, and coal industries would advise Bush to reverse his pledge on mandatory carbon caps. By the time Whitman returned from Italy, Bush had renounced his pledge on emissions, making Whitman's representations in Trieste seem foolish and uninformed. She met with the president to clarify the issue and tried to discuss the merits of an emissions cap, but Bush told her that the decision had already been made. Whitman recalls, "There really wasn't much discussion about climate change or how we could live up to the campaign promise or anything like that."[15]

Without the president's support, and facing open hostility from the vice president, a chastened and humiliated Whitman puttered about the EPA until her inevitable resignation in early 2003.

At an environmental conference held in Stockholm, U.S. Environmental
Protection Agency Administrator Christine Todd Whitman signs a 127-nation
agreement banning toxic chemicals such as PCBs and dioxin, May 22, 2001.
(AP Photo/Pressens Bild/Fredrik Persson)

Around the time of Whitman's 2001 trip to Trieste, Bush had received a stern letter from the European Union challenging him to find the "political courage" to confront the climate crisis. The letter said an agreement "leading to real reductions in greenhouse gas emissions is of the utmost importance. . . . The global and long-term importance of climate change and the need for a joint effort by all industrialized countries in this field makes it an integral part of relations between the USA and the EU."[16]

President Bush dismissed the EU's entreaty and six days later withdrew the United States entirely from the Kyoto Protocol, saying it was in America's economic interest.

CENSORSHIP AND SUPPRESSION

As a succession of scientific reports made it difficult for politicians to deny the reality of global warming, the Bush administration began a brazen campaign of scientific intimidation and censorship. One particularly prestigious report would become the center of controversy. Officially titled the "U.S. National Assessment of the Potential Consequences of Climate Variability and Change," but often referred to as the "National Assessment," this meticulously drafted and peer-reviewed document details the impacts of global warming on the various geographical regions and sectors of the United States. Its careful documentation of potential damage to a broad swath of America, including forests, grasslands, and coastlines, threatened to arouse popular concern on a level that would make inaction impossible. As a result, a concerted attack on the document was initiated by political conservatives and the fossil-fuel lobby.

First, Congress quietly passed a law—the Federal Data Quality Act—that would allow the suppression of federal reports if the technical information therein was not useful, reliable, and reproducible. The Center for Regulatory Effectiveness, a conservative think tank, promptly wrote to the Office of Management and Budget and the Office of Science and Technology Policy, citing the Data Quality Act and demanding that the National Assessment be withdrawn. When this demand failed, another conservative group tried direct legal action.

The Competitive Enterprise Institute (CEI) sued the White House's environmental arm, the Council on Environmental Quality, to have the National Assessment removed from circulation. The CEI explained, "These junk science reports are already being used . . . by global warming alarmists and states seeking to hobble those more competitive."[17]

A Freedom of Information Act (FOIA) request by the attorneys general of Maine and Connecticut subsequently acquired White House e-mails that revealed an extraordinary conspiracy. The Bush administration had secretly requested that the CEI sue the White House in order to have the National Assessment withdrawn! After the White House settled the suit with CEI, the federal Web site displaying the National Assessment was amended to include a warning that the document had not been subjected to the Data Quality Act requirements. The scientific community would, of course, disregard such a silly caveat, but the Bush administration used it as a pretext to discard the National Assessment and prohibit any further use of it in planning and policy making.

Joseph Romm, head of the Office of Energy Efficiency and Renewable Energy in the Clinton Administration, describes the shocking complicity of the Bush administration: "In short, the White House conspired with an oil-company-funded think tank to block a major government scientific report that sought to spell out the dangers of climate change to Americans. The failure of our government . . . to provide our people with a national assessment of the potential consequences of climate change denies Americans the information they need to make decisions."[18]

In June 2003, as the Environmental Protection Agency (EPA) was about to publish a report on the state of the environment, a former EPA official leaked a copy of an earlier draft of the report and an internal memo describing White House deletions from the climate section. The White House had removed all references to studies showing potential harm of global warming to health and ecosystems. Among the deletions were statements linking global warming to human activity such as industrial or automobile emissions. White House officials also deleted a reference to a study showing that global temperatures had risen more sharply in the past decade than in the previous 1,000 years. In its place was inserted a study financed by the American Petroleum Institute that questioned that conclusion.

Jeremy Symons, a climate expert at the National Wildlife Federation, said, "This is like the White House directing the secretary of labor to alter unemployment data to paint a rosy economic picture."[19]

As their research and counsel were ignored or censored, climate scientists within the Bush administration became disheartened, and many chose to leave government service. In March 2005, Rick Piltz, policy analyst at the U.S. Climate Change Science Program, resigned in protest over the Bush administration's manipulation of climate research. In a lengthy resignation letter, Piltz asked, "Why are administration officials who are not career science program managers, and whose job is essentially to satisfy the administration's constituencies on climate change politics and policy, participating in governing the Climate Change Science Program? In particular, why does a former oil industry lobbyist have the authority to edit scientific statements developed by career federal science professionals?"[20]

Piltz said the ability to make good decisions on climate change policy depended on "a free, accurate, honest, and unimpeded flow of communications about the findings of scientific research and scientifically based assessments of relevant issues. To block, distort or manipulate this flow . . . in order to further political agendas can be seen as analogous to interference with freedom of the press. The White House should not be in the business of pre-clearing scientific communications based on political impact."[21]

Perhaps the most heavy-handed White House censorship of climate science was imposed on NASA climatologist James Hansen, whose published warnings of the dangers of global warming infuriated the Bush administration. In 2005, the White House actually assigned a personal "minder" to follow Hansen and monitor his public communications. Hansen said that officials at NASA had been ordered to review his scheduled lectures, papers, postings on the Internet, and interviews with journalists. Dean Acosta, deputy administrator for public affairs at NASA, explained that "policy statements should be left to policy makers and appointed spokesmen."[22]

Hansen commented, "In my more than three decades in government, I have never seen anything approaching the degree to which information flow from scientists to the public has been screened and controlled as it is now."[23]

Hansen's "minder" was George Deutsch, a 24-year-old presidential appointee in NASA's press office who had worked as an intern in the "war room" of the 2004 Bush-Cheney reelection campaign. In 2006, Deutsch was forced to resign after it was discovered that he had fabricated information on the résumé submitted for the job at NASA, including his claim of a journalism degree from Texas A & M. After his resignation, Deutsch claimed, "Dr. Hansen and his supporters have a very partisan agenda. . . . Anyone perceived to be a Republican, a Bush supporter or a Christian is singled out and labeled a threat to their views. I encourage anyone interested in this story . . . to consider Dr. Hansen's true motivations and to consider the dangerous implications of only hearing out one side of the global warming debate."[24]

Donald Kennedy, editor of *Science*, called the White House actions against Hansen "bureaucratic stupidity," because Hansen's views on climate were long-standing and widely available. "For NASA to lock the stable door when this horse has been out on the range for years is just silly," said Kennedy. "The efforts by Acosta and Deutsch are reminiscent of the slapstick antics of Curley and Moe: a couple of guys stumbling off to gag someone who the audience knows will rip the gag right off."[25]

Indeed, Hansen would not be gagged. In an interview conducted shortly after NASA's attempt to silence him, Hansen said it would be irresponsible for him not to speak out, particularly because NASA's mission statement includes the phrase "to understand and protect our home planet."[26]

The White House response was extraordinary. If Hansen insisted on invoking NASA's mission statement, then the mission itself would have to be altered. In early 2006, unknown to NASA's scientists, the Bush administration submitted its annual budget request to Congress with an altered version of NASA's mission statement. The phrase "to understand and protect our home planet," originally adopted with advice from NASA's 19,000 employees, had been deleted by fiat. It seemed clear that the change was aimed at those parts of NASA whose focus was on Earth sciences, including global warming. Hansen explained, "They're making it clear that they have the authority to make this change, that the President sets objectives for NASA, and that they prefer that NASA work on something that's not causing them a problem."[27]

ENERGY POLITICS

James Hansen understands the formidable alliance of conservative politicians and energy companies that stands in the way of action on global warming. In a lecture before the American Geophysical Union, he explained, "[S]pecial interests have been a roadblock wielding undue influence over policymakers. The special interests seek to maintain short-term profits with little regard to either the long-term impact on the planet that will be inherited by our children and grandchildren or the long-term economic well-being of our country."[28]

Hansen left it to his audience to identify the particular corporations that exercise such influence, but Pulitzer Prize–winning climate-science author Ross Gelbspan was quite explicit: "Today, the White House has become the East Coast branch office of ExxonMobil and Peabody Coal, and climate change has become the preeminent case study in the contamination of our political system by money."[29]

The cozy relationship between the coal industry and the Bush administration demonstrates Gelbhorn's point. Coal interests donated $3.8 million to the presidential candidates in the 2000 race, and 88 percent of that went to the Republican Party. Within months of Bush's inauguration, an official of the West Virginia Coal Association told the association's members, "You did everything you could to elect a Republican President. Now you are already seeing in his actions the payback . . . for what we did."[30]

Bush quickly reneged on a campaign pledge to limit power-plant emissions, explaining that he was backing away from the cap because of the "incomplete state of scientific knowledge of the causes of, and solutions to, global climate change and storing carbon dioxide."[31]

Irl Engelhardt, chairman of the Peabody Group, the country's biggest coal company, had donated $250,000 to the Republican National Committee and had served as an adviser to the Bush-Cheney Energy Transition Team. Shortly after Bush was elected, Cheney formed his energy task force and turned to Peabody's chief lobbyist, Fred Palmer, to assist in forming the administration's energy plan. Palmer, who headed a coal consortium, had been relentless in attacking the science of global warming. He and other members of Peabody Energy met with the Cheney task force a number of times, and their meetings were closed to environmentalists.

Even before the final energy plan was announced, Cheney revealed his desire to increase coal production, ignoring the environmental impact and explaining, "Conservation may be a sign of personal virtue, but it is not a sufficient basis for a sound, comprehensive energy policy."[32]

When the energy plan was finalized on May 17, 2001, it called for the construction of between 1,300 and 1,900 power plants, most of them powered by coal and nuclear energy. Within a week after the Cheney plan was announced, Peabody Energy, a privately held company, went public, and its stock jumped from $24 to $36.

By 2001, ExxonMobil was replacing the coal industry as the most prominent and influential corporate "skeptic" on global warming. By 2003, ExxonMobil was giving more than $1 million a year to organizations opposing action on climate change, and its political influence on the Bush administration increased dramatically. As was documented earlier in this chapter, ExxonMobil lobbyist Randy Randol interceded with the White House to remove atmospheric scientist and IPCC chairman Robert Watson, complaining that his views on global warming were too similar to those of Al Gore. In effect, ExxonMobil picked up where Peabody Energy left off.

The tentacles of the energy industry reached deep into the Bush administration, including the following officials:

- Vice President Dick Cheney, former CEO of Halliburton, the country's largest oil services firm
- National Security Adviser Condoleezza Rice, who served on Chevron's board of directors
- Secretary of Commerce Donald L. Evans, who worked for the Denver oil and gas company Tom Brown, Inc.
- White House Chief of Staff Andrew Card, former president of the American Automobile Manufacturers Association
- Energy Secretary Spencer Abraham, who received over $700,000 in contributions from the auto industry for his 2000 Senate race
- Interior Secretary Gale Norton, who received more than $285,000 from energy industries for her 1996 race for the Colorado state senate, and then chaired the Coalition of Republican Environmental Advocates, which was funded by corporations such as BP, Amoco, and Ford.

The fact that energy companies played a major role in both of George W. Bush's presidential campaigns should not lead one to assume that energy politics is a purely partisan process. Within the coal industry, the corporations have influenced Republicans and the unions have influenced Democrats, all in an effort to increase coal production. The same pattern was true in the auto industry, where the corporations gave Republicans large campaign contributions while the unions gave Democrats strong electoral support. The results were the same: bipartisan support for policies friendly to the energy industries.

The effective and highly political use of advertising by the energy industry has been essential to its success in forestalling action on global warming. Sometimes the advertising campaigns appear to have an impossible task, selling a seemingly distasteful product. For example, as the entire industrial world seeks a way to prevent the disastrous consequences of rising carbon-dioxide levels in the Earth's atmosphere, the conservative Competitive Enterprise Institute has been running the following TV ad:

"It's what we breathe out and plants breathe in. Carbon dioxide: They call it pollution, we call it life."[33]

Similarly, the Western Fuels Association addressed the desirability of carbon dioxide in a documentary film that claimed, "A doubling of the CO_2 content of the atmosphere will produce a tremendous greening of planet earth." The film promised "a better world, a more productive world" as carbon-dioxide levels increase. Individuals who appeared to be farmers spoke on camera, declaring, "In terms of plant growth, it's nothing but beautiful," and "For citrus, it would be a very very positive thing."[34]

A climate scientist would find such gibberish laughable, but the global warming skeptics are mobilized to influence public opinion, not scientific research. Their strategies derive from the tobacco industry's advertising in the 1980s, which questioned the scientific evidence linking smoking and cancer. Today, a similar strategy is being used to cast doubt on climate science, and the playbook for that strategy was drafted in a memo by Republican strategist Frank Luntz, acquired in 2003 by the Environmental Working Group. Titled "Winning the Global Warming Debate—An Overview," the Luntz memo advised Republicans on how to address global warming, "particularly as Democrats and opinion leaders attack President Bush over Kyoto." Among its recommendations:

1. **The scientific debate remains open.** Voters believe that there is **no consensus** about global warming within the scientific community. Should the public come to believe that the scientific issues are settled, their views about global warming will change accordingly. Therefore, **you need to continue to make the lack of scientific certainty a primary issue in the debate**. . . .

2. **Americans want a free and open discussion.** . . . Emphasize the importance of **"acting only with all the facts in hand"** and **"making the right decision, not the quick decision."**

3. **Technology and innovation are the key in arguments on both sides.** Global warming alarmists use American superiority in technology and innovation quite effectively in responding to accusations that international agreements such as the Kyoto accord could cost the United States billions. . . . **We** need to emphasize how **voluntary** innovation and experimentation are preferable to bureaucratic or international intervention and regulation. . . .

   The scientific debate is closing [against us] but not yet closed. There is still a window of opportunity to challenge the science. Americans believe that all the strange weather that was associated with El Nino had something to do with global warming, and there is little you can do to convince them otherwise. However, only a handful of people believes the science of global warming is a closed question. Most Americans want more information so they can make an informed decision. It is our job to provide that information. . . .

   You need to be even more active in recruiting experts who are sympathetic to your view, and much more active in making them part of your message. People are willing to trust scientists, engineers, and other leading research professionals, and less willing to trust politicians.[35]

No one in Congress has followed the Luntz playbook more closely than Senator James Inhofe (R-OK). During his 2002 reelection race, Inhofe received most of his campaign donations from the oil, gas, and electric companies, and from his position as chairman of the Committee on Environment and Public Works he challenged the scientific basis of every environmental concern that came before him. In 2003, he was the driving force in defeating the Climate Stewardship Act, which would have created the first caps on greenhouse gas emissions approved by Congress.

On July 28, 2003, Inhofe delivered a 12,000-word Senate speech in which he rejected virtually all of the scientific consensus on global warming, characterizing global warming as a hoax. He later elaborated on his views:

As I said on the Senate floor on July 28, 2003, "much of the debate on global warming is predicated on fear, rather than science." I called the threat of catastrophic global warming the "greatest hoax ever perpetrated on the American people," a statement that, to put it mildly, was not viewed kindly by environmental extremists and their elitist organizations. . . . For these groups, the issue of catastrophic global warming is not just a favored fundraising tool. In truth, it's more fundamental than that. Put simply, man-induced global warming is an article of religious faith.[36]

The claim that the science of global warming is an article of religious faith may seem odd coming from a born-again Christian, but, in fact, it is precisely

Sen. James Inhofe (R-Oklahoma), then chairman of the Senate Committee on the Environment and Public Works, discusses pending energy legislation, July 30, 2003. (AP Photo/Dennis Cook)

the approach taken a few decades earlier when conservatives in Alabama, Florida, Kentucky, and Tennessee attempted to remove any public school books that taught evolution, sexual permissiveness, anti-biblical bias, anti–free enterprise economics, and a host of other ideas and policies. They coined the term *secular humanism* to describe the belief system of those who advocate teaching such dangerous ideas. Arguing that "secular humanism" was itself a *religion*, these people sued school boards for teaching the *religion* of secular humanism in violation of the establishment clause of the Constitution. In cases like *Grove v. Mead School District No. 354* (1985), *Mozert v. Hawkins County Board of Education* (1987), and *Smith v. Board of School Commissioners of Mobile (Ala.) County* (1987), the courts disposed of that claim, ruling that the disputed textbooks neither endorsed theistic religion nor discredited it, but rather promoted important secular values such as tolerance and logical decision-making.

Senator Inhofe frequently refers to his favorite author on global warming, science-fiction writer Michael Crichton. In his 2005 speech, Inhofe said, "[L]ast month, popular author Dr. Michael Crichton, who has questioned the wisdom of those who trumpet a 'scientific consensus,' released a new book called 'State of Fear,' which is premised on the global warming debate. I'm happy to report that Dr. Crichton's new book reached #3 on the *New York Times* bestseller list. . . . From what I can gather, Dr. Crichton's book is designed to bring some sanity to the global warming debate."[37]

Inhofe invited Crichton to testify before his Senate Committee on Energy and Environment as an "expert witness." Crichton, whose best-known novels are *Jurassic Park* and its sequel *The Lost World,* is hardly an expert on any aspect of science. Michael Meacher, a member of the British Parliament and former environmental minister, questions Crichton's credibility on climate science. "This is fairy land," he says. "You have a science fiction writer testifying before the United States Senate on global warming policy. . . . It's just ludicrous."[38]

Nevertheless, President Bush, himself a fan of Crichton's books, endorsed his views on global warming. Journalist David Remnick says that after reading *State of Fear*, the president was "so excited by the story, which pictures global warming as a hoax perpetuated by power-mad environmentalists, that he invited the author to the Oval Office. They talked for an hour and emerged in—surprise!—near-total agreement." Remnick concludes, "President Bush has made fantasy a guide to policy."[39]

Such preference for fiction over science has come to characterize the Bush administration. "You're talking about a president who says the jury is out on evolution, so what possible evidence would you need to muster to prove the existence of global warming?" says Robert F. Kennedy, Jr., author of *Crimes Against Nature.* "We've got polar ice caps melting, glaciers disappearing all over the world, ocean levels rising, coral reefs dying. But these people are flat-earthers."[40]

In January 2007, the Union of Concerned Scientists (UCS) and the Government Accountability Project (GAP) released the results of a joint investigation into political interference in federal climate science. UCS contributed an analysis of questionnaires it sent to over 1,600 climate scientists at seven federal agencies and to scientists at the nongovernmental National Center for Atmospheric Research (NCAR). GAP analyzed 40 in-depth interviews with climate scientists and other officials along with thousands of pages of government documents obtained through FOIA.

The joint report said federal climate science "has been increasingly tailored to reflect political goals rather than scientific fact." Noting that "unacceptably large numbers of federal climate scientists personally experienced instances of interference over the past five years,"[41] the report said:

- 46 percent of respondents perceived or personally experienced pressure to eliminate the words "climate change," "global warming," or similar terms from their communications.
- 43 percent perceived or personally experienced edits during review that changed the meaning of scientific findings.
- 37 percent perceived or personally experienced statements by agency officials that misrepresented scientists' findings.
- 38 percent perceived or personally experienced the disappearance or unusual delay of scientific information from Web sites, reports, or other science-based materials relating to climate.
- 46 percent perceived or personally experienced unusual administrative requirements that impair climate-related work.
- 25 percent perceived or personally experienced situations in which scientists objected to or removed themselves from a project because of pressure to change scientific findings.
- 150 scientists (58 percent) said they had personally experienced one or more incidents of political interference within the past five years.[42]

In contrast to this evidence of widespread interference in climate science at federal agencies, UCS reported "far fewer instances of interference" at the independent National Center for Atmospheric Research.[43]

The GAP interviews with climate scientists gave more personal views of political interference. One scientist said, "I believe the line has been crossed between science informing public policy and policy manipulating the science (and trying to influence its outcome). I have personally experienced this manipulation in the area of communicating the science many times."[44]

The joint report concluded:

Every day that the government chooses to ignore climate science is a day it fails to protect future generations from the consequences of global warming. Our government must commit to ensuring basic scientific freedoms and support scientists in their endeavors to bring scientific results to the policy arena, scientific fora, and a wide array of other audiences. Addressing climate change is a matter of national preparedness.[45]

STATE RESPONSES TO FEDERAL INTRANSIGENCE

As successive administrations have been unable to break the federal gridlock on global warming, state governments have had to address the problem on their own. In 2002, the Pew Center for Climate Change documented initiatives in more than half the states, including mandatory or voluntary programs to reduce emissions. Fifteen states, including Texas, had enacted legislation requiring utilities to increase their use of renewable energy sources such as wind power.

Among the state initiatives were:

- New regulations in California to reduce car and truck emissions by 2006
- A Texas requirement that 3 to 4 percent of its electricity will be generated from renewable energy sources by the end of the decade
- A formal target in Massachusetts to reduce power-plant emissions
- A New Hampshire law limiting emissions from the state's three coal-fired electric generating plants
- Nebraska legislation promoting the planting of trees to increase the absorption of carbon dioxide
- A New Jersey commitment to lower greenhouse gas emissions by 3.5 percent below 1990 levels by 2005 through the use of energy efficiency and renewable-energy programs.

In July 2002, the attorneys general of eleven states, including the chief legal officers of New York, California, Massachusetts, and Alaska, called on President Bush to address the issue by capping carbon emissions.

Later that year, at the U.S. Conference of Mayors, the chief executives of 250 cities called on Bush to act immediately on climate change, noting: "[T]he scientific community has reached a consensus that human activities are impacting the Earth's climate. . . . Mayors are uniquely situated to lead national climate protection efforts by taking action in a broad range of areas. . . . [M]any mayors are already pursuing programs and policies to reduce greenhouse gas emissions in their cities and communities, including more than 125 local governments that have committed to assessing emissions, setting a specific reduction target for greenhouse gas emissions and monitoring progress."[46]

When the Bush administration failed to respond to the concerns of state and city officials, the attorneys general of seven states filed a lawsuit against the federal government in early 2003 for refusing to regulate carbon dioxide through the Environmental Protection Agency. They expanded the suit eight months later when eleven states, along with the District of Columbia and American Samoa, claimed that the EPA is required by the U.S. Clean Air Act to regulate greenhouse gas emissions.

"Because the United States is already dealing with the harmful effects of global warming, the American people want less talk and more action now," said Rhode Island attorney general Patrick Lynch. Massachusetts attorney general Thomas Reilly said the carbon emissions were causing real environmental and health problems, adding, "You're seeing the erosion of our beaches. You're seeing saltwater contaminating our drinking water. You see damage to our infrastructure, to our roads and our causeways and our bridges."[47]

In 2003, more than 100 U.S. cities in 30 states initiated plans to reduce their own carbon emissions. Meanwhile, that same year, the governors of Washington, Oregon, and California announced that they were pooling their resources to buy high-efficiency vehicles, develop renewable sources of electricity, and institute a verifiable system of measuring and reporting on greenhouse gas emissions.

K. C. Golden of the Washington-based group Climate Solutions noted, "We can't afford to wait while the federal government fiddles. We have too much to lose as the climate becomes unstable, and too much to gain by taking a leadership role in developing climate solutions. The rest of the world's advanced economies have already begun to retool for a successful, prosperous transition to clean energy sources and efficient energy systems. With this announcement, the Governors are clearly signaling that the federal government won't stop America's most forward-looking states from taking action."[48]

The state of Texas recently became the focus of a political battle over coal-fired energy plants when the Dallas-based utility TXU said it would build eleven new coal-fired power plants, a plan that was fast-tracked by Texas governor Whit Perry. Farmers in Texas, who were concerned about the consequences of extreme heat and drought on their land, joined with environmental groups in a suit to stop the coal plants from being built. Mayors across the state joined the fight, backing the "cowboys against coal."

"We are alarmed that the state of Texas is considering doubling the coal-fired plants in our state," said Dallas mayor Laura Miller. "And, worse than that, our Governor has decided that he wants to fast-track all of it and get it up and built as soon as possible. It just seems contrary to the direction that the rest of the country is going."[49]

Surprisingly it was big business that played the major role in resolving the Texas battle over the coal plants. Two Wall Street private-equity firms decided to buy TXU, the largest power provider in Texas, and negotiated an unusual agreement with environmental groups. They pledged to cancel construction of eight of the eleven planned coal plants, reduce emissions by 20 percent, and invest heavily in wind power. The agreement was brokered by former EPA director William Reilly, who predicted that the negotiated plan would prove to be "green" in both senses of the word. It would make money and protect the environment.

When asked if this represented a new model for the energy industry, Reilly said, "I would hesitate to characterize it as a new model until it really plays out and we see how successful we are, but certainly it has been described by the environmentalists as a game-changer, and based upon the calls I'm getting from other energy companies, I think it may be."[50]

As the effects of global warming became more evident in localities around the country, local and state politicians took action. In 2005, California governor

Arnold Schwarzenegger told a United Nations conference on the environment, "Today, California will be a leader in the fight against global warming. I say the debate is over. We know the science, we see the threat, and we know the time for action is now."[51] Schwarzenegger's plan called for reducing the state's greenhouse emissions to 2000 levels by 2010, 1990 levels by 2020, and 80 percent below 1990 levels by 2050.

In 2006, Schwarzenegger signed landmark climate change legislation, the nation's first law imposing mandatory caps on carbon-dioxide emissions. Then, in an unprecedented act of state autonomy, Schwarzenegger signed a historic agreement with British prime minister Tony Blair, linking the climate strategies of California and England. At the signing ceremony on July 31, 2006, Schwarzenegger said:

You can build a great economy and you can take care of the environment at the same time. . . . And we do not want to wait for the Federal Government to create that action; We want to create it and we want to be the leaders in that. And this is why . . . we have taken the unprecedented step by signing an agreement between California and the United Kingdom. We are collaborating on a long-term challenge that Prime Minister Tony Blair has correctly called the single most important issue we face as a global community.

The international partnership is what is exactly needed in order to fight the global warming, and that is what we are seeing here today. California, after all, is like a nation state, and when we act, the world takes notice and it has a tremendous impact. Our state has been at the forefront of environmental protection and on energy efficiency for the last three decades. The agreement that we are signing here with Prime Minister Blair means that we will share best practices on emission trading to speed up the transition to a low carbon economy.[52]

Terry Tamminen, the governor's former environmental adviser and current roving environmental ambassador to the other states, says, "On the climate-change issue in particular, the mistake most environmental groups are making is going to Washington and looking for the national solution first. . . . If you let some of these state and regional solutions percolate up and get some success, you can build on them and allow for some flexibility and adaptation."[53]

Tamminen recalled a conversation he had with Tony Blair when Schwarzenegger signed a climate agreement with the British prime minister: "[Blair] said, 'I'm imploring you to get other states to do what California has done.' We had to explain, 'We're trying to build a de facto national climate plan one state at a time.'"[54]

California has led the way in energy-efficiency programs, including new standards for homes and commercial buildings. From 1976 to 2005, as electricity consumption per capita grew 60 percent in the rest of the nation, it stayed flat in fast-growing California. This impressive result was accomplished by adopting an aggressive energy-efficiency strategy. Most utilities in the United States can only make money by selling more power, and they lose money if they sell less. Under California's new regulations, a utility's profits are not determined solely by how much electricity it sells. Utilities now receive a share of any energy savings they help consumers and businesses achieve.

The California Energy Commission directly supports efforts to boost energy efficiency, including building codes that specify efficiency requirements for new constructions. California's electricity rates are about 50 percent higher than the national average, yet its annual electric bill per person is about the same as the rest of the nation because it wastes less electricity. The average Californian generates under one-third of the carbon-dioxide emissions of the average American while paying the same average bill.

Helping Californians use electricity more wisely is far cheaper than building new power plants. By 2004, the average cost of the efficiency programs had dropped in half, to under 1.4 cents per kilowatt-hour, cheaper than any form of new power supply in this country. California's success has led other states to take similar action. A 2006 report of the Western Governors' Association confirmed that a variety of energy-efficiency programs in western states have delivered comparable savings at similarly low cost.

Surely the most dramatic conflict between federal and state authority on climate policy came in 2007, when California passed its own emissions standards but was prevented by federal order from implementing them. The new California law required a 30 percent reduction in emissions by 2016, raising California's fuel-efficiency standards to 43.7 miles per gallon for passenger cars. The federal Clean Air Act allows other states to adopt California's standards, but the act prevents implementation of *any* state emissions standard unless the Environmental Protection Agency (EPA) grants a waiver exempting the state from federal regulation.

One would expect the EPA waiver to be routinely granted if the state standard is more rigorous than the current federal regulation, but, in this case, the administration argued that carbon dioxide is not a pollutant that California can regulate and that this law illegally preempted federal authority in setting mileage standards for cars. President Bush defended the denial, asking, "Is it more effective to let each state make a decision as to how to proceed in curbing greenhouse gases? Or is it more effective to have a national strategy?"[55]

Governor Schwarzenegger responded, "It's another example of the administration's failure to treat global warming with the seriousness that it actually demands."[56]

California promptly initiated a suit against the EPA to uphold the right of states to regulate greenhouse gas pollution from automobiles. During the next few months, the EPA's conflict with California extended to other states hoping to adopt California's emissions standards. By January 2008, fifteen states had joined California's suit, filed in the U.S. Court of Appeals for the Ninth Circuit. In addition to California, those states are: Massachusetts, Arizona, Connecticut, Delaware, Illinois, Maine, New Jersey, New Mexico, New York, Oregon, Pennsylvania, Rhode Island, Vermont, and Washington. Further details and the current status of this suit are discussed in Chapter 10.

The most promising state project to combat global warming was inaugurated on September 29, 2008, when six states in the Regional Greenhouse Gas Initiative (RGGI) held the nation's first cap-and-trade auction for greenhouse gas reduction. The ten states in the RGGI (Connecticut, Delaware, Maine, Maryland, Massachusetts, New Hampshire, New Jersey, New York, Rhode Island, and Vermont) did an end-run around the federal government's refusal to cap emissions by setting their own limits and asking local power plants to pay for any pollution above those limits.

"This will be the first time that a price will be put on greenhouse gases," said David Littell, commissioner of Maine's Department of Environmental Protection.[57]

This historic state initiative, conducted by Connecticut, Maine, Maryland, Massachusetts, Rhode Island, and Vermont, raised nearly $40 million to spend on renewable technologies and energy-efficient programs, and it will be followed by auctions in the other RGGI states in 2009. Ned Raynolds of the Union of Concerned Scientists said, "This shows it is possible to put a price on polluting and the sky won't fall. What was a concept now is a reality."[58]

Some critics have charged that the RGGI emissions cap is set too high and the penalty fees too low to make a major dent in short-term pollution, but the cap will drop by 2.5 percent per year starting in 2015. Shari Wilson, Maryland's environmental secretary, said, "We're off to a really strong start, and we couldn't be more pleased. We want to make steady progress, but we want it to be a very technically and financially sound program."[59]

NOTES

1. "Hot Politics," *Frontline* transcript, PBS, April 24, 2007, 2, www.pbs.org/wgbh/pages/frontline/hotpolitics/etc/script.html.
2. Testimony of James Hansen, U.S. Senate Committee on Environment and Public Works, June 23, 1988. http://epw.senate.gov/public/index.cfm?FuseAction=Minority.Blogs&ContentRecord_id=b6a8baa3-802a-23ad-4650-cb6a01303a65.
3. "Hot Politics," *Frontline* transcript, PBS, April 24, 2007, 3, www.pbs.org/wgbh/pages/frontline/hotpolitics/etc/script.html.
4. Ibid., 4.
5. Ibid., 5.
6. James E. Hansen, "Climate Changes: Understanding the Global Warming," *in The Health and Survival of the Human Species in the 21st Century*, ed. Robert Lanza (Santa Fe, NM: Health Press, 1996), 173–190.
7. Intergovernmental Panel on Climate Change, "IPCC Second Assessment: Climate Change 1995," www.ipcc.ch/pub/sa(E).pdf.
8. "Hot Politics," *Frontline*, PBS, April 22, 2008.
9. "Scientists Issue Dire Prediction on Warming," *Washington Post*, January 23, 2001.
10. American Petroleum Institute memo, acquired by the Environmental Defense Fund and available online at www.environmentaldefense.org/documents/3860_GlobalClimateSciencePlanMemo.pdf.

11. Committee on the Science of Climate Change, National Research Council, "Climate Change Science: An Analysis of Some Key Questions" (Washington, D.C.: National Academy Press, 2001), www.nap.edu/catalog/10139.html?onpi_webextra6.

12. "Bush and Kerry Offer Their Views on Science," *Science*, September 16, 2004, www.sciencemag.org/cgi/rapidpdf/1104420v1.pdf.

13. "U.S. Aims to Pull Out of Warming Treaty, 'No Interest' in Implementing Kyoto Pact, Whitman," *Washington Post*, March 28, 2001.

14. CNN Late Edition with Wolf Blitzer, March 25, 2001, CNN.com Transcripts. http://transcripts.cnn.com/TRANSCRIPTS/0103/25/le.00.html

15. "Hot Politics," *Frontline*, PBS, April 22, 2008.

16. Duncan Campbell, "Europe Pleads with Bush to Show 'Political Courage' on Global Warming," CommonDreams.org, March 24, 2001. www.commondreams.org/headlines01/0324-02.htm.

17. Competitive Enterprise Institute press release, "Group Sues to Enforce Sound Science Law," August 13, 2003.

18. Joseph Romm, *Hell and High Water* (New York: Harper Collins, 2007), 118.

19. Ibid.

20. Rick Piltz, resignation memo to U.S. Climate Change Science Program, June 1, 2005, http://pubs.acs.org.

21. Ibid.

22. Andrew Revkin, "Climate Expert Says NASA Tried to Silence Him," *New York Times*, January 29, 2006, A1.

23. Bruce E. Johansen, "A Man with a Mission: James Hansen," *Omaha Magazine*, October/November 2005, 52.

24. Juliet Eilperin, "Censorship Is Alleged at NOAA; Scientists Afraid to Speak Out, NASA Climate Expert Reports," *Washington Post*, February 7, 2006, A11.

25. Donald Kennedy, "The New Gag Rules," editorial, *Science* 311, February 17, 2006, 917.

26. Andrew Revkin, "Climate Expert Says NASA Tried to Silence Him," *New York Times*, January 29, 2006, A1.

27. Andrew Revkin, "NASA's Goals Delete Mention of Home Planet," *New York Times*, July 22, 2006, A10.

28. James E. Hansen, "Is There Still Time to Avoid 'Dangerous Anthropogenic Interference' with Global Climate?" (paper delivered to the American Geophysical Union, San Francisco, CA, December 6, 2005), www.columbia.edu/~jeh1/kneeling_talk_and_slides.pdf.

29. Ross Gelbspan, *Boiling Point* (New York: Basic Books, 2004), 38.

30. "A Coal-Fired Crusade Helped Bring Bush a Crucial Victory," *Wall Street Journal*, June 13, 2001.

31. Ross Gellspan, *Boiling Point* (New York: Basic Books, 2004), 45.

32. "Cheney Promises Increasing Supply as Energy Policy," *New York Times*, May 1, 2001.

33. Competitive Enterprise Institute, television advertisement, May 2006, http://gristmill.grist.org/story/2006/5/17/15336/5459.

34. Western Fuels Association, *The Great Global Warming Swindle*, 2007, http://video.google.com/videosearch?q=%22global+warming+swindle%22.

35. "PR Versus Science: the Luntz Memo," *Lightbucket*, April 9, 2008, http://lightbucket.wordpress.com/2008/04/09/pr-versus-science-the-luntz-memo/.

36. Senate Floor Statement by Senator James M. Inhofe, "Climate Change Update," press release, January 4, 2005. http://inhofe.senate.gov/pressreleases/climateupdate.html.

37. Ibid.

38. Mark Hertsgaard, "While Washington Slept," *Vanity Fair*, May 2006, 241.

39. David Remnick, "Ozone Man," *The New Yorker*, April 24, 2006, 48.

40. Katherine Mieszkowski, "Bush: Global Warming is Just Hot Air," Salon.com, September 10, 2004, http://dir.salon.com/tech/feature/2004/09/10/bush.

41. Union of Concerned Scientists and Government Accountability Project, "Atmosphere of Pressure: Political Interference in Federal Climate Science: Executive Summary," January 2007, 1, www/ucusa.org/scientific_integrity/interference/atmosphere-of-pressure.html.

42. Ibid.

43. Ibid., 2.

44. Ibid.

45. Ibid., 5.

46. "Proposed Resolutions," 70th Annual Conference of Mayors, Madison, Wisconsin, June 14–18, 2002, 63. http://usmayors.org/70thAnnualMeeting/2002resolutions.pdf.

47. "States Sue the Federal Government to Control Greenhouse Emissions," *Wall Street Journal*, October 23, 2003.

48. Office of the Governors, "Statement of the Governors of California, Oregon and Washington on Regional Action to Address Global Warming," September 22, 2003, www.oregon.gov/ENERGY/GBLWRM/docs/2ab-GovernorsStatementonGlobal-Warming.pdf.

49. "Hot Politics," *Frontline*, PBS, April 22, 2008.

50. Ibid.

51. "Arnold Targets Global Warming," CBS News, June 2, 2005, www.cbsnews.com/stories/2005/06/02/tech/main699281.shtml.

52. California Office of the Governor, "Gov. Schwarzenegger, British Prime Minister Tony Blair Sign Historic Agreement to Collaborate on Climate Change," July 31, 2006, http://gov.ca.gov/index.php/speech/2918/.

53. "One Nation, Under Terry," Grist Environment News and Commentary, January 4, 2007, www.grist.org/news/maindish/2007/01/04/tamminen/.

54. Ibid.

55. "Schwarzenegger: California Will Sue Federal Government," CNN.com, December 20, 2007, www.cnn.com/2007/POLITICS/12/20/.

56. Ibid.

57. "Emission Rights for Sale in Auction," *Washington Post*, September 25, 2008, A3.

58. "Carbon Sale Raises $40 Million," *Washington Post*, September 30, 2008, A4.

59. Ibid.

6

The Politics of Nature

A victim of Hurricane Katrina is evacuated by helicopter from his devastated neighborhood, August 30, 2005. New Orleans mayor Ray Nagin estimated that 80% of the city was flooded. (AP Photo/Vincent Laforet/POOL)

ENVIRONMENTAL CORRUPTION

The federal responsibility for protecting the nation's environment is assigned primarily to the Environmental Protection Agency (EPA), but it is shared by a number of other agencies, including the Department of Energy (DOE) and the

Federal Emergency Management Agency (FEMA). Together, these agencies must protect America's natural resources, its land, its air, its water, its flora, and its fauna. When politics intrudes on environmental protection, these precious natural resources are placed at risk.

The EPA is charged "to protect human health and the environment," yet the Union of Concerned Scientists (UCS) reports that under the Bush administration "political appointees used tainted science to justify weaker protections of public health and the environment."[1] A recent survey conducted by the UCS documented persistent political interference with scientific decisions at the EPA. The 44-question survey of nearly 5,500 EPA scientists asked for information about political interference in their scientific work, barriers to communication, employee morale, and the agency's effectiveness.

The UCS survey report concludes: "The results of these investigations show an agency under siege from political pressures. On numerous issues—ranging from mercury pollution to groundwater contamination to climate change—political appointees of the George W. Bush administration have edited scientific documents, manipulated scientific assessments, and generally sought to undermine the science behind dozens of EPA regulations."[2]

Among the specific findings of the survey were:

- 889 scientists personally experienced at least one incident of political interference during the past five years.
- Among EPA veteran scientists, 409 said interference occurred more often in the past five years than in the previous five-year period.
- 94 scientists were frequently or occasionally "directed to inappropriately exclude or alter technical information from an EPA scientific document."
- 191 scientists personally experienced frequent or occasional "situations in which scientists have actively objected to, resigned from, or removed themselves from a project because of pressure to change scientific findings."
- 232 scientists personally experienced frequent or occasional "changes or edits during review that change the meaning of scientific findings."
- 285 scientists personally experienced frequent or occasional "selective or incomplete use of data to justify a specific regulatory outcome."
- 153 scientists personally experienced frequent or occasional "pressure to ignore impacts of a regulation on sensitive populations."
- 299 scientists personally experienced frequent or occasional "disappearance or unusual delay in the release of web sites, press releases, reports, or other science-based materials."
- 394 scientists personally experienced frequent or occasional "statements by EPA officials that misrepresent scientists' findings."
- 555 scientists agreed or strongly agreed with the statement, "recent changes and closures in the EPA library system have impaired my ability to do my job."[3]

Respondents to the USC survey indicated that political interference came from both internal and external sources, including political appointees, commercial interests, and nongovernmental or advocacy groups. Nearly 100 scientists identified the White House Office of Management and Budget (OMB) as the primary source of external interference.

The dramatic decline in EPA investigations and prosecutions of polluters in recent years—down by one-third—suggests that the political interference described in the UCS survey may have had a direct effect on the agency's ability to protect the environment. Eric Schaeffer, who resigned as director of EPA's Office of Civil Enforcement to protest the administration's lax enforcement of environmental regulations, says, "You don't get cleanup, and you don't get deterrence. I don't think this is a problem with agents in the field. . . . They lack the political support they used to be able to count on, especially in the White House."[4]

The EPA currently employs 172 criminal investigators, less than the legal minimum required by the 1990 Pollution Prosecution Act, signed by President George W. Bush's father. The second Bush administration's reduction in support for the EPA goes far beyond investigative staff, extending to communications and access to materials and services in the EPA's library network. As indicated in the UCS survey, EPA scientists believe that such reductions have impaired their ability to do their jobs.

During 2006, the White House sought to reduce the EPA library budget by 80 percent, forcing many of its regional libraries to close. Jeff Ruch, executive director of Public Employees for Environmental Responsibility, says, "We view this as another example of the Bush administration marginalizing EPA research so that the agency scientists and other specialists can't do their jobs. And then in the absence of information, plans by industries and others that have environmental implications go forward."[5]

When the EPA proceeded to cut the headquarters library, the Chemical Library in Washington, D.C. and three regional libraries, Congress approved an additional $1 million to reopen the libraries, but the libraries remain closed. Representative Bart Gordon, chairman of the House Science and Technology Committee, complained, "As a result, EPA library services are impaired, employees will have a harder time doing their jobs and the public has lost access to government information."[6]

The EPA is not the only environmental agency that has endured scandal and charges of corruption. The Department of Energy has been dogged by the controversy surrounding Vice President Cheney's energy task force, the National Energy Policy Development Group. As explained in Chapter 5, Cheney's task force met in secret with representatives of the energy industry to craft a global warming strategy that contradicted the public positions of President Bush and his EPA administrator, Christine Whitman.

Beginning in 2002, environmental groups like the Sierra Club brought suit to acquire the membership rolls and meeting schedules of Cheney's task force, alleging that Cheney met improperly with the energy industry, which determined his energy policy. The Bush administration claimed executive privilege in withholding the information, and the suits eventually reached the Supreme

Court. In 2004, the high court affirmed the administration's position, ruling that internal deliberations within the executive branch can be shielded from the public.

Finally, in 2007, the *Washington Post* acquired the confidential list of task-force attendees from a former White House official. The list, which was compiled in the summer of 2001, shows that James T. Rouse, then vice president of Exxon Mobil and a major donor to the Bush inauguration, was the first visitor. A week later, Kenneth Lay, then head of Enron Corporation, attended the first of two task-force meetings, exerting major influence on the creation of the administration's energy policy. Lay would later be prosecuted and brought down for the illegal profiteering that sparked the energy crisis in California.

Following Lay came the leaders of some of the country's biggest electric utilities, including Duke Energy and the Constellation Energy Group. Next came representatives from about 20 oil and drilling companies, followed by 36 energy associations, including the Interstate Natural Gas Association, the American Petroleum Institute, and the National Mining Association. Jack Gerard, representing the National Mining Association, urged the administration to remove responsibility for climate issues from the EPA, which was empowered to impose regulations on greenhouse gas emissions, and assign it instead to the DOE. The administration soon did just that.

Mystery continues to surround Cheney's energy task force and the covert means by which it determined America's energy policy. David Hawkins, a climate expert at the Natural Resources Defense Council, concludes, "Cheney had his finger on a critical issue. He just pushed it in the wrong direction."[7]

No federal agency has been more criticized than the Federal Emergency Management Agency, which is best known for its inadequate and incompetent response to the Katrina disaster in late August 2005. The storm killed 1,330 people, displaced 1 million families, swamped 80 percent of New Orleans, and led to $100 billion in federal assistance. The following year, a bipartisan national inquiry into the storm faulted FEMA for failing to fund and coordinate disaster readiness efforts after the September 11 terrorist attacks, emphasizing terrorism at the expense of natural-disaster preparedness, and neglecting warnings about the inadequacy of the New Orleans levee system to survive Katrina.

As if FEMA's bungling of the storm response was not bad enough, the agency attempted to control and manipulate press accounts of flood relief, creating a stained public image that remains to this day. During Katrina, FEMA asked the press not to photograph any of the bodies recovered in Louisiana and Mississippi. *Washington Post* reporter Timothy Dwyer says he heard security officials in flooded New Orleans tell a camera crew, "If we catch you photographing one body, we're going to bring you back in and throw you off the boat."[8] Another report from New Orleans describes a police officer who raised the muzzle of her weapon and aimed it at members of the media, who were armed only with note pads.

Rebecca Daugherty of the Reporters Committee for Freedom of the Press complained that it was impossible to give the public a realistic idea of the horrors of Katrina "if you don't see that there [were] bodies as well."[9]

Alex Jones, who runs the Shorenstein Media Center at Harvard, described the politics surrounding press coverage of Katrina: "There's a reasonable belief that part of the wish to restrict access is rooted in image and public relations. The history of this administration has been very intensely to control the information and control the message."[10]

Why did FEMA fail to anticipate the vulnerability of the New Orleans levee system to the Katrina storms? In the wake of Katrina, why did FEMA fail to respond to the plight of hundreds of thousands of displaced and homeless, allowing many to die and placing others indefinitely in dangerous trailers laced with formaldehyde? The American public demanded answers, but FEMA obscured or misrepresented its relief programs while reassuring critics that the agency would handle things better when the next emergency hit the nation. In the fall of 2007, FEMA had a chance to redeem itself when massive wildfires throughout much of California were designated a national emergency.

FEMA quickly announced that the effectiveness and transparency of its response to the fires would demonstrate that this was a "new FEMA." As proof, Harvey Johnson, FEMA's deputy administrator, called a rare news briefing on October 23, 2007, as the California fires raged on. Reporters were given only 15 minutes notice of the briefing, making it unlikely that many would show up, but they were given an 800 number to connect with the briefing. Unfortunately, the phone connection was a "listen-only" line, with no questions allowed. Despite these restraints, parts of the briefing were carried live on Fox News, MSNBC, and other outlets.

Harvey Johnson stood at the lectern and delivered a confident overview for those able to attend the press briefing, after which he solicited questions. Johnson seemed to know the reporters, often addressing them by first name.

One reporter inquired about "lessons learned from Katrina," and another asked, "Are you happy with FEMA's response so far?"

"I'm very happy with FEMA's response so far," answered Johnson, who complemented the "very smoothly, very efficiently performing team" and added, "I think what you're really seeing here is the benefit of experience and the benefit of good partnership, none of which were present in Katrina."[11]

Judging from the press briefing, this certainly was a new FEMA. No questions were asked about those trailers reeking of formaldehyde in which the homeless from both Katrina and the wildfires were placed, but, in general, things seemed to be going very smoothly. Perhaps that was because all of the questions were coming from FEMA staffers pretending to be reporters. There was no press at the press briefing.

When the deception was discovered, Homeland Security Secretary Michael Chertoff called it, "[O]ne of the dumbest and most inappropriate things I've seen since I've been in government."[12]

An investigation into the hoax found that FEMA's press secretary had directed aides to pose as reporters and secretly coached them during the briefing. FEMA chief R. David Paulison apologized for the bad judgment of his staff, explaining, "These are career people. They should have stepped up and said something. . . . But their bosses said, 'Do this,' and they did it."[13]

A *Washington Post* editorial recalled FEMA's "disgraceful performance during Hurricane Katrina" and concluded, "FEMA personnel who participated in this hoax undermined the agency's still-tattered credibility smack in the middle of an emergency."[14]

MOUNTAINTOP REMOVAL

The process of extracting coal from the Earth has always torn the land, often leaving terrible environmental damage, but nothing comparable to the most recent form of strip-mining: mountaintop removal. The process uses huge machines to shear away the tops of mountain ridges, exposing coal seams. After removing the coal, millions of tons of waste rock and dirt are dumped into nearby hollows, burying mountain headwater streams under these "valley fills." Between 1985 and 2001, these practices have cut down 7 percent of Appalachian forests and buried or polluted more than 1,200 miles of streams across the region.

The environmental danger posed by such massive alteration of the land was acknowledged in a 1998 court settlement in which the federal government agreed to preceding mountaintop removal with an Environmental Impact Statement (EIS) that would analyze the effects and offer environmentally benign alternatives. Scientists at the Department of the Interior (DOI) worked for almost four years to prepare the required EIS, but in 2001, J. Stephen Griles, Bush's deputy secretary of the interior, instructed agency scientists to ignore the EIS and drop consideration of any environmentally beneficial alternatives to mountaintop removal. Griles, a former lobbyist for the National Mining Association, also edited technical language in the EIS to remove the impact classifications of "significant" and "severe."

A recently released memo from Griles to the White House Council on Environmental Quality shows that Griles pressed for a new EIS that would "focus on centralizing and streamlining coal-mining permitting" rather than studying ways to limit environmental damage.[15]

Many agency scientists were outraged at the manipulation of the EIS. Cindy Tibbot, a Fish and Wildlife Service biologist involved in the EIS process, said, "It's hard to stay quiet about this when I really believe we're doing the public and the heart of the Clean Water Act a great disservice." Tibbot said the only alternatives that would remain in Griles's EIS would be "alternative locations to house the rubber stamp that issues the [mining] permits."[16]

An internal memo from the Fish and Wildlife Service staff gave a critical review of the draft EIS: "The alternatives and actions, as currently written, belie four years of work and the accumulated evidence of environmental harms, and would substitute permit process tinkering for meaningful and measurable change. Publication of a draft EIS with this approach, especially when the public has seen earlier drafts, will further damage the credibility of the agencies involved."[17]

Jim Hecker of Trial Lawyers for Public Justice, who filed the Freedom of Information Act (FOIA) request that acquired the internal documents related to the EIS, says, "In this case, the administration eliminated all environmental protective alternatives from consideration. The simple fact is: that is scientifically and intellectually dishonest."[18]

The obvious conflict of interest represented by Griles's longstanding association with the mining industry led the U.S. Senate to demand that he sign a "statement of disqualification," committing him to avoid all issues affecting his former clients. Nonetheless, documents obtained under the FOIA showed that Griles met a dozen times with coal industry representatives to discuss the EIS and mountaintop removal at the very time that Griles ordered a change of direction on the EIS.[19]

Representatives from fifty environmental organizations wrote a letter to President Bush and the EPA charging that the draft EIS violated the National Environmental Protection Act: "We find the draft EIS's failure to provide alternative proposals that would provide better regulation of mountaintop removal mining to protect the environment unacceptable and inappropriate."[20]

In October 2008, President Bush concluded his second term with a significant change to environmental regulations by way of a rule issued by the Department of the Interior that made it easier for mountaintop-mining companies to dump their waste near rivers and streams. The revised rule, which would take effect after a 30-day review by the EPA, calls on mining companies to minimize harming streams "to the extent practicable." Previous rules had prohibited dumping valley fills within 100 feet of any stream if the debris harms the stream's water quality or reduces its flow.[21]

Joan Mulhern, counsel for the environmental law firm Earthjustice, said, "I can't imagine a circumstance in which this is not going to be challenged by environmental groups. . . . It didn't even include the alternative of actually enforcing the rule on the books. The implications of this ruling are devastating, they're widespread and they're irreversible."[22]

On June 11, 2009, the new Obama administration announced plans to tighten scrutiny of mountaintop mining. After months of discussions between the White House Council on Environmental Quality (CEQ) and coal industry leaders, an agreement was reached requiring applications for mining permits to undergo a more detailed environmental review. Federal oversight of state regulators would also be required, including checks on their work for lax scrutiny, but the practice of mountaintop removal would not be prohibited. "It is allowed under current federal law," explained CEQ chair Nancy Sutley. "And until that changes, we have to use the tools that we have."[23]

WATER POLLUTION

Water is the true elixir of life—and death. It must be protected and protected against. The latter function is performed by the U.S. Army Corps of Engineers, a little-known contingent linked to FEMA and tainted by it. The Corps, as it is usually called, has been around for a long time. It began as an engineering regiment during the Revolutionary War, building fortifications at Bunker Hill. It is still run by army officers, but today most of its 35,000 employees are civilians working on civilian projects such a draining wetlands for agriculture and development; deepening ports; replenishing beaches; and controlling rivers for barge traffic, flood control, and hydropower.

Officially, the Corps is a Pentagon agency, but it functions at the whim of Congress, its civil works budget consisting almost entirely of earmarks requested by individual members of Congress. The result is a pork-barrel water resources agency that undertakes politically determined projects in congressional districts around the country.

Executive branch officials have long complained that Corps leaders exploit their congressional connections to secure funding for clients in the shipping, dredging, farming, and building industries. The Corps can endorse projects whenever it calculates that the economic benefits to private interests will exceed the cost to taxpayers, but without executive-branch oversight, the Corps has traditionally inflated benefits and underestimated costs in order to keep its employees busy and its congressional patrons happy.

The Corps set the stage for the Katrina disaster decades ago by surrounding the Mississippi River behind giant levees, reducing the wetlands that serve as buffers to hurricanes. During Katrina, levees with natural buffers had much higher survival rates than those that did not. The floodwalls built around New Orleans by the Corps collapsed in the face of a storm they were designed to withstand.

Investigative reporter Michael Grunwald explains, "The Corps put most of its levees around undeveloped and highly vulnerable flood plains . . . partly because Corps cost-benefit analyses did not consider the cost of human life or environmental degradation, and partly because powerful developers owned swampland in those vulnerable flood plains."[24]

Whether through corruption or politics, the Corps clearly failed the American public during Katrina and deserves to share the blame with FEMA.

The failures of FEMA and the Corps of Engineers to protect the public from floodwater may have smaller long-term consequences than the failure of the federal government to protect water itself. The water in our lakes, rivers, and aquifers has been contaminated by man-made toxins: synthetic substances that have become fundamental to modern commerce. When these chemicals show up in our drinking water, even politicians take notice. A good example is the current debate over perchlorate contamination of drinking water in many states around the nation. Perchlorate is an ingredient in rocket fuel and munitions that has been found in groundwater in 33 states. Exposure to perchlorate increases risks of brain damage in fetuses and thyroid disorders in adults, yet the EPA has refused to set a safe drinking-water standard for the chemical.

Perchlorate contamination is particularly acute in California because of its many military bases and defense contractors. One particular Pentagon contractor, Aerojet, has disposed of residual rocket fuel for decades by dumping it in unlined pits, allowing the toxic chemicals to seep through the soil into the groundwater. In response to a clear public-health threat, the state of California established its own maximum allowable level for perchlorate in drinking water. Massachusetts adopted a similar statutory standard for perchlorate, but the EPA still refused to take action, leaving most of the nation's states unprotected.

On May 6, 2008, the Senate Committee on Environment and Public Works, chaired by Senator Barbara Boxer (D-CA), held a hearing to investigate the EPA's inaction on perchlorate contamination. Boxer began by declaring, "EPA is trying to shunt the scientists to the back, put the [defense] contractors to the front. We want to see action by the scientists. We want to see a standard set."[25]

Benjamin Grumbles, the EPA's assistant administrator for water, acknowledged the potential dangers posed by perchlorate in drinking water, but said the EPA would not establish a standard for the chemical unless it could be shown that regulation would meaningfully reduce those risks.

Richard Wiles, executive director for the Environmental Working Group, told the Senate committee of White House interference in the decision-making process at EPA and the National Academy of Sciences (NAS) with respect to toxic chemical regulation. Wiles, a former employee at NAS, testified, "I can say from experience that the influence that politics and the vested interests are having on the process now is unprecedented. . . . It's a very serious problem, but the corruption of the NAS process or the influence of industry interests on the process is just a small part of the overall corruption of science that we've seen in this administration."[26]

Wiles said the perchlorate problem:

provides a textbook example of a corrupted health protection system where polluters, the Pentagon, the White House, the EPA have conspired to block health protections in order to pad budgets, curry political favor, and protect corporate profits. With perchlorate, we have reached that rare environmental moment when there is nothing left to do but act. Contamination of food, tap water, and breast milk are wide-spread and well-documented. We have a clear understanding of the dangers to infants, children, and women of child-bearing age. . . . It is rare that science provides us with such a clear picture of a pollutant's harmful effects, which have been termed 'consistent with causality' by the CDC [Centers for Disease Control and Prevention]. It is even more unusual to have this level of evidence and to do nothing. Yet this administration has failed to act.[27]

Wiles described "secret White House reviews of science and a shift of public health decision-making away from agencies with the expertise to agencies responsible for the pollution." He concluded, "Simply put, perchlorate is an environmental and public health nightmare of epic proportions for the Department of Defense and its contractors, and rather than address it head-on and protect the public health, they have spent 50 years and millions of dollars trying to avoid it."[28]

In a prepared statement, Chairman Boxer promised legislative action.

While the federal EPA delays—or does worse, rolls back safeguards—children and families are exposed to dangerous toxic chemicals. I told EPA last week that if the Bush administration failed to protect our people, Congress would step in. I have two bills to protect people from perchlorate contamination. The first bill, the "Perchlorate Monitoring and Right to Know Act," S.24, says that EPA is to restore the rule requiring that drinking water be tested for perchlorate, and that the results of those tests must be disclosed to the public.

My second bill, the "Protecting Pregnant Women and Children from Perchlorate Act," S.150, requires EPA to quickly set a perchorate standard for drinking water that protects pregnant women and children. . . . Congress will not sit idle while EPA fails to adequately protect our children. We must step in to require action that will ensure that our children and families can turn on their taps and be assured that what comes out is safe to drink.[29]

On October 3, 2008, the EPA issued a news release saying it had found that in more than 99 percent of public drinking-water systems, perchlorate was "not at levels of public health concern." The EPA therefore concluded that there was "not a meaningful opportunity for health risk reduction through a national drinking water regulation." In its news release, the EPA assumed the maximum safe perchlorate contamination level to be 15 times higher than what the agency had suggested in 2002.[30]

Senator Barbara Boxer, chair of the Environment and Public Works Committee, said, "The Bush EPA's failure to set a standard for perchlorate, a dangerous contaminant found in drinking water, is outrageous, and I will do everything in my power to reverse it."[31]

The environmental law firm Earthjustice quickly said it would file suit to overturn the EPA decision, explaining, "Weapons makers will benefit at the expense of millions of Americans drinking water spiked with rocket fuel."[32]

Even the EPA's own scientific advisers expressed doubt about the agency's decision. The heads of the EPA's Science Advisory Board and its drinking-water committee wrote to EPA administrator Stephen Johnson urging him to extend the public commentary period on the decision. The chairs of those two groups wrote, "Given perchlorate's wide occurrence and well-documented toxicity to humans, the [Science Advisory Board] strongly believes that there must be a compelling scientific basis to support a scientific conclusion not to regulate perchlorate as a national drinking water contaminant."[33]

And what of the contamination of our soil by toxic chemicals that, though never occurring naturally on Earth, are now found virtually everywhere and represent a threat to animate and inanimate life? One such widely distributed toxin,

Soon after Sen. Barbara Boxer (D-California) assumed the chair
of the Senate's Environment and Public Works Committee, she held field
hearings in New Orleans on the lagging recovery efforts following Hurricane
Katrina, February 27, 2007. (Courtesy of the U.S. Senate)

dioxin, is so potent that one drop, distributed among 1,200 people, can kill all
of them. Dioxin was the active ingredient in Agent Orange, the herbicide
sprayed by U.S forces over vast tracts of Southeast Asia during the Vietnam
War. Initially, the U.S. Army dismissed reports of cancers among American
troops who handled Agent Orange, but by 2001 the Department of Veterans

Affairs was paying compensation to Vietnam veterans for a wide variety of disabilities, including Hodgkin's disease, multiple myeloma, non-Hodgkin's lymphoma, soft-tissue sarcoma, and prostate cancer.

Today, dioxins are mainly by-products of industrial processes, including smelting, chlorine bleaching, and the production of herbicides and pesticides. During the summer of 2000, the Environmental Protection Agency released its *Draft Dioxin Reassessment*, which concluded that dioxin and other structurally related chemicals "are carcinogenic to humans and can cause immune system alterations; reproductive, developmental, and nervous system effects; endocrine disruption, altered lipid metabolism; liver damage; and skin lesions."[34]

Dioxins are now contaminating soil and water in the United States, primarily through the waste-disposal processes of chemical plants, but also by way of commercial herbicides and other widely sold products. Despite its publicly stated concerns about dioxins, the EPA has done little to regulate them, focusing instead on cleaning up already contaminated sites. A rough cleanup standard of around 90 parts per trillion has been established, despite the fact that dioxin is toxic at *any* detectable concentration. Even under this loose standard, the EPA has had great difficulty getting the chemical industry to cooperate in cleanups.

The politically charged process within which the EPA works was seen recently when Mary Gade, a senior EPA official in Chicago, was forced to resign after she pressed Dow Chemical to clean up a Michigan river system near a Dow plant. She called for more dredging after tests found dioxin levels of 1.6 million parts per billion, the highest concentration ever recorded in the United States. Gade, who headed the EPA's Midwest regional office, said that aides to EPA Administrator Stephen Johnson stripped her of her power and told her to resign or be fired. "There's no question this is about Dow," she told the *Chicago Tribune*. "I stand behind what I did and what my staff did."[35]

In a speech on the Senate floor, Sheldon Whitehouse (D-RI) called Gade's forced resignation "just the latest in a growing pile of evidence of a troubling and destructive force at work within our government, one with serious consequences for our environment, our natural resources and our public health." He said the Bush administration "values compliance with a political agenda over the best interests of the American people."[36]

AIR POLLUTION

Much of the EPA's action, or inaction, on air pollution has been analyzed in the context of global warming. This is understandable given the urgency of the current debate over climate change, but air pollution was an environmental concern long before global warming showed up on the political radar. In Chapter 5, we examined the central role of carbon-dioxide emissions in creating the "greenhouse effect," which traps heat in the Earth's atmosphere. But the EPA's failure to regulate emissions has allowed the air that we breathe today to reach contamination levels that represent an immediate public-health threat. This may represent the greatest environmental failure of the Bush administration.

Eric Schaeffer, former director of the EPA's Office of Regulatory Enforcement, resigned during Bush's first term, declaring, "As happened under Ronald Reagan . . . the process of environmental enforcement has once again been intensely politicized." Schaeffer explained the disappointment that led to his resignation: "In a matter of weeks, the Bush administration was able to undo the environmental progress we had worked years to secure. Millions of tons of unnecessary pollution continue to pour from these power plants each year as a result. . . . It became clear that Bush had little regard for the environment—and even less for enforcing the laws that protect it."[37]

In a report titled *America's Dirtiest Power Plants: Plugged Into the Bush Administration*, Schaeffer revealed that the nation's biggest polluters were also the largest contributors to George W. Bush's 2000 and 2004 presidential campaigns. Since 1999, the 30 utility companies that own the nation's most-polluting power plants have contributed $6.6 million to the Bush campaigns and the Republican National Committee. Many of these contributors were invited to join Bush's transition teams and serve on the committees that nominated officials in the new administrations.

The electric utilities pressed the Bush administration to soften the provisions of the Clean Air Act, particularly the requirement that power plants use less-polluting technology when they modernize. Indeed, when the time came to modernize, many power plants disobeyed the law and refused to implement the required pollution controls. At the same time, the Bush administration pressed the Justice Department to drop EPA suits against noncompliant electric utility companies, but the Justice Department ruled that the law suits were legitimate and could proceed. In response, Bush introduced his Clear Skies Initiative in February 2002, intended to replace the Clean Air Act regulations with a cap-and-trade market system that would allow 50 percent more sulfur dioxide, nearly 40 percent more nitrogen oxides, and three times more mercury than the Clean Air Act allowed.

In 2003, Congress made an attempt to stem the attack on the Clean Air Act by proposing an amendment to the president's Clear Skies Act that would control emissions of carbon dioxide, sulfur dioxide, nitrogen oxides, and mercury. EPA scientists evaluated the amendment and prepared a report estimating that it would reduce pollutants far earlier and in larger amounts than under the Clear Skies Act.

Jeffrey R. Holmstead, EPA's assistant administrator for air and radiation, met with staff members to discuss the unreleased EPA report and told staffers, "How can we justify Clear Skies if this gets out?"[38]

Indeed, Holmstead withheld publication of the report, but Bush's Clear Skies plan stalled in committee and never came to a vote. At this point, the Bush administration had to use some sleight of hand to avoid the New Source Review

(NSR) provisions of the Clean Air Act, which required power plants to employ the best environmental technology whenever they modernized. Once again, Jeffrey Holmstead found a way around the law. He simply redefined what "plant modernization" meant. Earlier, the EPA's enforcement administrator had formally stated that modernization of a power plant occurs whenever renovation costs exceed 0.75 percent of the value of a generating unit. Anything less would be considered routine maintenance. Instead, Holmstead ruled that utilities could spend up to 20 *percent* of a generating unit's replacement costs without triggering the NSR requirements!

Former EPA enforcement official Eric Schaeffer said, "Five percent would have been too high, but 20? I don't think the industry expected that in its wildest dreams."[39]

In 2006, the EPA adopted a rule prohibiting states and local governments from imposing stricter monitoring of pollution generated by power plants than is required by the federal government. Environmental groups, including the Sierra Club and the Natural Resources Defense Council, filed suit, and in August 2008 the U.S. Court of Appeals for the D.C. Circuit struck down the EPA rule, saying it violated the Clean Air Act.

Keri Powell, a lawyer for the environmental groups, said the court's ruling "affects every major stationary air-pollution source in the country. . . . This is a very important case, just in terms of the public's right to know and guarding the public's opportunity to keep tabs" on polluters.[40]

It was precisely this failure to enforce environmental law that precipitated an unprecedented Supreme Court case in 2007. In *Massachusetts v. Environmental Protection Agency*, 549 U.S. 547 (2007), the high court chastised the EPA for its failure to regulate auto emissions under the Clean Air Act. The high court's decision was a strong rebuke to the Bush administration, which had maintained that the EPA does not have the authority to regulate carbon dioxide and other gases under the Clean Air Act and that, even if it did, it would not exercise that authority.

Justice John Paul Stevens, joined by Justices Kennedy, Souter, Ginsburg, and Bryer, said that by offering nothing more than a "laundry list of reasons not to regulate," the EPA had defied the Clean Air Act's "clear statutory command." He said a refusal to regulate must be based on science and reasoned justification, and that the agency's claimed right to exercise its judgment on the issue was not "a roving license to ignore the statutory text."[41]

The case against the EPA had been brought by a broad coalition of states, cities, and environmental groups, signaling local dissatisfaction with federal enforcement of environmental law. As added emphasis to its ruling, the Supreme Court followed with a second decision on the Clean Air Act, issuing an expansive reading of the EPA's authority to regulate emissions from factories and power plants. The unanimous ruling in *Environmental Defense v. Duke Energy Corp.* resulted in reopening a federal enforcement effort against the Duke Energy Corporation under the Clean Air Act.

In December 2007, the EPA responded to the Supreme Court ruling by proposing a rule limiting greenhouse gas emissions from new vehicles. The proposed rule was sent to the White House Office of Management and Budget (OMB) by the EPA's associate deputy administrator, Jason Burnett. White House officials had pressured Burnett not to issue the new rule, and when he emailed the order to OMB, the White House intervened once more, demanding that the email be recalled.

Burnett chose to resign, explaining that he left because the White House was preventing the EPA from responding to the Supreme Court's decision. In his resignation statement, he described the actions that must be taken to address the risk of climate change. "The White House made it clear they did not want to address the ramifications of that finding and have decided to leave the challenge to the next administration. Some [at the White House] thought that EPA had mistakenly concluded that climate change endangers the public. It was no mistake."[42]

Having withdrawn Burnett's proposal, the Bush administration charged EPA Administrator Stephen Johnson with the responsibility for a new draft. According to one EPA official, Johnson and his top aides had been in intense negotiations with the White House on revising the original draft. S. William Becker, executive director of the National Association of Clean Air Agencies, said the White House found the EPA's original draft unacceptable: "It demonstrates that the Transportation Department's proposed fuel economy standards fall far short of what is technologically feasible and cost effective."[43]

The Bush administration thus prevented the EPA from responding to the Supreme Court's ruling. Indeed, at this point, a cowered EPA seemed intent on imposing its own passivity on state governments. In December 2007, the state of California, disappointed with the EPA's lax standards on vehicle emissions, created its own tough standards. Because federal law authorizes the EPA to establish national emissions standards, California needed a waiver from the EPA to establish its own. Granting such a waiver was considered a mere formality—California had been granted such waivers numerous times over the years—but, under pressure from the White House, the EPA denied the waiver request.

As described in Chapter 5, California governor Arnold Schwarzenegger initiated a suit to overcome the EPA's waiver denial, and the suit was joined by 16 other states that wished to adopt California's emissions standards. EPA Administrator Johnson was called before House and Senate committees to explain why he overruled the agency's science advisers, who were in favor of granting California and 16 other states permission to mandate strict vehicle emissions standards. In his testimony, Johnson refused to discuss the White House role in his decision, leading Representative Henry Waxman (D-NY), chairman of the House Oversight and Government Reform Committee, to subpoena documents about White House communications with the EPA.

Among the documents obtained was a briefing prepared for the EPA's general counsel that said, "[W]e don't believe there are any good arguments against granting the waiver. . . . All of the arguments . . . are likely to lose in court if we are sued."[44]

Embarrassed by the appearance of political influence on the EPA's final decision, the Bush administration invoked executive privilege and refused to release any other documents. Waxman responded, "Administrator Johnson has repeatedly insisted he reached his decision on California's petition and the new ozone standard on his own. . . . Today's assertion of executive privilege raises serious questions about Administrator Johnson's credibility and the involvement of the president."[45]

Johnson was similarly unresponsive in his appearance before the Senate Committee on Environment and Public Works, after which Chair Barbara Boxer introduced a bill that would direct the EPA to grant California a waiver to regulate vehicle emissions under the Clean Air Act. Boxer declared: "Administrator Johnson's decision to deny the waiver was not supported by the facts, by the law, by the science, or by precedent."[46]

Senator Diane Feinstein (D-CA) said, "It's become clear that Administrator Johnson's denial of California's waiver was based on politics, not science. Even the EPA's own experts have said that there was a compelling need for action. So, today, Senator Boxer and I have introduced legislation to take this decision out of the hands of the EPA—and allow California to move ahead with curbing tailpipe emissions."[47]

Senator Patrick Leahy (D-VT) said, "The Bush administration has been AWOL or worse on air quality issues, and now they even want to undermine states like California and Vermont that are trying to pick up the slack. They won't lead and they won't follow."[48] In May 2009, the new Obama administration pledged that, beginning in 2012, the federal government would impose its own limits on tailpipe emissions. The following month, Obama's EPA granted California's request to set its own limits on emissions until the federal limits kick in.[49]

WILDERNESS AND WILDLIFE

The definition of "wilderness" has been established by statute, but the federal government's obligation to protect it has shifted with the political winds. The National Wilderness Preservation System was created on September 3, 1964, when President Lyndon Johnson signed the Wilderness Act. The preservation system created by the act was to protect those lands, already owned by the American people, that were "untrammeled by man, where man himself is a visitor who does not remain."[50]

Such lands were to be managed "for the use and enjoyment of the American people in such manner as will leave them unimpaired for future use and enjoyment as wilderness." No roads or structures were to be built there, and vehicles and other mechanical equipment were not to be used. Although 9.1 million acres of national forest were immediately designated by the act, much more was to be added after the federal land-managing agencies surveyed their territory and made recommendations to Congress as to which areas qualified as "wilderness."[51]

During the Clinton administration, the state of Utah set in motion a conflict over wilderness lands that would eventually allow the Bush administration to declare that the Department of the Interior could no longer identify and protect wilderness as it had in the past. After the Clinton Interior Department designated 2.6 million acres of land in Utah for wilderness consideration, Utah sued in 1996, arguing that only Congress could designate wilderness lands. Utah lost the case in federal appeals court in 1998, with the court ruling that the "plain language" of the Federal Land Policy Management Act required the Interior Department's Bureau of Land Management to continually review land under its control and determine its suitability for wilderness protection.

Utah filed an amended complaint in 2003, and the Bush administration quietly settled the Utah suit behind closed doors, giving the state all that it had asked while using the settlement as a pretext for declaring a radical new land-use agenda. That agenda was spelled out by Utah's lead lawyer in a memo issued shortly before the settlement.

"We need a clear statement," the lawyer, Connie Brooks, wrote to the Bush Interior Department. "No more wilderness."[52]

Bush's Interior Secretary Gail Norton responded by declaring that the Interior Department would henceforth be barred from identifying and protecting wilderness. Environmental groups challenged the Utah settlement and the new wilderness policy, saying the accord was an illegal backroom deal that allowed Norton and Utah governor Mike Leavitt to emasculate federal protection of pristine lands. Bush revealed his position on the controversy by appointing Leavitt as head of the EPA.

In a related development, the Bush administration announced a plan to reverse longstanding "roadless area" protections for national forests located in Idaho, Colorado, and Alaska. The "roadless rule," established during the Clinton administration, had placed nearly a third of the national forests off-limits to development. During Bush's first term, timber companies challenged the rule in court, losing on appeal. In 2005, the administration issued a new rule allowing state governors to decide which land in national forests may be opened to development, but that rule was overturned by the federal courts, reinstating the Clinton-era roadless rule.

Unable to alter national policy on roadless areas, the Bush administration circumvented federal court rulings by creating a piecemeal policy in three states. "The Bush administration is just dedicated in its last months to go after the roadless rule one forest at a time,"[53] said Franz Matzner of the Natural Resources Defense Council. "The roadless rule and the courts have sheltered many of the last, best places in our national forests, even during an administration hostile to forest protection. Now, with one foot out the door, Bush officials are looking for whichever way they can to give away the family silver."[54]

Opening up national forests to logging and other development not only puts a "for sale" sign on the trees but also puts the wildlife in vast wilderness areas at risk. Trish Rolphe of the Alaska Sierra Club describes Alaska's Tongass Forest as "the crown jewel of our nation's roadless wildlands." She says, "Wild salmon, bears, eagles, and wolves thrive there among moss-draped ancient trees, along crystalline fjords and untamed rivers. It has nine million acres of roadless areas that lack permanent protection. The Bush administration has just put some of the best of them on the chopping block."[55]

On May 28, 2009, the new Obama administration took action to impose a "timeout" on incursions into roadless wildlands. Agriculture Secretary Tom Vilsack issued a temporary order requiring all new projects in roadless areas to be approved by him personally. A spokesman for the department said, "We're raising the level of scrutiny. From this moment . . . we are going to make sure that our forests are protected in all projects that we approve."[56]

Despite such setbacks, the political winds have begun to shift in Congress. For years, Representative Richard Pombo (R-CA) fiercely opposed designating any new wilderness areas. As a result, by early 2008, the Bush administration had offered more than 40 million acres in the Rockies for oil and gas drilling and 70 million acres in the Alaskan Arctic for similar "extractive" uses. During this period, the Forest Service estimated that development was eliminating 6,000 acres of open space every day.

When Pombo lost his seat and committee chairmanship, his successor, Representative Nick Rahall (D-WV), began shepherding numerous bills to extend wilderness protection. Rahall declared, "To those critics who say, 'Why do we need new wilderness?' I say these areas are already wilderness. We simply want to preserve them . . . for future generations."[57]

Representative Jay Inslee (D-WA), another member of the Natural Resources Committee, said one man had prevented the will of the American people from being fulfilled. "What you're seeing right how is this one-man dam has broken," said Inslee.[58]

As protection for wilderness areas diminished during the Bush administration, the survival of animal species within those areas depended increasingly on the Endangered Species Act (ESA). Unfortunately, the ESA itself is among the more politically manipulated of all the federal environmental statutes. In 2005, a survey of scientists conducted by the Union of Concerned Scientists (UCS) and Public Employees for Environmental Responsibility (PEER) revealed how political interference was perverting the Endangered Species Act. In particular, the survey showed that political intervention to alter scientific results had become pervasive with the U.S. Fish and Wildlife Service (FWS).

Among the survey results were:

- Nearly half of all respondents whose work is related to endangered species reported that "they have been directed, for non-scientific reasons, to refrain from making jeopardy or other findings that are protective of species." One in five agency scientists said they had been "directed to inappropriately exclude or alter technical information from a FWS scientific document."

- More than half of all respondents reported cases where "commercial interests [had] inappropriately induced the reversal or withdrawal of scientific conclusions or decisions through political intervention."
- More than a third said they could not openly express "concerns about the biological needs of species and habitats without fear of retaliation."

Some of the respondents attached explanatory statements to the survey form. One such statement from a biologist from Alaska described the climate of fear within the agency. "Recently, [DOI] officials have forced changes in Service documents, and worse, they have forced upper level managers to say things that are incorrect," he wrote. "It's one thing for the Department to dismiss our recommendations, it's quite another to be forced (under veiled threat of removal) to say something that is counter our best professional judgment."[59]

Spokespersons for the two organizations that conducted the survey were understandably shocked at the extent of political manipulations revealed in the responses.

Lexi Shultz of the Union for Concerned Scientists said, "The survey results illustrate an alarming disregard for scientific facts among political appointees entrusted to protect threatened and endangered species. Employing scientists only to undermine their findings is at best a mismanagement of public resources and at worst a serious betrayal of the public trust."[60]

PEER Program Director Rebecca Roose said, "Political science, not biology, has become the dominant discipline in today's Fish and Wildlife Service."[61]

The Bush administration's policy on endangered species may be the most disturbing example of its indifference to wildlife, having listed only 25 species as endangered during the entire first term, all forced by court order. Compare that to the Clinton administration, which listed an average of 65 species *per year*, or even Bush Senior's administration, which listed an average of 58 species per year.[62]

During George W. Bush's first term, Craig Manson, assistant secretary for fish, wildlife, and parks, led the attack on the Endangered Species Act, often suppressing or manipulating scientific studies that recommended listing a species. Manson made no secret of his disdain for protecting endangered species. "If we are saying that the loss of species in and of itself is inherently bad, I don't think we know enough about how the world works to say that," declared Manson. "The orthodoxy is that every species had a place in the ecosystem and therefore the loss of any species diminishes us in some negative way. But it's a presumptuous thing to suggest that we know for sure that that is a fact."[63]

During Bush's second term, Julie MacDonald, deputy assistant secretary at the Department of the Interior, continued to discourage the listing of endangered species. In early 2007, following an internal DOI investigation, MacDonald was found guilty of editing scientific decisions on endangered species, altering scientific content in the agency's documents, violating ethics rules, forcing scientists at the U.S. Fish and Wildlife Services to alter their findings, and leaking confidential agency information to lobbyists for farm and industry groups.

MacDonald resigned after the results of the investigation were made public, but Democrats in Congress pursued the matter. A hearing before Representative Nick Rahall's House Committee on Natural Resources heard testimony on the Bush administration's efforts to revise the ESA by rewriting the law's enforcement regulations.

"From changes in regulations to poorly developed legal reviews . . . the evidence of a systematic effort to undermine the law and species protection is quite clear," said Rahall.[64]

The Fish and Wildlife Service soon began reviewing any Endangered Species Act decisions influenced by MacDonald, revisiting seven rulings that denied endangered species listings or critical habitat designations. The Government Accountability Office (GAO) said the scope of the review was too narrow, and Robin Nazzaro, head of the GAO's natural resources and environment division, told the House Committee on Natural Resources, "Questions remain about the extent to which Interior officials other than MacDonald may have inappropriately influenced ESA decisions and whether broader ESA policies should be revisited."[65] Indeed, in interviews and surveys with the GAO, FWS employees cited at least four other Interior Department political appointees who may have inappropriately influenced decisions.

Committee Chairman Rahall was more explicit in his criticism. "The agency's well-publicized post-MacDonald review, ostensibly designed to correct listing and critical habitat decisions—decisions tainted by politics—was a boondoggle; it is fixing nothing," said Rahall. "As a result, we can have no confidence that political tinkering with the ESA program is being addressed any better now than it was under the MacDonald reign. At this point, the best hope for endangered species may simply be to cling to life until after January when this president and his cronies . . . hit the unemployment line."[66]

Even a new administration may not be able to overcome a last-minute strategy by the Bush administration to issue new agency "rules" affecting endangered species. One example concerns the polar bear, a species listed as "threatened" only after environmental groups sued the Interior Department in 2005. When the department missed the stipulated deadline for listing the polar bear, another suit finally forced the listing on May 15, 2008. What made the determination particularly significant was its justification, which, for the first time, said a species was imperiled because of global warming and the resultant melting of arctic ice.

In announcing the listing of the polar bear, administration officials sought to minimize the policy consequences of the decision. Dick Hall, head of the Fish and Wildlife Service, said no regulations designed to reduce global warming would be justified by the listing unless a direct connection between human activity and the polar bear's plight could be proved. "We have to be able to connect the dots," he said. "We don't have the science today to do that."[67]

Jamie Rappaport Clark, head of FWS during the Clinton administration, said, "The administration has been brought kicking and screaming to this decision. This decision isn't over by a long shot."[68]

Indeed, on August 12, 2008, the Bush administration played its last card in the contest over protecting the polar bear, proposing a rule to overhaul the Endangered Species Act, eliminating the previously required independent scientific reviews of federal projects that might imperil protected species. The new rule would thus prevent any review of climate change policies in drafting the recovery plan for polar bears. The ultimate fate of that rule is examined in detail in Chapter 10.

NOTES

1. Union of Concerned Scientists, "Interference at the EPA," April 2008, 1, www.uscusa .org/scientific_integrity/interference-at-the-epa.html.
2. Ibid., 2.
3. Ibid., 2–3.
4. "Bush's EPA Is Pursuing Fewer Polluters," *Washington Post*, September 30, 2007, A1, A19.
5. "Budget Cut Would Shutter EPA Libraries," *Washington Post*, May 15, 2006, A15.
6. "EPA Closure of Libraries Faulted for Curbing Access to Key Data," *Washington Post*, March 14, 2008, A15.
7. "Papers Detail Industry's Role in Cheney's Energy Report," *Washington Post*, July 18, 2007, A8.
8. "Standing in the Way of a Good Story," *Washington Post*, September 9, 2005, C7.
9. Ibid.
10. Ibid.
11. "FEMA Meets the Press, Which Happens to Be . . . FEMA," *Washington Post*, October 26, 2007, A19.
12. Al Kamen, "You Messed Up, Now Here's Your Promotion," *Washington Post*, November 8, 2007, A19.
13. "FEMA Press Secretary Directed Fake News Briefing, Inquiry Finds," *Washington Post*, November 9, 2007, A19.
14. "The Ghost of Brownie," editorial, *Washington Post*, October 30, 2007, A14.
15. J. Stephen Griles to James L. Connaughton, chairman, Council on Environmental Quality, memorandum, October 5, 2001, www.tlpj.org.
16. Cindy Tibbot, U.S. Fish and Wildlife Service, October 30, 2002, email correspondence circulated internally. Part of FOIA request documents available at www.tlpj.org.
17. David Densmore, Supervisor, Pennsylvania Field Office, U.S. Fish and Wildlife Service, "FWS Comments on 9/20/02 Draft of Chapter IV (Alternatives)," memorandum, September 30, 2002, available at www.tlpj.org.
18. Seth Shulman, *Undermining Science: Suppression and Distortion in the Bush Administration* (Berkeley: University of California Press, 2006), 80.

19. "Leveling a Mountain of Research on Mountaintop Removal Strip Mining," Union of Concerned Scientists, July 2004, www.ucusa.org/scientific_integrity/abuses_of _science/case_studies_and_evidence/mountaintop-removal.

20. Gerald Winegrad et al. to President George W. Bush and John Forren, Environmental Protection Agency, January 2, 2004, available at www.ohvec.org.

21. "Mines Get Freer Hand to Dump Waste," *Washington Post*, October 18, 2008, A6.

22. Ibid.

23. David Fahrenthold, "Mountaintop Mining to Get More Scrutiny," *Washington Post*, June 11, 2009, A6.

24. Michael Grunwald, "The Scandal Came before Katrina Hit," *Washington Post*, May 14, 2006, A5.

25. U.S. Senate Committee on Environment and Public Works, full committee hearing, *Perchlorate and TCE in Water*, May 6, 2008, http://epw.senate.gov/public/index .cfm?FuseAction=Hearings.Hearing&Hearing_ID=9cb06bed-802a-2.

26. Ibid.

27. Ibid.

28. Ibid.

29. Senator Barbara Boxer, "Perchlorate and TCE in the Nation's Waters," prepared statement, press release, May 6, 2008, http://epw.senate.gov/public/index.cfm?FuseAction= PressRoom.PressReleases&ContentRecord_id.

30. "EPA Makes No Rule on Chemical in Water," *Washington Post*, October 4, 2008, A3.

31. Ibid.

32. "EPA Advisers Seek Perchlorate Review," *Washington Post*, November 14, 2008, A8.

33. Ibid.

34. Quoted in Bruce E. Johansen, *The Dirty Dozen: Toxic Chemicals and the Earth's Future* (Westport, CT: Praeger, 2003), 27.

35. "Administration Reportedly Forces Out EPA Official," *Washington Post*, May 3, 2008, A2.

36. Ibid.

37. Eric Schaeffer, "Clearing the Air," *Washington Monthly*, July/August 2002, 2, 7, www.washingtonmonthly.com/features/2001/0207.schaeffer.html.

38. J. Lee, "Critics Say E.P.A. Won't Analyze Clean Air Proposals Conflicting with President's Politics," *New York Times*, July 14, 2003.

39. Bruce Barcott, "Up in Smoke," *New York Times Sunday Magazine*, April 4, 2004.

40. "Bush Administration Rule on Pollution Struck Down," *Washington Post*, August 20, 2008, A2.

41. "Justices Say E.P.A. Has Power to Act on Harmful Gases," *New York Times*, April 3, 2007, www.nytimes.com/2007/04/03/washington/03scotus.html?_r=1.

42. "White House Tried to Silence EPA Proposal on Car Emissions," *Washington Post*, June 26, 2008, A2

43. Ibid.

44. "Official: White House Influenced EPA Ruling on California Emissions," McClatchy Washington Bureau, May 19, 2008, www.mcclatchydc.com/homepage/ story/37681.html.

45. "White House Refuses to Release Documents on Air-Quality Policy," *Washington Post*, June 21, 2008, A4.

46. Senate Committee on Environment and Public Works, "Boxer Introduces Bill to Reverse EPA Waiver Decision," January 24, 2008.

47. Ibid.
48. Ibid. http://epw.senate.gov/public/index.cfm?FuseAction=Majority.PressReleases.
49. David Fahrenthold, "EPA to Let Calif. Set Own Auto Emissions Limits," *Washington Post*, July 1, 2009, A2.
50. The Wilderness Society, "The Wilderness Act of 1964," www.wilderness.org/OurIssues/Wilderness/act.cfm.
51. Ibid.
52. "Recasting Wilderness As Open for Business," *Los Angeles Times*, October 25, 2004, 2, www.latimes.com/new/nationworld/politics/scotus/la-na-wild25oct25,1,4217675.story?ctrack=.
53. "Administration Forest Plan Assailed," *Washington Post*, January 26, 2008, A4.
54. Natural Resources Defense Council, "Bush Administration Strips Protections from America's Largest Forest," January 25, 2008, www.nrdc.org/media/2008/080125a.asp.
55. Ibid.
56. David Fahrenthold, "'Roadless' Forest Areas Now under Vilsack," *Washington Post*, May 29, 2009, A15.
57. "Congress Pushes to Keep Land Untamed," *Washington Post*, June 16, 2008, A10.
58. Ibid.
59. Public Employees for Environmental Responsibility, "Politics Trumps Science at U.S. Fish and Wildlife Service," February 9, 2005, http://peer.org/news/news_id.php?row_id=474.
60. Ibid.
61. Ibid.
62. Defenders of Wildlife, "Sabotaging the Endangered Species Act," December 3, 2003, www.defenders.org.
63. Amanda Griscom, "Craig's List: An Interview with Bush's Point Person on Species and Parks," *Grist Magazine*, April 15, 2004, www.grist.org.
64. "Endangered Species Act: Politics Endangers Science," Environmental Science & Technology Online News, June 4, 2007, http://pubs.acs.org/subscribe/journals/esthag-w/2007/june/policy/rc_endangered.html.
65. "Endangered Species: Political Influence May Be Wider Than MacDonald," E & E News PM, May 21, 2008, www.americanlands.org/news.php.
66. Ibid.
67. "Polar Bear Is Named 'Threatened' Species," *Washington Post*, May 15, 2008, A1.
68. Ibid.

7

The Politics of Public Health

Surgeon General C. Everett Koop takes reporters' questions after releasing a report on smoking that branded nicotine as an addictive drug, May 16, 1988. (AP Photo/Susan Walsh)

Protecting the health and safety of the American public may be the most significant service rendered by the federal government, but political interference has often undercut or perverted the performance of that responsibility. The tarnished reputation of the Department of Health and Human Services (HHS) can be traced to the shabby treatment accorded to our surgeons general by a succession of administrations, both Republican and Democrat.

THE NATION'S DOCTOR

Known popularly as "The Nation's Doctor," the U.S. surgeon general is charged with the responsibility to protect, promote, and advance the health, safety, and security of the nation, and, in practice, the surgeon general is the chief public-health educator for the United States. In an unprecedented congressional hearing in 2007, three former attorneys general of the United States gave examples of political restraints on their communications. Representative Henry Waxman (D-CA), who chaired the hearing, said:

Political interference is compromising the independence of the Office. On key public health issues the Surgeon General has been muzzled. This probably will not solve itself. . . . As we will hear this morning, political interference with the work of the Surgeon General appears to have reached a new level in this administration. We will hear how reports were blocked, speeches were censored and travel restricted. We will also hear how the Surgeon General had to resist repeated efforts to enlist his office to advance partisan political agendas."[1]

Former Surgeon General C. Everett Koop, who served under Presidents Ronald Reagan and George Bush, Senior, told the House committee that Reagan was pressured by members of his cabinet to fire him because his findings on the transmission of HIV went against the conservative view that "those who had AIDS deserved what they got."[2]

When asked to identify the source of political pressure on scientists, Koop said, "I suppose it was 'they and them.' My Chief of Staff frequently had calls from the White House—you all know what that means—This is the White House calling. My boss doesn't like what your boss said yesterday."[3] Koop concluded, "I believe that the Surgeon General should not be a political appointment."[4]

Following Koop's testimony, former Surgeon General David Satcher, who served from February 1998 until 2002, told of his uneasiness in the wake of the firing of Joycelyn Elders, who had preceded him as surgeon general. President Clinton had forced Elders to resign in 1994 after she remarked that public schools should consider teaching about masturbation.

Satcher said Elders was fired "because of comments she made having to do with sexuality," and he reflected, "It was a difficult time—the nature of Dr. Elders' firing created a difficult situation, and one that undermined the Office of the Surgeon General."[5]

Satcher testified that while working under President Bill Clinton, he was prevented from releasing a report on sexuality and public health, in part because of sensitivities triggered by the Monica Lewinski scandal.

The final witness was former Surgeon General Richard Carmona, who began serving in August 2002 and was forced out unceremoniously just a few days before the end of his first term. He began by saying, "My fellow U.S. Surgeons General warned me that partisan political agendas often undermine the public health and well-being of our nation. . . . As I witnessed partisanship and political manipulation, I was astounded but also unsure of what I was witnessing—for I had no reference point."[6]

Faced with unexpected political pressures early in his tenure, Carmona turned to previous attorneys general for insight into the process and how it could be navigated. What he learned from his predecessors was disturbing.

"[N]ever had they seen Washington, D.C. so partisan, or a new Surgeon General so politically challenged and marginalized as during my tenure," recalled Carmona. He continued:

[T]he reality is that the nation's doctor has been marginalized and relegated to a position with no independent budget, and with supervisors who are political appointees with partisan agendas. Anything that doesn't fit into the political appointees' ideological, theological, or political agenda is ignored, marginalized, or simply buried. The problem with this approach is that in public health, as in a democracy, there is nothing worse than ignoring science, or marginalizing the voice of science for reasons driven by changing political winds. The job of Surgeon General is to be "the doctor of the nation"—not "the doctor of a political party."[7]

Carmona said the Bush administration made it extremely difficult to discuss the science behind issues like stem cell research. "Much of the discussion was being driven by theology, ideology, and preconceived beliefs that were scientifically incorrect. I approached leadership to say the Surgeon General should . . . make sure the American public, and our elected officials, our appointed officials are all knowledgeable about the science. I was blocked at every turn. I was told the decision had already been made, stand down, don't talk about it. That information was removed from my speeches."[8]

When Chairman Waxman asked if Carmona had other speeches censored, Carmona answered, "Repeatedly."[9]

Carmona was constantly pressured to alter his reports and communications. "The vetting was done by political appointees who were specifically there to be able to spin, if you will, my words in such a way that would be preferable to a political or an ideologically preconceived notion that had nothing to do with science," he said. "[T]hings were put into my speeches. . . . I told the staff, let them put in whatever they want, I will not say it anyway."[10]

Camona said he was pressured to mention the president's name throughout his speeches: "I was told it should be mentioned . . . at least three times on every page. I said I am not going to do that. I said I will mention any politician when

participants at the meeting that Mosholder was being removed from the schedule because his work was not "finalized."

Subsequent investigations revealed that Mosholder's FDA supervisors had not only censored his research, but had threatened him with criminal prosecution if he discussed his findings with anyone. Ultimately, those findings would be fully corroborated, leading to warning labels on antidepressants and dramatic decreases in their use by children.

A similar, more highly publicized FDA scandal occurred in late 2004, when Dr. David Graham, an associate director in the FDA's Office of Drug Safety, told his supervisors of disturbing findings about cardiovascular risks in patients taking the popular painkiller Vioxx. Graham's research showed that taking Vioxx could triple a patient's risk of a heart attack. As in the Mosholder case, the FDA muzzled Graham, prevented him from publishing his research, and even tried to force him to resign.

Fearing for his job, Graham contacted the Government Accountability Project (GAP), a nonprofit whistle-blower support group. GAP's legal director, Tom Devine, says he received an anonymous phone call disparaging Graham's research and urging him to disregard Graham's account of his treatment. Devine traced the call and discovered that it came from the offices of top FDA management.

Graham submitted his work to the medical journal *The Lancet*, but FDA managers tried to force him to withdraw the article, claiming that he hadn't submitted it for an internal review. In reality, he had sought clearance weeks earlier. Meanwhile, Bush appointees at the FDA tried to denigrate his research, characterizing it with the pejorative term of choice, "junk science."

In November 2004, Graham appeared before a Senate Finance Committee hearing on Vioxx. He described the large epidemiological study he performed with Kaiser Permanente that concluded that high-dose Vioxx significantly increased the risk of heart attacks and sudden death. "This conclusion triggered an explosive response from the Office of New Drugs, which approved Vioxx in the first place and was responsible for regulating it post-marketing," said Graham. "The response from senior management in my office, the Office of Drug Safety, was equally stressful. I was pressured to change my conclusions and recommendations, and basically threatened that if I did not change them, I would not be permitted to present the paper at the conference. . . . This is similar to what Dr. Mosholder went through earlier this year when he reached his conclusion that most SSRIs [antidepressants] should not be used by children."[17]

Graham concluded, "Vioxx is a terrible tragedy and a profound regulatory failure. I would argue that the FDA, as currently configured, is incapable of protecting America against another Vioxx. We are virtually defenseless. It is important that this Committee and the American people understand that what has happened with Vioxx is really a symptom of something far more dangerous to the safety of the American people. Simply put, FDA and its Center for Drug Evaluation and Research are broken."[18]

Such testimony was unpopular with the pharmaceutical industry, and particularly with Merck, the firm that was grossing over $1 billion in annual sales of Vioxx. Still, when other researchers corroborated Graham's findings, Merck decided to remove Vioxx from the market.

More recently, the FDA has been involved in a controversy over two chemicals that pose particular danger to infants and young children. In September 2008, the FDA issued a draft report on bisphenol-A (BPA), a plastic hardener used in manufacturing baby bottles, linings on aluminum cans, and other food containers. The draft report concluded that BPA was safe for food storage, but a subcommittee of scientists from government and academia was assigned responsibility for researching the issue and making a formal recommendation to accept or reject the draft.

On October 30, the agency panel found that the FDA had ignored scientific evidence and used flawed methods when it declared BPA to be safe. The panel criticized the FDA for not taking into consideration scores of studies that have linked BPA to prostate cancer, diabetes, and other health problems in animals, and it concluded that the agency's margin of safety was "inadequate."

Sarah Janssen, a reproductive biologist at the Natural Resources Defense Council, said, "The current levels of exposure [to BPA] are not safe. We should get rid of it in food containers."[19]

Facing persistent charges that it had relied too heavily on industry-funded studies, an embarrassed FDA spokesperson responded, "FDA agrees that due to the uncertainties raised in some studies relating to the potential effects of low doses of bisphenol-A, that additional research would be valuable."[20]

Just weeks later, a similar dispute arose over the dangers of the contaminant melamine. Once more, the FDA said that consuming small doses of the chemical posed no serious risk to humans. The agency acknowledged that it was unable to determine what a safe amount of melamine in baby formula would be, but it set 2.5 parts per million as the maximum "tolerable" level in other foods.

Representative Rosa DeLauro (D-CT), head of the House subcommittee that oversees FDA funding, criticized the agency for accepting melamine in American food. "While other countries throughout the world, including the European Union, are acting to ban melamine-contaminated products . . . the FDA has chosen to establish an acceptable level of melamine in food in an attempt to convince customers that it is not harmful," said DeLauro. "Not only is this an insult to customers, but it would appear that the FDA is condoning the intentional contamination of food."[21]

After melamine was found in infant formula made by Nestle and Mead Johnson, DeLauro declared, "This FDA, this Bush administration, instead of protecting the public health, is protecting industry. We're talking about babies, about the most vulnerable. This really makes me angry."[22]

FDA spokesperson Judy Leon said, "We know trace levels [of melamine] do not pose a risk whatsoever," but critics pointed out that the FDA had said the same thing about bisphenol-A, making such assurances unconvincing. Ken

Cook, president of Environmental Working Group, said, "When FDA claims there isn't any reason to worry, that's exactly what the consumer should do. The once-revered public health agency has morphed into a taxpayer-funded public relations arm for the very industries it was created to oversee."[23]

HIV/AIDS

It is estimated that over 25 million people have lost their lives to the disease known as AIDS (Acquired Immune Deficiency Syndrome), despite the fact that the disease was first detected only thirty years ago. How could such a deadly disease spread so rapidly, and how have politics and cultivated ignorance contributed to the epidemic?

The HIV (Human Immonodeficiency Virus) retrovirus that causes AIDS was first isolated in 1984, and subsequent tests revealed a strong connection between the amount of HIV in the blood and the decline of a type of red blood cells (CD4+ T cells) that are essential to the normal function of the human immune system. In 1982, the Centers for Disease Control (CDC) formally established the term *AIDS* to describe the HIV-related syndrome and declared the new disease an epidemic.

In the early 1980s, people associated the disease with homosexuals, hemophiliacs, and intravenous drug users, allowing most politicians to conclude that their constituencies were not at risk. Only when the disease began to appear in women and children was it feared that transmission could occur through casual contact. In New York City, cab drivers wouldn't pick up people who looked sick. People stopped using public bathrooms.

The assumption of casual transmission was, of course, false, but in the absence of medical information and federal leadership, panic spread throughout the United States. Today, it is known that HIV can be transmitted through blood, semen, vaginal fluid, or even breast milk, but not through casual contact. Nonetheless, by 1994, AIDS had become the leading cause of death in the United States among 25- to 45-year-olds.

Although it normally takes years between the time of HIV infection and the development of full-blown AIDS, survival time following an AIDS diagnosis has been less than two years. Despite the alarming death rate from AIDS, the search for a cure has been a low federal priority since the Reagan administration. President Ronald Reagan didn't publicly mention the word "AIDS" until 1987, halfway through his second term. He briefly and generally referred to the problem in a press conference late in his first term, by which time the epidemic had taken the lives of more than 12,000 Americans.

Meanwhile, those suffering from AIDS were subject to discrimination, routinely evicted from their homes, fired from their jobs, and denied health insurance. Reagan's silence on the AIDS epidemic was encouraged by social conservatives such as domestic policy adviser Gary Bauer, who was offended at the idea of educating the public about "safe sex" or condoms to prevent

AIDS. Surgeon General C. Everett Koop was prevented from saying anything about AIDS during Reagan's entire first term. In his memoir, Koop recalled, "I have never understood why these peculiar restraints were placed on me."[24]

Dr. Michael Gottlieb, the immunologist who first recognized the looming AIDS epidemic, recalls, "In the first years of AIDS, I imagine we felt like the folks on the rooftops during Katrina, waiting for help." Epidemiologist Donald Francis of the CDC recalls the political opposition to his requests for funding an AIDS-prevention campaign. "It went up to Washington and they said f— off," says Francis, who subsequently resigned from the CDC in protest.[25]

The Reagan White House seemed dismissive, even contemptuous, of the AIDS threat. In a 1982 press conference, Reagan press spokesman Larry Speakes responded awkwardly to several questions.

Question: Does the President have any reaction to the announcement from the Center for Disease Control in Atlanta that AIDS is now an epidemic?
Speakes: What's AIDS?
Question: . . . It's a pretty serious thing that one in every three people that get this have died. And I wonder if the President is aware of it?
Speakes: I don't have it. Do you?
Question: . . . In other words, the White House looks on this as a great joke?
Speakes: No, I don't know anything about it. . . .
Question: Does the President, does anyone in the White House know about this epidemic?
Speakes: I don't think so. I don't think so, I don't think there's been any . . .
Question: Nobody knows?[26]

Many conservatives in the Reagan administration felt that AIDS was a homosexual disease and that homosexuals were being punished by God for their sinful lifestyle. In 1983, Reagan adviser Pat Buchanan editorialized, "The poor homosexuals—they have declared war against nature, and now nature is exacting an awful retribution."[27]

In the twenty years since the Reagan administration, there have been dramatic improvements in the treatment of HIV/AIDS patients, but the politics of the disease has not significantly changed. The Bush administration's AIDS policies were strongly influenced by conservative religious politics, and funding was often denied to medical programs that did not conform to the administration's point of view. Abstinence-only HIV-prevention programs were promoted to the exclusion of such proven strategies as sex education, needle exchange programs, and condom distribution. As we saw in Chapter 3, the Bush administration decided to remove the condom fact sheets from the "Programs That Work" section of the HHS Web site.

Despite the federal government's inaction on AIDS, there was growing public support for greater federal spending to treat the disease and prevent the spread of HIV. By 2006, two-thirds of Americans said the government was spending too little to fight HIV/AIDS, up from 52 percent in 2004. In addition,

60 percent of Americans said the United States had a responsibility to fight HIV/AIDS in developing countries.[28]

Such public pressure led the Centers for Disease Control (CDC) to recommend that all teenagers and most adults have routine HIV tests as part of routine medical care. The tests would be voluntary and would not require submission of a consent form. The Bush administration soon allocated federal funds for HIV vaccine research, although federal awards were restricted to a small group of researchers. In July 2008, Bush signed a bill committing the United States to spending about $40 billion over the next five years to fight AIDS overseas. The legislation extends an implicit pledge to continue funding for the purchase of lifesaving drugs for millions of people in developing countries.

The Bush administration has been widely praised for its international AIDS programs, but it should be noted that at least one-third of all U.S. government funds spent to prevent AIDS worldwide has been restricted to abstinence education. As a result, according to a 2006 Government Accountability Office (GAO) study, the policy has actually weakened the global fight against AIDS, because in order to receive any aid, officials in some countries have had to reduce spending on programs to prevent the transmission of HIV from women to their newborn babies. And, of course, prevention strategies stressing condom use have been ineligible for U.S. funding.

In the final analysis, Bush's AIDS policy will probably be judged on its willingness to fund and support social programs to prevent the spread of HIV in the United States. The most politically contentious of these programs is the needle exchange program (NEP). Because intravenous drug users, particularly those in poor urban areas, tend to share their needles, the likelihood of spreading HIV through contaminated needles is extremely high.

The number of AIDS cases directly attributed to intravenous drug use has climbed annually since the epidemic began. By 2003, an estimated 218,000 individuals had been infected with HIV/AIDS through their IV drug use, and another 93,000 cases were indirectly attributable to IV drug use. The number of such cases continues to increase annually. In response, many local communities around the country introduced programs to provide clean needles to drug users, thus eliminating HIV contamination. Conservative politicians who claimed that such programs may encourage drug use responded by passing federal legislation banning needle exchange programs.

The original statutory basis for the ban on NEPs came with the political agenda of the War on Drugs, which included the Model Drug Paraphernalia Act of 1979 (MDPA). The act made it unlawful to manufacture, sell, or distribute a wide range of devices if they could be used to introduce a controlled substance into the human body. Hypodermic syringes and needles were on the top of the prohibition list. In the 1980s, Congress passed a series of bills that further prohibited federal funding for the distribution of sterile syringes. The Anti-Drug Abuse Act of 1986 provided federal authority to strictly prohibit the sale and transportation of drug paraphernalia. In 1990 and 1991 appropriation acts, HHS specifically banned the funding of NEPs unless the surgeon general or president certified that such programs were effective in preventing HIV *and* did not encourage the use of illegal drugs. By 2009, five presidents and six surgeons general later, the federal funding ban on NEPs is still in effect.

Studies by the National Institutes of Health (NIH), the World Health Organization (WHO), the Centers for Disease Control, and other prominent health agencies and organizations have established that needle exchange programs not only prevent the transmission of HIV/AIDS, but do *not* encourage drug use. A 1995 National Academy of Sciences report affirmed that "well-implemented needle exchange programs can be effective in preventing the spread of HIV and do not increase the use of illegal drugs."[29]

In 1998, President Clinton's HHS secretary Donna Shalala announced, "We have concluded that needle-exchange programs, as part of a comprehensive HIV-prevention program, will decrease the transmission of HIV and will not encourage the use of illegal drugs." Yet, to the dismay and confusion of the public health community, Shalala followed with an awkward admission that this effective program would not be supported by the administration. "We had to make a choice," she said apologetically. "It was a decision. It was a decision to leave it to local communities."[30]

The Bush administration that succeeded Clinton was less apologetic in its rejection of NEPs. In 2005, Bush claimed that current medical research had "cast doubt on the pro-exchange consensus," and the White House referred a reporter to a number of scientists who were said to hold such doubts. When the reporter actually contacted those scientists, he discovered that they did not oppose needle exchange programs at all.

Despite the unambiguous scientific evidence supporting NEPs, Congress and the White House have ignored, dismissed, or disputed the research. Today, the United States remains the only country in the world to directly oppose the use of NEPs to prevent HIV/AIDS. Nonetheless, state funding and private philanthropy have allowed a patchwork of NEPs across the country to distribute millions of sterile syringes. Such programs have contributed to a 68 percent decline in the number of AIDS cases attributable to IV drug use since 1994.

SMOKING IS DANGEROUS TO YOUR HEALTH

The National Library of Medicine refers to cigarette smoking as "the leading cause of preventable death and disability in the United States."[31] It is sufficiently alarming to simply note that it causes death and disability, but to say that all of this medical misfortune is *preventable* suggests a high level of personal and political culpability.

By the 1950s, epidemiologists had established a link between smoking and the increase in lung cancer mortality. Pathologists soon confirmed the statistical relationship of smoking to lung cancer as well as to other serious diseases,

related to smoking and health. In return, the states would drop all claims against the companies and grant the industry immunity from future class action suits.

Because the settlement required changes in federal law before taking effect, the entire matter was left in the hands of the politicians. Unfortunately, most politicians in both parties were beholden to the tobacco industry. House members had received $1.67 million in tobacco contributions during the 1995–1996 election cycle, and senators had received $1.32 million between 1991 and 1996. Both parties had received an additional $6.6 million in soft money contributions from the tobacco industry in the 1995–1996 cycle.[34]

The consumer advocacy organization Public Citizen analyzed the tobacco-related votes in Congress during 1997, assigning each member a "pro-consumer" score based on the number of times the member voted *against* the big tobacco position. Those votes were then compared to campaign contributions from the tobacco industry. The analysis showed that on the Senate votes on tobacco issues during 1997, the 12 senators who voted most often for the tobacco industry position received an average of $32,258 in tobacco contributions from 1991 to 1996, an amount that was over 15 times greater than what was received by the 16 senators who voted consistently against the industry position.[35]

In the House, there were three votes on tobacco issues in 1997, and the members who voted for the tobacco industry position received over 9 times the campaign contributions from the industry than those who voted against the industry position.

In this highly politicized atmosphere, various members of Congress introduced their own bills designed to implement the tobacco settlement, but each of the bills failed. By the end of 1997, the potential settlement had unraveled, and the politics of tobacco returned to the status quo.

Federal regulation of tobacco and smoking had been headed off at the pass, but the already existing restraints on advertising and the ban on the sale of cigarettes to those under 18 years of age made it unlikely that future generations of Americans would be a reliable market for cigarette manufacturers. As smoking among young Americans declined dramatically, tobacco companies relied increasingly on overseas sales and the relatively stable domestic market among already addicted smokers.

But a growing wave of scientific research was suggesting a new public-health threat that would require the federal government to protect nonsmokers from smokers. What disturbed the tobacco industry was that this would require restraints on the inveterate smoker, the backbone of the domestic cigarette market. "Ambient smoke," or "second-hand smoke," was implicated in the same kinds of diseases, death, and disability as direct smoking. Many communities around the country had already designated restaurants and workplaces as "smoke free," and that trend soon became a tidal wave. But it was just the tip of the iceberg. Entire families were now at risk if a family member smoked in the home, in the automobile, or wherever second-hand smoke could be inhaled by a spouse, child, or friend.

Back in the early 1980s, epidemiological reports had begun to appear indicating that wives of smokers had increased cancer risks due to "environmental tobacco smoke." In 1992, an EPA "risk assessment" report estimated that second-hand smoke causes some 3,000 lung-cancer deaths each year. The EPA classified second-hand smoke as a human lung carcinogen, a conclusion already reached by a number of prominent health organizations. Now the EPA was in a position to impose second-hand smoke regulations and federal bans on smoking in public places.

The Tobacco Institute responded by characterizing the EPA's conclusions as "another step in a long process characterized by a preference for political correctness over sound science."[36] The tobacco industry attacked the research through a conservative advocacy group, The Advancement of Sound Science Coalition (TASSC), headed by former New Mexico governor Garrey Carruthers. The tobacco giant Philip Morris had decided to form such a group the moment the EPA had issued its report on second-hand smoke. In a February 17, 1993, memo to Philip Morris president William Campbell, the company's vice president Ellen Merlo wrote, "Our overriding objective is to discredit the EPA report." She said that Philip Morris had hired the PR firm APCO "to form local coalitions to help us educate about the danger of 'junk science.'"[37]

In the autumn of 1993, when TASSC was ready to launch its public face, its PR firm wrote Philip Morris that "the groundwork we conduct to complete the launch will enable the TASSC to expand and assist Philip Morris in its efforts with issues in targeted states in 1994."[38]

The science on second-hand smoke was clear, but a well-funded group of political contrarians held off federal action by casting doubt on the data. A 1998 analysis of over 100 review articles on the health risks of ambient smoke, published in the *Journal of the American Medical Association*, found that the likelihood of an article reaching a "not harmful" conclusion was "88.4 times higher" if the authors had tobacco industry affiliations. Often, the study noted, such authors had not disclosed their industry backers.[39]

Such action succeeded in delaying federal action until 2006, when Surgeon General Richard Carmona released a report that was unambiguous on the dangers of second-hand smoke. Carmona was interviewed by public television news anchor Jim Lehrer, who asked if the debate over second-hand smoke had finally been resolved.

"The debate is over," answered Carmona. "It causes disease and kills people. . . . It is clear now that we have enough science to say that it causes significant disease, as well as death, across the board, from birth to the senior population."[40]

Carmona said 126 million Americans are exposed to second-hand smoke, and he predicted that "every day that they're exposed, it's another day toward added risk for disease, cardiovascular disease, cancer, lung disease. . . . Even small exposure, just a few minutes of exposure, begins cellular changes that start to harm your cells."

When asked for a concluding message, Carmona said, "Stay away from second hand smoke. There's no safe amount of second hand smoke and it will hurt you."[41]

It seemed that science had closed every door to the tobacco industry. Smoking could no longer be considered a bad habit, but a personal choice. The smoking environment was a public-health danger to everyone. Congressional action seemed imminent.

In 2007, Congress held hearings on the Family Smoking Prevention and Tobacco Act, a bill that would grant the FDA the authority to regulate tobacco products and smoking. Identical versions of the bill in the House and Senate would give the FDA the same authority over tobacco that it has over drugs, medical devices, and many foods. Under the bill, the agency could regulate the levels of tar, nicotine, and other harmful ingredients in cigarettes and smoke.

At the House hearing, FDA Commissioner Andrew von Eschenbach surprised committee members by claiming that "the bill could undermine the public health role of FDA." The Bush administration had never supported the bill, but the FDA's argument against it was unusual. Von Eschenbach noted that the FDA is required to promote the public health, and he claimed that the bill would inappropriately "apply this framework to tobacco products that, when used as intended, produce disease rather than promote health." He concluded, "[W]e are concerned that the public will believe that products 'approved' by the Agency are safe and that this will actually encourage individuals to smoke more rather than less."[42]

Given the Bush administration's support for the tobacco industry, von Eschenbach's explanation seemed disingenuous to supporters of the bill. The legislation had the support of 200 sponsors in the House, 55 in the Senate, and more than 500 public advocacy groups, yet the threat of a presidential veto delayed a vote on it.

In 2008, Michael Leavitt, Bush's secretary of health and human services, said, "The administration would strongly oppose this legislation." In a letter to Representative Joe Barton of Texas, the ranking Republican member of the House committee that had approved the bill, Leavitt complained about the cost of enforcing the regulations proposed in the bill and said, "Unlike the medical products FDA regulates, tobacco products cannot be made safe, and there is no medically established public health benefit associated with tobacco. Adding tobacco to FDA's regulatory responsibilities could also leave the public with the misperception that tobacco products are safe, or at least safer, with the FDA regulating them."[43]

On July 30, 2008, the House voted 326 to 102 to approve the bill giving the FDA the power to ban the marketing of cigarettes to children, require disclosure of tobacco ingredients, reduce or eliminate harmful ingredients, mandate more-specific health warnings, and ban candy- or fruit-flavored cigarettes. The White House signaled that President Bush would veto the bill if it passed the Senate.

On June 11, 2009, a new Senate bill regulating tobacco was passed by a 79 to 17 vote. The bill then went back to the House, where it passed by a wide margin. New President Obama, himself a smoker struggling to quit, said he would sign the bill, which gives sweeping new powers to the federal government to oversee tobacco products. Matthew Myers, president of the Campaign for Tobacco-Free Kids, said, "A bill this broad, comprehensive, this strong would have been unimaginable even five years ago."[44]

AMERICA'S OBESITY EPIDEMIC

The medical data documenting an obesity epidemic in America and linking it to disease and death is indisputable. A 2009 study revealed:

- About 32% of American adults are obese.
- The incidence of obesity has more than doubled in the past 30 years.
- Each obese patient costs health insurers and government programs $1,429, or 42% more, a year than a normal-weight individual.
- Without obesity, spending by Medicaid would be 8.5% less and Medicare would be lowered by 11.8%.[45]

Being obese, or just overweight, increases the risk of developing a host of diseases. Obesity is an independent risk factor for coronary heart disease, high blood pressure, and elevated cholesterol. It has been causally linked to many other diseases, including diabetes, vascular disease, sleep apnea, liver disease, gall bladder disease, degenerative joint disease, osteoarthritis, and certain types of cancer. Over the past two decades, obesity has doubled among adults, and the number of overweight children has tripled.

The political battle over obesity is reminiscent of the very early days of the "tobacco wars," when smoking was regarded as a personal choice, not to be limited by the public interest. Obesity may be an even more difficult public-health issue to confront than was smoking, because, unlike smoking, obesity is not an unhealthy *activity*. It is a *condition* caused by unhealthy eating habits. States can ban smoking in public places, but can they ban excessive eating in restaurants? It took decades of scientific debate and political struggle to impose modest limits on the tobacco industry. The fast-food industry may be an even more formidable foe.

The federal government did not officially acknowledge the connection between diet and disease until 1969, when a White House conference on food, health, and nutrition addressed the issue. The first authoritative evidence of alarming increases in obesity rates came from the National Institutes of Health in the 1970s. It would be almost 25 years before the U.S. surgeon general's "Call to Action" in 2001 declared obesity to be an American epidemic. Perhaps the most significant change in attitude came in 2004, when the Department of Health and Human Services officially classified obesity as a disease. But this appeared to be a disease caused by personal self-indulgence, fueled by corporate greed, and enabled by political corruption.

About 31 percent of Americans were obese in 2000, according to the CDC, up dramatically from 14.5 percent in 1971. In 2000, women consumed 1,877 calories daily, and men consumed 2,618, both up dramatically over 1971, when the average consumption rates were 1,542 and 2,450 calories respectively. What could possibly have caused Americans to begin eating much more food, food their bodies clearly didn't require?

The problem of obesity in the United States is primarily a function of over-production of food, which is then aggressively marketed toward overconsumption. Food companies market primarily to children, promoting high-calorie, highly sweetened foods. They also encourage consumption of larger portions of those foods through "super-size" and "two-for-one" promotions and larger bottles of soft drinks. The agriculture, food product, restaurant, diet, and drug industries all profit when people eat more than they need, and their lobby groups discourage the government from taking action that would inhibit the production and marketing of food. To make matters worse, the fast-food industry is aggressively marketing ingredients that contribute directly to obesity: fat, salt, and sugar.

The primary sources of fat in the American diet are red meats, plant oils, and dairy products, and the government heavily subsidizes all three. Federal farm subsidies also tend to encourage the production of less-nutritious foods. No federal or state regulations control the production or consumption of low-nutrition, high-fat foods. This seeming indifference to the health consequences of poor diet can be seen even in government-approved school-lunch programs, which provide food with a fat content far above recommended guidelines.

It has been known for decades that salt consumption can lead to high blood pressure, heart disease, and stroke. In response, the American Medical Association recently asked the FDA to regulate salt as a food additive, which would require packaged-food companies to adhere to limits on sodium levels in a variety of foods. The Salt Institute has predictably lobbied against salt regulation, and to date, the FDA has shown little inclination to act on the issue.

Medical evidence clearly shows that consumption of sugar-sweetened foods and beverages is the most significant factor in the obesity epidemic, yet the sugar industry has waged an effective campaign to prevent any restraints on America's sweet tooth. The Bush administration's ties to the sugar industry have always been extensive. During President Bush's 2004 campaign, sugar magnate Pepe Fanjul was listed among the campaign's "Rangers"—fundraisers who raise at least $200,000. Among the campaign's "Pioneers"—those who raised a minimum of $100,000—was Robert Coker, a U.S. Sugar Corporation senior vice president. Other Rangers and Pioneers included executives from Coca Cola and Nestle.

One example of this political power was seen in 2003, when a United Nations panel on diet, nutrition, and disease reviewed the evidence linking poor diet to obesity, diabetes, and cancer. After examining the available research and soliciting comments from scientists, government officials, health organizations, and industry groups, the panel issued a World Health Organization and Food and Agriculture Organization (WHO/FAO) report documenting their conclusions.

The report's recommendations were simple: eat more fruits and vegetables, and cut back on sugars and fats. Despite these unexceptional conclusions, the report was immediately attacked by the U.S. Sugar Association because of its recommendations to limit sugars to 10 percent of daily calories. On April 23, 2003, Andrew Briscoe, chairman and CEO of the Sugar Association, held his own press conference to criticize the report, warning the WHO that the association would "exercise every avenue available" to challenge the study, including asking Congress to block U.S. funding for the WHO.[46]

A lobbying alliance consisting of the sugar manufacturers, the Corn Refiners Association (whose members manufacture high-fructose corn syrup, the most common soft-drink sweetener), and other food-industry groups requested HHS Secretary Tommy Thompson to personally intervene to have the draft of the WHO/FAO report removed from the WHO Web site. Political allies like Senators Larry Craig (R-ID) and John Breaux (D-LA), both members of the "U.S. Senate Sweetener Caucus," also pressed Thompson to cease any promotion of the report.

Meanwhile, the WHO produced a follow-up report calling on governments worldwide to battle obesity through taxes on junk foods, subsidies for healthier foods, and controls on advertising to children. The U.S. government responded with horror.

William R. Steiger, director of the Office of Global Health Affairs at President Bush's HHS, wrote to WHO director-general Lee Jong-wook, invoking the conservative buzz words "sound science" and stating that the United States had a different "interpretation of the science" than did the WHO. Steiger questioned the link between specific foods, such as those with high sugar content, and obesity, and criticized the WHO for its failure to emphasize "personal responsibility" on matters of diet.[47] As we saw earlier in this chapter, Steiger was the political appointee who squelched Surgeon General Carmona's report on global health because it did not sufficiently highlight the Bush administration's policy accomplishments.

In 2004, the Bush administration announced an unprecedented policy that would control which American health scientists could participate in WHO activities and deliberations. Once more, it was William Steiger who delivered the new policy, stating that, effective immediately, the WHO could no longer invite specific U.S. experts to serve as scientific or technical advisers. Instead, Steiger's office would identify an "appropriate expert" to participate. Steiger's letter also stated that American scientists must represent the United States "at all times and advocate U.S. Government policies." This contrasted with WHO guidelines, which require the WHO's scientific experts to serve independently of the governments for which they work and not to represent official policy positions.[48]

Despite such White House efforts to protect the American food industry from embarrassing international research, the most overt political support is found in the halls of the U.S. Congress. The best example of such support is "the cheese-burger bill," an attempt to insulate the food industry from any obligation to inform customers of the content of its food. Indeed, the bill would remove all legal liability for the nutrition-related consequences of restaurant food.

The Commonsense Consumption Act of 2005, popularly known as "the cheese-burger bill," would ban "frivolous" lawsuits against the food industry for making people fat. In particular, the bill protects the industry against any "claims of injury relating to a person's weight gain, obesity, or any health condition associated with weight gain or obesity." Shortly after the bill was introduced, food-industry groups, including the American Frozen Food Institute, The National Association of Wheat Growers, and the American Bakers Association, wrote to Senate Majority Leader Bill Frist (R-TN), urging him to cosponsor the bill. The letter said, "Over the last three years we have seen lawsuits claiming the plaintiff's weight gain is the respon-sibility of those selling food. . . . Litigation that blames the consequences of one's eating habits on another erodes personal responsibility and threatens business with substantial legal costs."[49]

Opponents of the bill say it is up to the courts, not Congress, to decide whether a lawsuit is frivolous. The food industry and its congressional support-ers say that matters of personal responsibility, such as poor eating habits, don't belong in the courts, and they warn that obesity lawsuits are threatening the food industry. Yet only a handful of cases blaming restaurants for obesity have ever been filed, and only one major case remains open: a 2002 case alleging that misleading advertising by McDonalds restaurants led teenagers to eat food high in fat, salt, sugar, and cholesterol, leading to obesity.

Senator Mitch McConnell, who introduced the cheeseburger bill in 2005, says the McDonalds case, "and the threat of many more like it," will drive up insurance costs for the food industry, which will then pass the costs on to the consumer. In a 2007 press conference, McConnell said, "The latest trend among unprincipled trial lawyers, aided and abetted by certain academics and overzealous public-health advocates, is to turn people who overindulge in food into victims. . . . [B]y pinning the blame on restaurants, obesity lawyers under-mine the basic truth that we all must take personal responsibility for what we put into our mouths."[50]

Senator Patrick Leahy (D-VT), who opposes the bill, says, "This legisla-tion favors the interests of corporations over the health of our children and the health of their parents. . . . The handful of lawsuits that would have been barred by this legislation actually resulted in settlements providing for more nutritious food in our schools, more accurate labeling for consumers and the removal of harmful transfats from some of the foods we eat. A blanket ban on such measures would lead to more serious health problems like increases in heart disease and diabetes and other chronic conditions that are taxing this nation's health system."[51]

Despite strong support from the Bush White House, the Commonsense Con-sumption Act never became law.

The new administration of President Barack Obama made health care reform its top legislative priority, but it quickly became the most contentious political issue since President Clinton attempted the same thing more than a decade earlier. During the hot summer of 2009, the debate became even hotter. Angry protesters took over "town-hall meetings" on health care, brandishing signs showing Obama as Adolph Hitler and burning him in effigy. Democrats offered evidence that the protests were staged by conservative political organization, but Republicans insisted it was simply the voice of the people.

In describing Obama's health care proposal, Republican Senator James Inhofe (OK) said, "I just hope the President keeps talking about it, keeps trying to rush it through. We can stall it. And that's going to be a huge gain for those of us who want to turn this thing over in the 2010 elections. . . . But I just, frankly for political reasons, I kind of like the idea of keeping this thing alive. Look what it did for us in 1994."[52]

The politicized debate on health care reform became so acrimonious that the media soon reported on nothing but the squabbles, ignoring the public health issues and even the content of the pending legislation.

In July 2009, at the height of the health care debate, Republican Senator Jim DeMint (SC) declared, "If we're able to stop Obama on this, it will be his Waterloo, it will break him."[53]

President Obama responded, "Just the other day, one Republican senator said . . . 'If we're able to stop Obama on this, it will be his Waterloo. It will break him.' Think about that. This isn't about me. This isn't about politics. This is about a health care system that is breaking America's families, breaking America's businesses, and breaking America's economy."[54]

In the face of such political hysteria, Congress backed away from any significant health care reform legislation in 2009.

NOTES

1. "The Surgeon General's Vital Mission: Challenges for the Future," Hearing before the Committee on Oversight and Government Reform, House of Representatives, 11th Congress, 1st Session, July 10, 2007, pp. 5, 7. http://oversight.house.gov/documents/20071127162330.pdf.
2. Ibid., p. 20.
3. Ibid., p. 22.
4. Ibid., p. 23.
5. Ibid., pp. 30–31.
6. Ibid., p. 38.
7. Ibid., p. 39.
8. Ibid., p. 45.
9. Ibid., p. 47.
10. Ibid., p. 61.
11. Ibid.
12. "Bush Aide Blocked Global Health Report," *Washington Post*, July 29, 2007, A5.

13. Ibid.
14. House Oversight and Reform Committee, "Rep. Waxman to Introduce the Surgeon General Independence Act," July 12, 2007, http://oversight.house.gov/story .asp?ID=1409.
15. "Surgeon General Nominee Grilled," Time.com, July 12, 2007, www.time.com/time/ health/article/0,8599,1643181,00.html.
16. Vivien Labaton, "Acting Surgeon General Galson Fumbled Plan B," RHRealityCheck .org, September 27, 2007, www.rhrealitycheck.org/print/49230,8599,1643181 ,00.html.
17. Dr. David J. Graham, testimony before the Senate Finance Committee, November 18, 2004, www.senate.gov/~finance/hearings/testimony/2004test/111804.
18. Ibid.
19. "BPA Ruling Flawed, Panel Says," *Washington Post*, October 29, 2008, A13.
20. Ibid.
21. "FDA Sets Safety Threshold for Contaminant Melamine," *Washington Post*, October 4, 2008, A5.
22. "FDA Draws Fire Over Chemicals in Baby Formula," *Washington Post*, November 27, 2008, A2.
23. Ibid.
24. Chris Mooney, *The Republican War on* Science (New York: Basic Books, 2005), 36.
25. "How AIDS Changed America," *Newsweek*, May 15, 2006, www.newsweek .com/id/47748?tid=relatedcl.
26. "The Great Communicator," Dangerous Chunky Notebook, June 29, 2004, http://dangerouschunky.com/notebook/?m=200406.
27. "How AIDS Changed America," *Newsweek*, May 15, 2006, www.newsweek .com/id/47748?tid=relatedcl.
28. Madelon Lubin Finkel, *Truth, Lies, and Public Health* (Westport, CT: Praeger, 2007), 54.
29. Institute of Medicine, *Preventing HIV Transmission: The Role of Sterile Needles and Bleach* (Washington, DC: National Academies Press, 1995), 6.
30. Lauran Neergaard, "U.S. Won't Fund Needle Exchanges," Associated Press, April 20, 1998.
31. National Library of Medicine, "Profiles in Science: The C. Everett Koop Papers," http://profiles.nlm.nih.gov/QQ/Views/Exhibit/narrative/tobacco.html.
32. National Library of Medicine, "The 1964 Report on Smoking and Health," http://profiles.nlm.nih.gov/NN/Views/Exhibit/narrative/smoking.html.
33. Ibid.
34. "Sweethearts of Big Tobacco—Tobacco PAC Contributions and 1997 Tobacco Votes," Net Industries, 2008, www.libraryindex.com/pages/2134/Government-SUING -TOBACCO-COMPANIES.html.
35. Ibid.
36. Chris Mooney, *The Republican War on* Science (New York: Basic Books, 2005), 66.
37. Ibid.
38. Ibid., 68.
39. Deborah Barnes and Lisa Bero, "Why Review Articles on the Health Effects of Passive Smoking Reach Different Conclusions," *Journal of the American Medical Association* 279, no. 19 (May 20, 1998).

40. "Surgeon General Concludes There Is No Safe Level of Second-Hand Smoke," *NewsHour with Jim Lehrer*, PBS, June 27, 2006, www.pbs.org/newshour/bb/health/jan-june06/smoke_06-27.html.

41. "Surgeon General Concludes There Is No Safe Level of Second-Hand Smoke," *NewsHour with Jim Lehrer*, PBS, June 27, 2006, www.pbs.org/newshour/bb/health/jan-june06/smoke_06-27.html.

42. "H. R. 1108, Family Smoking Prevention and Tobacco Control Act," Testimony of Andrew C. von Eschenbach, Commissioner of Food and Drugs, October 3, 2007, U.S. Department of Health and Human Services, FDA, www.fda.gov/NewsEvents/Testimony/ucm/09873.htm.

43. "Bush Administration Opposes Tobacco Regulation," *Seattle Times*, July 22, 2008, http://seattletimes/nwsource/com/html/politics/2008066116_apfdtobacco.html.

44. Lyndsey Layton, "Senate Passes Bill to Let FDA Regulate Tobacco," *Washington Post*, June 12, 2009, A1.

45. Shannon Pettypiece, "Obesity Medical Costs Balloon to $147 Billion, Study Finds," Bloomberg.com, July 27, 2009, www.bloomberg.com/apps/news?pid=20601124&sid=aTy59DsnA3Wg.

46. Sugar Association to the World Health Organization, April 14, 2003, www.commercialalert.org/sugarthreat.pdf.

47. Ibid, 128.

48. William Steiger to Denis G. Aitken, assistant director general, World Health Organization, April 15, 2004.

49. "Congressional 'Cheeseburger Bill' Gains Support," Heartland Institute, November 2005, www.heartland.org/Article.cfm?artId=17952.

50. Office of Senator Mitch McConnell, press release, May 10, 2007, http://mcconnell.senate.gov/record.cfm?id=273993&start=1.

51. Office of U.S. Senator Patrick Leahy, press release, June 19, 2006, http://leahy.senate.gov/press/200606/061906a.html.

52. "White House Plans to Assail As 'Politics' Another GOP Senator's Remarks about Health Care Reform Fight," ABC News, July 23, 2009, http://blogs.abcnews.com/politicalpunch/2009/07/white-house-plans-to-assail-as-politics-another-gop-senators-remarks-about-health-care-reform-fight.html.

53. "President Obama Finds DeMint Fresh," ABC News, July 20, 2009, http://blogs.abcnews.com/politicalpunch/2009/07/president-obama-finds-demint-fresh.html.

54. Ibid.

8

The Politics of Evolution

Charles Darwin was photographed by Julia Margaret Cameron shortly before the publication of his controversial book *The Descent of Man* (1871). (Library of Congress, Prints & Photographs Division, LC–USZ62-52389)

Since the appearance of Charles Darwin's *Origin of the Species* in 1859, the scientific community has been virtually unanimous in embracing evolution as the natural explanation for the origin and development of life forms on Earth. Nonetheless, the American public has been slow in accepting the proposition that all life forms, including *Homo sapiens*, evolved from lower organisms. Indeed, a 2005 Gallup poll, conducted almost 150 years after the publication of Darwin's groundbreaking book, found that 53 percent of Americans believed that "God created human beings in their present form exactly as the Bible describes it."[1]

Even more striking was a 2005 *Newsweek* poll revealing that 80 percent of Americans believed "that God created the universe."[2]

DARWIN, EVOLUTION, AND CREATIONISM

The process by which American science left the public—and its elected representatives—behind is disturbing but instructive. Surprisingly, the early creationist opposition to evolution was more concerned with reconciling science and scripture than it was with disproving evolution. Calling themselves "creation scientists," they sought to attribute the undeniable fossil record to the Biblical flood and its aftermath. They believed that the plants and animals buried sequentially in the stratified rocks once lived together in the antediluvian world. The fossils were thus not evidence of successive populations of flora and fauna, as evolutionists claimed.

In this regard, the book *Scientific Creationism* declared: "If the system of flood geology can be established on a sound scientific basis, and be effectively promoted and publicized, then the entire evolutionary cosmology . . . will collapse."[3]

These "flood geologists" had trouble demonstrating that all animal and plant fossils could be dated to the Biblical flood, and they were soon replaced by a new group of Christian Darwinists. Led by G. Frederick Wright, they accepted virtually all of evolutionary science but maintained that God intervened from time to time. Such a view, according to Wright, "allows us to retain our conceptions of reality in the forces of nature, makes room for miracles, and leaves us free whenever necessary, as in the case of the special endowments of man's moral nature, to supplement natural selection with the direct interference of the Creator."[4]

Wright explained, "The Creator first breathed life into one, or, more probably, four or five distinct forms," after which a combination of miracles and natural selection produced the various families, genera, and species. Thus, said Wright, "the miraculous creation of man might no more disprove the general theory of natural selection than an ordinary miracle of Christ would disprove the general reign of natural law."[5]

As the American church sought common ground with Darwinism, its flock was much more likely to cling to a literal interpretation of the scriptures that was incompatible with evolution. Such popular religious conservatism was initially reflected in local ordinances and school-board regulations, and it would be many years before it found national political expression through William

Jennings Bryan, three-time presidential candidate and former secretary of state under Woodrow Wilson.

Bryan was a populist Democrat and fundamentalist Christian who campaigned against evolution as society's "great evil." In speaking engagements around the country, Bryan delivered thundering denunciations of Darwin and scientists who insisted that the Earth was far older than the Biblical chronology suggested. Bryan urged his supporters to "trust in the Rock of Ages, not the age of rocks."[6] Over the course of several years, Bryan's movement inspired the introduction of anti-evolution legislation in more than two-thirds of the nation's states.

Bryan personally applauded Tennessee governor John Butler for signing the Butler Act, the most prominent of such laws. Butler had easily won election to the governorship by campaigning on one issue: getting evolution out of the schools. He then wrote the anti-evolution law that was passed overwhelmingly by the Tennessee legislature in 1925. The law barred any publicly supported grade school, high school, or university from teaching "any theory that denies the story of the Divine Creation of man as taught in the Bible" or "that man has descended from a lower order of animals." The Butler Act criminalized the teaching of evolution, making it punishable by a fine of $100 to $500.[7]

Renowned orator and political candidate William Jennings Bryan (right) testified for the prosecution at the Scopes "Monkey" trial, July 1925. He was subjected to withering cross-examination by defense attorney Clarence Darrow (left). (AP Photo)

John Butler acknowledged that he found his inspiration in the fire-and-brimstone anti-evolution crusade of William Jennings Bryan. Indeed, Bryan's pamphlet, *The Menace of Evolution*, provided a template for anti-evolution legislators:

Now that the legislatures of the various states are in session, I beg to call attention of the legislators to a much needed reform, viz., the elimination of the teaching of atheism and agnosticism from schools, colleges and universities supported by taxation. Under the pretense of teaching science, instructors who draw their salaries from the public treasury are undermining the religious faith of students by substituting belief in Darwinism for belief in the Bible. . . .

The tendency of Darwinianism, although unsupported by any substantial fact in nature . . . is to destroy faith in a personal God, faith in the Bible as an inspired Book, and faith in Christ as Son and Saviour. . . .

When the Christians of the nation understand the demoralizing influence of this godless doctrine, they will refuse to allow it to be taught at public expense.

A resolution without penalties will be sufficient—a resolution passed by the legislature declaring it unlawful for any teacher, principal, superintendent, trustee, director, member of a school board, or any other person exercising authority in or over a public school, college or university, whether holding office by election or appointment, to teach or permit to be taught in any institution of learning, supported by public taxation, atheism, agnosticism, Darwinism, or any other hypothesis that links man in blood relationship to any other form of life.[8]

The close connection between Bryan and Butler would soon propel Bryan into the most sensational court case of the 20th century, *Tennessee vs. John Scopes*, known as "The Monkey Trial."

John Scopes, a high school biology teacher and part-time football coach in Dayton, Tennessee, had been teaching from a textbook that included readings on evolution, a clear violation of Tennessee's Butler Act. Scopes actually initiated the case in an attempt to test the constitutionality of the law, and when William Jennings Bryan offered to join the prosecution team—despite not having practiced law for over 30 years—celebrated trial lawyer Clarence Darrow jumped at the chance to defend Scopes.

Nearly a thousand people jammed the county courthouse on July 10, 1925, when the trial opened. Judge John T. Raulston had proposed moving the trial to a tent that would hold 20,000 people, but the trial proceeded in the steaming courtroom. Nationwide press coverage was augmented by the first live radio broadcast from a courtroom.

A jury of twelve men, eleven of them regular churchgoers, was quickly selected, and the trial adjourned for the weekend. On Sunday, Bryan delivered the sermon at Dayton's Methodist Church, using the occasion to attack the Scopes defense team. Judge Raulston and his family listened attentively from their first-pew seats.

On the first business day of the trial, the defense moved to quash the indictment on both state and federal constitutional grounds, but Judge Raulston denied the motion. The prosecution opened its case by presenting testimony showing that Scopes had admitted to teaching evolution in violation of state law. A number of Scopes's students then testified that he had told them that man had evolved from one-celled organisms. Darrow gently cross-examined the students, but there was little in dispute. The prosecution rested its case.

The defense called its first witness: Dr. Maynard Metcalf, a zoologist who attempted to explain the theory of evolution. Bryan responded with an extended speech in which he mocked the evolutionists for claiming that man descended "not even from American monkeys, but Old World monkeys."[9] But the dispute over evolution became meaningless when Judge Raulston ruled Dr. Metcalf's expert testimony irrelevant to Scopes's guilt or innocence and therefore inadmissible.

At this point, Judge Raulston transferred the proceedings to the lawn outside the courthouse, expressing concern that the courtroom floor might collapse from the weight of the many spectators. On the seventh day of the trial, before a crowd that had swelled to about 5,000, came what the *New York Times* described as "the most amazing court scene on Anglo-Saxon history."[10] Against the advice of his prosecution colleagues, William Jennings Bryan agreed to a defense request that he testify as an expert on the Bible.

Darrow began his interrogation of Bryan with a series of questions designed to undermine a literal interpretation of the Bible. Bryan was pressed on Biblical accounts of the whale that swallowed Jonah, Joshua making the sun stand still, Noah and the great flood, Adam in the Garden of Eden, and the creation according to Genesis. An exasperated Bryan shook his fist at Darrow, saying, "I want the world to know that this man, who does not believe in God, is trying to use a court in Tennessee . . ." Darrow interrupted, saying he objected to Bryan's statement and his "fool ideas that no intelligent Christian on earth believes."[11]

As the battle between Bryan and Darrow became increasingly incendiary, Judge Raulston declared the court adjourned, and on the following day he ordered that Bryan not be allowed to return to the stand and that all of his previous testimony be stricken from evidence. Once more, the court had removed all discussion of science and religion from consideration by the jury, leaving only the issue of Scopes's guilt or innocence. Darrow asked the jury to return a verdict of guilty against his client so that the case could be appealed to the Tennessee Supreme Court. The jury complied with Darrow's request, and Judge Raulston concluded the proceedings by fining Scopes $100.

Six days after the trial, Bryan died in his sleep. A year later, the Tennessee Supreme Court reversed the decision of the Dayton court on a technicality—not the constitutional grounds that Darrow had sought—and dismissed the case with the comment, "Nothing is to be gained by prolonging the life of this bizarre case."[12]

Despite the dismissal, the court chose in its commentary to endorse the constitutionality of the Butler Act, declaring, "We are not able to see how the prohibition of teaching the theory that man has descended from a lower order of animals gives preference to any religious establishment or mode of worship. So far as we know, the denial or affirmation of such a theory does not enter into any recognized mode of worship."[13]

The sensational Scopes trial had a mixed effect on the teaching of evolution in Tennessee and nationwide. Perhaps because of the notoriety of the trial, Tennessee chose to voluntarily repeal the Butler Act, but little had changed in the politics of evolution. One year after the Scopes trial, the next edition of the book Scopes had used had almost all mention of Darwin removed. Other states continued to adopt anti-evolution laws, and textbook publishers began to omit evolution from their biology books.

It would be almost 40 years before the constitutionality of anti-evolution laws would be decided in court. The state of Arkansas had a statutory prohibition against teaching evolution that dated back to 1928, yet no one had ever been prosecuted under the statute. Then, in 1967, Susan Epperson, a Little Rock science teacher, challenged the law, and a trial court in Little Rock overturned the ban. The state of Arkansas appealed, and the case reached the U.S. Supreme Court in October 1968.

On November 12, 1968, Justice Abe Fortas, writing for the high court, concluded:

Government in our democracy, state and national, must be neutral in matters of religious theory, doctrine, and practice. It may not be hostile to any religion or to the advocacy of non-religion; and it may not foster or promote one religion or religious theory against another or even against the militant opposite. . . . In the present case, there can be no doubt that Arkansas has sought to prevent its teachers from discussing the theory of evolution because it is contrary to the belief of some that the Book of genesis must be the exclusive source of doctrine as to the origin of man. . . . Arkansas' law cannot be defended as an act of religious neutrality. Arkansas did not seek to excise from the curricula of its schools and universities all discussion of the origin of man. The law's effort was confined to an attempt to blot out a particular theory because of its supposed conflict with the Biblical account literally read. Plainly, the law is contrary to the mandate of the First, and in violation of the Fourteenth, Amendment to the Constitution.[14]

Epperson seemed to be the death knell for state legislation banning the teaching of evolution in public schools, but did it prohibit the teaching of creationism? That would depend on whether such teaching was an unvarnished attempt to advance Christianity, or any other religion.

THE NEW AND IMPROVED CREATIONISM

The post-*Epperson* legal realities led conservative state legislators to undertake a new legislative initiative against evolution, the "balanced treatment" approach. Such laws would require schools to spend equal time teaching creationism and evolution. In 1973, Tennessee adopted a balanced treatment law requiring all biology textbooks and lesson plans that discussed evolution to give equal time and space to alternatives, which were defined as "including, but not limited to" the biblical Genesis account. To protect the Bible from any of the statute's restraints, the bill declared that "the Holy Bible shall not be defined as a textbook, but is hereby declared to be a reference work and shall not be required to carry the disclaimer above provided for textbooks."[15]

Because the bill's undefined category of "alternatives" seemed to open the door to an unlimited number of religious sects and cults, the statute exempted occult or satanic teachings from inclusion in the textbooks. The statute also made clear that the absence of both evolution and creationism from the curriculum qualified as balanced treatment.

The Tennessee Textbook Commission was charged under the statute with the task of choosing properly balanced teaching materials. A group of Tennessee science teachers sued the textbook commission, asking that the law be overturned for the same reasons cited in *Epperson*. The case, *Daniel v. Waters*, eventually found its way to the U.S. Court of Appeals for the Sixth Circuit, one rung below the U.S. Supreme Court, and in 1975 that court ruled that such balanced treatment laws still violated the constitutional ban on establishment of religion.

The court made it clear that truly scientific alternatives to evolution could always be taught, but primarily religious ones could not. Indeed, the court found the broad category of required alternatives to evolution to be absurd, declaring, "Throughout human history the God of some men has frequently been regarded as the Devil incarnate by men of other religious persuasions. It would be utterly impossible for the Tennessee Textbook Commission to determine which religious theories were 'occult' or 'satanical' without seeking to resolve the theological arguments which have embroiled and frustrated theologians through the years."[16]

The court concluded, "The result of this legislation is a clearly defined preferential position for the Biblical version of creation as opposed to any account of the development of man based on scientific research and reasoning. For a state to seek to enforce such a preference by law is to seek to accomplish the very establishment of religion which the First Amendment to the Constitution of the United States squarely forbids."[17]

Daniel v. Waters once more affirmed the persistent constitutional flaw in creationist challenges to evolution, and that flaw is the overtly religious purpose. A new approach, called "creation science," emerged in the 1980s. Still claiming to seek balanced treatment of evolution and creationism in public schools, creation science offered Bible-friendly scientific explanations of natural phenomena.

It was no accident that the proliferation of state laws mandating the teaching of creationism alongside evolution occurred during President Ronald Reagan's administration. During his earlier California governorship, Reagan's state board of education had discouraged the teaching of evolution and endorsed creationism.

During his 1980 presidential campaign, Reagan complained of the "great flaws" in the theory of evolution and said schools should therefore teach the "biblical story of creation" as well. He declared that evolution was a "theory only, and it has in recent years been challenged in the world of science and is not yet believed in the scientific community to be as infallible as it once was believed. But if it was going to be taught in the schools, then I think that also the Biblical theory of creation . . . should also be taught."[18]

An editorial in *Science* magazine said, "Reagan's sympathy with the creationists was common knowledge when he was governor. Reagan supported an unsuccessful 1972 suit brought by the state school board . . . to bring the teaching of creationism to public schools."[19]

After Reagan's election as president, his science adviser, George Keyworth, when questioned about his views on evolution, refused to repudiate the teaching of creationism in the public schools. Reagan's secretary of the interior, James Watt, was more explicit in declaring, "We believers in the Old Testament want the theories of both evolution and Creation taught. . . . Unfortunately, in many school systems, the liberals have now censored the treating of Creation."[20]

It was in this political atmosphere that Louisiana lawmakers crafted the Balanced Treatment for Creation Science and Evolutionary Science Act that banned the teaching of evolution unless accompanied by instruction in the theory of creation science. The bill claimed there was far more scientific evidence to support a theory of supernatural creation than there was to support the theory of evolution; that evolution was being taught as a fact, not a theory; that it had become a kind of religion, allowing a small group of scientists to brainwash teachers into suppressing information on creation science; and that teaching evolution as fact while "censoring" creation science trampled on the religious beliefs of students.

The law was challenged by a group of Louisiana parents and teachers, and the case, *Edwards v. Aguillard*, went all the way to the Supreme Court in 1987. The court found that the Louisiana legislature had a religious motive in passing the act and said the scientific language in the act could not obscure the fact that the law "endorses religion by advancing the religious belief that a supernatural being created humankind." It concluded, "The Act's primary purpose was to change the public school science curriculum to provide persuasive advantage to a particular religious doctrine that rejects the factual basis of evolution in its entirety. Thus, the Act is designed either to promote the theory of creation science that embodies a particular religious tenet or to prohibit the teaching of a scientific theory disfavored by certain religious sects. In either case, the Act violates the First amendment."[21]

Looking back at the *Edwards* decision, it is the dissent by Justice Antonin Scalia, less than eight months into his tenure on the Supreme Court, that stands out. Scalia not only accused the majority of antireligious reasoning, but declared that it really didn't matter if the Louisiana lawmakers had religious motives in passing the law.

"We do not presume that the sole purpose of a law is to advance religion merely because it was supported strongly by organized religions or by adherents of particular faiths," said Scalia. "To do so would deprive religious men and women of their right to participate in the political process."[22]

Scalia had little sympathy for the science teachers who challenged the law, concluding, "If the Louisiana Legislature sincerely believed that the State's science teachers were being hostile to religion, our cases indicate that it could act to eliminate that hostility. . . . The people of Louisiana, including those who are Christian fundamentalists, are quite entitled, as a secular matter, to have whatever scientific evidence there may be against evolution presented in their schools, just as Mr. Scopes was entitled to present whatever scientific evidence there was for it."[23]

Thus, the strong majority of the Supreme Court rejected the teaching of creationism in public schools, but Scalia's embrace of "balanced treatment" promised that the legal battle would continue. Indeed, the advocates of creation science further refined their arguments, choosing language that avoided explicit mention of God or the Bible. They argued instead that the complexity of higher forms of life implied an undefined master designer. This new form of creationism, called Intelligent Design (ID), quickly became the preferred framework for the ongoing war against evolution.

INTELLIGENT DESIGN AND THE DOVER CASE

The conservative embrace of Intelligent Design as the legal and political basis for opposing the teaching of evolution was a pragmatic decision, borne of the excesses of traditional creationism and its persistent failure to pass constitutional muster. Perhaps the last political gasp of anti-evolution fundamentalism came in 1999, when the Kansas state board of education voted to strip not only evolution, but most of modern cosmology, including the big bang theory, from Kansas teaching standards. After a national outcry, most of the offending school board members lost their seats in the next election, leaving an opportunity for ID proponents.

The same phenomenon occurred in school districts around the country, as conservative opponents of evolution realized that advocating the teaching of the biblical story of creation instead of or alongside evolution was not a practical legal strategy. The new approach would target the scientific gaps or weaknesses in evolutionary theory without explicitly advocating creationism.

The initial call from ID proponents was to "teach the controversy," the notion that schools should be required to educate their students on the scientific doubts and controversies concerning evolutionary theory. The legal advantage of this approach was the absence of overt support for teaching religious doctrine. The weakness was the absence of the alleged controversy within the scientific community.

Following the *Edwards v. Aguillard* decision, the Institute for Creation Research (ICR) recommended that "school boards and teachers should be strongly encouraged at least to stress the scientific evidences and arguments against evolution in their classes . . . even if they don't wish to recognize these as evidences or arguments for creationism."[24]

A prominent example of this approach appeared in Ohio in early 2004, when the state board of education adopted a model lesson plan that invited students to "critically analyze five different aspects of evolutionary theory."[25] To guide the students in their criticism, the lesson plan provided its own critiques, all of which were later explicitly rejected by the National Academy of Sciences.

Meanwhile, in Dover, Pennsylvania, the school district went even further by teaching Intelligent Design in its science classes. In late 2004, the ACLU sued the Dover district, touching off a legal conflict that will be discussed later in this chapter.

The Seattle-based Discovery Institute has provided the intellectual power and credibility behind ID, formulating the anti-evolution position in secular and sometimes scientific language. In fact, the institute has recruited a handful of professional scientists to tout the legitimacy of ID. The most prominent of them is biochemist Michael Behe, who declares that the alleged scientific revolution known as Intelligent Design "rivals those of Newton and Einstein, Lavoisier and Schrodinger, Pasteur and Darwin."[26]

Of course, simply saying that ID is a scientific breakthrough does not make it so. In the scientific community, such claims must be established through peer-reviewed, published research, something that has been conspicuously absent from ID. Indeed, a recent literature search failed to find scientific papers that present research supporting ID in peer-reviewed journals. Brown University's Kenneth Miller explains, "The scientific community has not embraced the explanation of design because it is quite clear on the basis of the evidence, that it is wrong."[27]

ID's fundamental claim is that living organisms show detectable evidence of being designed by a rational agent, presumably God, but not so identified. The Discovery Institute claims that evolution inculcates atheism and destroys moral values, but it has been cautious about espousing religion. Nonetheless, behind the organization's secular appearance is a clearly religious purpose, as revealed in a strategy document leaked to the Web in 1999. The seven-page paper, known as the Wedge Document, outlines a strategy "to replace materialistic explanations with the theistic understanding that nature and human beings are created by God." The document states that Intelligent Design "promises to reverse the stifling dominance of the materialist worldview and to replace it with a science consonant with Christian and theistic convictions." Toward this objective, ID will "function as a 'wedge'" that will split the trunk of scientific materialism.[28]

In addition to its underlying religious motivation, ID functions as part of the religious right, the political movement that gained national influence during President Reagan's administration. Today, ID is endorsed by conservative organizations like Focus on the Family, the Eagle Forum, Conservative Women for America, Coral Ridge Ministries, the American Family Association, and the Alliance Defense Fund. Conservative members of Congress have also joined the ID crusade against evolution.

In 2001, Senator Rick Santorum (R-PA) teamed up with ID proponents to introduce a "teach the controversy" amendment to the No Child Left Behind Act. The origin of Santorum's amendment can be traced back to 2000, when the Discovery Institute held a briefing with Santorum and other congressional supporters of ID. In fact, Phillip E. Johnson, founding adviser of the Discovery Institute's Center for Science and Culture, claims that he authored the original Santorum amendment.

Santorum's amendment was a non-binding "Sense of the Senate" resolution designed to put the Senate on record without statutory implications. In describing his amendment, Santorum said it addressed "the subject of intellectual freedom with respect to the teaching of science in the classroom in primary and secondary education. It is a sense of the Senate that does not try to dictate curriculum to anybody; quite the contrary, it says there should be freedom to discuss and air good scientific debate within the classroom. In fact, students will do better and will learn more if there is this intellectual freedom to discuss."[29]

The brief amendment reads: "It is the sense of the Senate that—

1) good science education should prepare students to distinguish the data or testable theories of science from philosophical or religious claims that are made in the name of science; and
2) where biological evolution is taught, the curriculum should help students to understand why this subject generates so much continuing controversy and should prepare the students to be informed participants in public discussions regarding the subject."[30]

On June 14, 2001, the amendment was passed by the Senate as part of the education funding bill. The Discovery Institute immediately sent out a triumphant e-mail newsletter declaring, "Undoubtedly this will change the face of the debate over the theories of evolution and intelligent design in America. . . . It also seems that the Darwinian monopoly on public science education, and perhaps the biological sciences in general, is ending."[31]

The Discovery Institute's celebration was premature. When the House of Representatives passed the education bill, it removed the Santorum amendment. As always, it was left to a conference committee to reconcile the differences between the Senate and House bills. During the committee's deliberations, a coalition of 96 scientific and educational organizations issued a letter urging the committee to strike the amendment from the final bill. Indeed, the committee did just that, but a shortened version of the amendment's language remained in the conference report as explanatory text concerning the history and purposes of the bill. That text reads:

The conferees recognize that a quality science education should prepare students to distinguish the data and testable theories of science from religious or philosophical claims that are made in the name of science. Where topics are taught that may generate controversy (such as biological evolution), the curriculum should help students to understand the full range of scientific views that exist, why such topics may generate controversy, and how scientific discoveries can profoundly affect society.[32]

Despite the fact that the Santorum amendment does not appear in the final legislation and therefore has no legal force, ID supporters continue to celebrate the related text in the conference report. The Discovery Institute persisted in claiming that the text in the conference report implies federal acceptance of Intelligent Design. In 2003, ID's three most prominent congressional supporters, John Boehner, Judd Gregg, and Santorum, sent a letter to the Discovery Institute urging it to invoke the conference report as evidence of "Congress's rejection of the idea that students only need to learn about the dominant scientific view of controversial topics."[33] The letter was sent to several state boards of education that were considering campaigns in support of Intelligent Design.

THE DOVER DECISION AND BEYOND

According to the National Center for Science Education (NCSE), between 2001 and 2004, Republican state political parties embraced anti-evolution strategies, with seven state parties adopting such platforms or public policy statements. At the same time, according to an NCSE survey, 43 U.S. states saw significant anti-evolution activity, and the political strategies employed by local legislators were, in large part, borrowed from the Discovery Institute.

In 2004, a school board in Dover, Pennsylvania, rejected a biology textbook, claiming that it was "laced with evolution." The board recommended that a book supporting the creationist doctrine of Intelligent Design replace or accompany the regular text. The board's action directly affected only the teachers and students at Dover High School. Even the federal court case that ensued was, technically, lacking in precedential authority outside the Dover area. Yet this local controversy has had a powerful effect on the national debate over evolution.

In many ways, the Dover controversy initially resembled a censorship case—an attempt to restrict access to a textbook on evolution and impose a religious doctrine, Intelligent Design, on ninth-grade science classes.

The commonly invoked axiom, "All politics is local," may be an overstatement, but it is certainly true that most politically imposed censorship is local. This was documented in my earlier book, *Banned in the USA: A Reference Guide to Book Censorship in Schools and Public Libraries*, where I wrote:

Today . . . the overwhelming majority of bookbanning is local, not federal. Community censorship, particularly in schools and libraries, . . . prohibits or restricts access to books already published, distributed, and even approved by school or library boards. Such materials may already be on library shelves or part of the teaching curriculum, and the pressure to remove them usually comes from groups outside the institution in question. All too often, the strident demands of a well-organized minority are accommodated by politically sensitive school and library boards or harried teachers.[34]

In the Dover controversy, the "outside" group was the Discovery Institute, a Seattle-based think tank devoted primarily to propagating the theory of Intelligent Design. The "strident demands of a well-organized minority" came from religious fundamentalists in the community and on the school board, who not only subverted the Dover High School science curriculum by secret and duplicitous means, but also issued death threats to local science teachers and the federal judge who eventually ruled on the case. The fact that *all* of the offending school board members were removed in the election immediately following the court case makes clear that they were a minority in the Dover community.

The conflict in Dover began in the spring of 2003 when science teachers at Dover High School were told by the assistant superintendent that a school board member, Alan Bonsell, wanted them to teach creationism along with evolution. At a subsequent school board meeting, Bill Buckingham, head of the board's curriculum committee, complained that the standard biology textbook was "laced with evolution" and would therefore need to be replaced by a textbook that would include creationism.[35]

Buckingham then contacted two outside groups: a Michigan law firm called the Thomas More Law Center and a Seattle-based think tank named the Discovery Institute. The groups recommended that Buckingham use a book titled *Of Pandas and People*, published by the Discovery Institute. The book presents the theory of Intelligent Design, which claims that the various forms of life on Earth began abruptly, through "an intelligent agency." The word *God* is not explicitly mentioned in the book.

Buckingham went back to the Dover science teachers and presented them with an ultimatum: accept *Of Pandas and People* as a companion book to the standard biology text or he would not approve the current text. The outraged teachers rejected the proposal, and when Buckingham made the same proposal to the school board, he came up two votes short. When the board chose to purchase only the standard text, the dispute seemed to have ended. However, a few weeks later, sixty copies of *Pandas* arrived at the school as a gift from an anonymous donor. Without consulting the teachers, Buckingham drafted a new policy proposal for the school board, mandating that all students taking ninth-grade biology be read a one-minute statement declaring Darwin's theory to be flawed and suggesting Intelligent Design as an alternative. The sixty copies of *Pandas* would be a reference book for the students.

This time, the majority of the board agreed to the policy change, while the minority resigned in protest. Tammy Kitzmiller, the mother of a ninth-grade student who would be read the one-minute statement, called Vic Walczak at the Pennsylvania ACLU. Walczak recalls, "We had parents, we had students, we had teachers, all calling us and saying, 'There's a problem here, can you help us?'"[36]

On December 14, 2004, Kitzmiller, joined by ten other Dover parents and two Dover biology teachers, filed a lawsuit alleging that the elected school board was violating their constitutional rights by introducing religion into science class. The plaintiffs would be represented by the ACLU and the law firm

Pepper Hamilton. The school board would be represented by the Thomas More Law Center, the firm that had referred Buckingham to the Discovery Institute and to *Of Pandas and People.*

By the time the trial began, other challenges to evolution had emerged in dozens of other states, and Intelligent Design had become a national political issue. Rick Santorum, the conservative Republican senator from Pennsylvania, publicly praised the Dover school board for its actions. Even President George W. Bush threw his support behind Intelligent Design, saying it should be taught alongside evolution. The presiding judge in the Dover case, John Jones III, carried his own widely publicized political baggage. Judge Jones had been recommended for his position on the bench by Senator Santorum, who aggressively supported the Dover school board, and Jones had been appointed by President Bush, who advocated the teaching of Intelligent Design.

On September 26, 2005, testimony began in *Kitzmiller v. Dover Area School District.* Eric Rothschild, the lead attorney for the ACLU, began, "Dover school board members announced their interest in the topic of evolution in starkly religious terms. They looked for a book that could provide a religious alternative to evolution, and they found one in *Of Pandas and People.* They did everything you would do if you wanted to incorporate a religious topic in a science class and cared nothing about its scientific validity."[37]

Patrick Gillen of the Thomas More Law Center opened for the defense: "Defendants' experts will show this court that Intelligent Design theory is science, it is not religion. This expert testimony will also demonstrate that making students aware of gaps and problems in evolutionary theory is good science education."[38]

The attorneys for the school board repeatedly declared that evolution was only a theory, not a fact, but the plaintiffs' first witness, biologist Ken Miller, coauthor of the very textbook rejected by the school board, explained that in the world of science, a theory is not a supposition. It is a well-tested hypothesis that provides the best available explanation for natural phenomena. On the other hand, a fact is little more than an isolated piece of data to be organized by scientific theory.

When the attorney for the school board claimed that modern scientific research had cast doubt on Darwin's theory, Miller insisted that the opposite was true. He noted a recent genetics paper that had confirmed the most contentious part of Darwin's theory, the common ancestry of humans and apes. Miller concluded, "You could say that when modern genetics came into being, everything in Darwin's theory was at risk. It could have been overturned if it turned out that genetics contradicted the essential elements of evolutionary theory. But it didn't contradict them. It confirmed them in great detail. . . . Not a single experimental result has ever emerged in 150 years that contradicts the general outlines of the theory of evolution. Any theory that can stand up to 150 years of contentious testing is a pretty darn good theory, and that's what evolution is."[39]

The most prominent expert witness for the defense was Michael Behe, a scientist and senior fellow at the Discovery Institute and author of the popular Intelligent Design book *Darwin's Black Box*. Behe testified, "Intelligent Design is a scientific theory that proposes that some aspects of life are best explained as the result of design, and that the strong appearance of design in life is real and not just apparent." Behe denied that Intelligent Design was based on any religious beliefs, declaring, "It is based entirely on observable, empirical physical evidence from nature, plus logical inferences."[40]

Judge Jones listened attentively to hours of expert testimony on the issue of whether Intelligent Design was science and therefore an appropriate subject for a biology class. But he would be ruling on a second issue as well, the question of whether the school board had been *motivated* by religion when it introduced Intelligent Design into the Dover classroom. On that issue, the National Center for Science Education would play a decisive role.

Nick Matzke of the NCSE began investigating the origins of *Of Pandas and People*. He came across a creationist newspaper from 19981 that carried a brief story announcing that Charles Thaxton, a fellow at the Discovery Institute, was working on a book presenting both creationism and evolution. Thaxton would become the editor of *Pandas*, and it became clear to Matzke that the original draft of that book was about creationism, only later called Intelligent Design.

Matzke e-mailed the information to Eric Rothschild at Pepper Hamilton, who immediately issued a subpoena to the publishers of *Pandas* for all preliminary drafts of the book. Rothschild soon received two boxes of material, which were assigned to Barbara Forrest, a professor who had been tracking Intelligent Design for years. Buried within the documents were two drafts of *Pandas* straddling the 1987 *Edwards v. Aguillard* case, in which the Supreme Court ruled it unconstitutional to teach creationism in public-school science classes. One draft of *Pandas* was written before the decision and the other was revised immediately after the decision.

The first draft said, "Creation means that various forms of life began abruptly through the agency of an intelligent creator." After the *Edwards* decision, the same sentence was changed to read, "Intelligent Design means that various forms of life began abruptly through an intelligent agency." The only difference between the two was that, in response to the *Edwards* decision, "creation" was replaced with "Intelligent Design."

When Barbara Forrest carefully examined the two drafts, she discovered something bizarre. The authors had intended to replace the word "creationists" with the phrase "design proponents" throughout the second draft, but in their haste they left a hybrid term, "c design proponentsists." Ironically, this was the missing link—a transitional fossil, if you will—between creationism and Intelligent Design.

Barbara Forrest's testimony on the creationist lineage of *Pandas* was crucial to the case against the school board, but she also revealed some important history on the Discovery Institute, the publisher of *Pandas*. Forrest presented a previously secret paper known as the Wedge Document—written by the Discovery Institute's Center for the Renewal of Science and Culture—which spelled out the following goals:

Governing Goals
- To defeat scientific materialism and its destructive moral, cultural and political legacies.
- To replace materialistic explanations with the theistic understanding that nature and human beings are created by God.

Five Year Goals
- To see intelligent design theory as an accepted alternative in the sciences and scientific research being done from the perspective of design theory.
- To see the beginning of the influence of design theory in spheres other than natural science.
- To see major new debates in education, life issues, legal and personal responsibility pushed to the front of the national agenda.

Twenty Year Goals
- To see intelligent design theory as the dominant perspective in science.
- To see design theory application in specific fields, including molecular biology, biochemistry, paleontology, physics and cosmology in the natural sciences, psychology, ethics, politics, theology and philosophy in the humanities; to see its influence in the fine arts.
- To see design theory permeate our religious, cultural, moral and political life.[41]

Forrest's testimony and evidence strongly suggested that *Of Pandas and People* was originally conceived as a creationist text and that the Discovery Institute itself had a religious motivation for assisting the Dover school board. But what motivated Bill Buckingham and Alan Bonsell, the school board members who introduced the Intelligent Design policy? On the witness stand, Buckingham admitted that, contrary to the claim that *Of Pandas and People* arrived at the school from an anonymous donor, he had given a check to Bonsell to purchase the books. This contradicted statements that Buckingham and Bonsell had made in their sworn depositions. They had both lied under oath.

After six weeks of testimony, the trial concluded with closing arguments. The prosecution said, "This trial has established that Intelligent Design is unconstitutional because it is an inherently religious proposition, a modern form of creationism. It is not just a product of religious people, it does not just have religious implications, it is in its essence religious. The shell game has got to stop."[42]

The defense concluded, "I respectfully submit that the evidence shows that the plaintiffs have failed to prove that the primary purpose or primary effect of the reading of a four paragraph statement on Intelligent Design . . . [threatens] the harm which the Establishment Clause of the First Amendment to the United States Constitution prohibits. . . . The defendant's policy has the primary purpose and primary effect of advancing science education by making students aware of a new scientific theory, one which may well open a fascinating prospect to a new scientific paradigm."[43]

Judge John E. Jones, III, presided over *Kitzmiller v. Dover Area School District,* ruling on December 20, 2005, that the school district's mandated teaching of intelligent design in the public school system was unconstitutional. (U.S. District Court of Middle Pennsylvania.)

On December 20, 2005, Judge Jones issued a 139-page opinion, ruling that "ID is not science" and that it is "unconstitutional to teach ID" in Dover science classes. The opinion concluded:

Those who disagree with our holding will likely mark it as the product of an activist judge. If so, they will have erred as this is manifestly not an activist Court. Rather, this came to us as the result of the activism of an ill-informed faction on a school board, aided by a national public interest law firm eager to find a constitutional test case on ID, who in combination drove the Board to adopt an imprudent and ultimately unconstitutional policy.

The breathtaking inanity of the Board's decision is evident when considered against the factual backdrop which has now been fully revealed through this trial. The students, parents, and teachers of the Dover Area School District deserved better than to be dragged into this legal maelstrom, with its resulting utter waste of monetary and personal resources.[44]

Jones pointedly noted that several members of the board had lied to cover their tracks and "disguise the real purpose" behind the Intelligent Design policy, and he recommended that the U.S. attorney consider perjury charges against Buckingham and Bonsell.

Shortly after the trial concluded, Judge Jones appeared on public television and explained how the actions of a few local officials in a small Pennsylvania town could have violated the U.S. Constitution. Jones paraphrased the Establishment Clause of the First Amendment, which forbids Congress from passing any law that favors one religion over another: "And that trickles down to the actions of a school board, in this case, through the Fourteenth Amendment to the Constitution, . . . so the school board is just as subject to it as the United States Congress is."[45]

Judge Jones said he wrote the opinion in a comprehensive way because he knew the dispute would be replicated elsewhere. "It's not precedential outside of the middle district of Pennsylvania, but I thought that if other school boards and other boards of education could read it, they would possibly be more enlightened about what the dispute was all about. And, in fact, in Ohio, in Kansas, in California, and some other places, it was reacted to in a positive way."[46]

Jones knew that politics, science, and religion would continue their adversarial dance for years to come. "I think history tells us that there is an enduring disagreement and dispute in the United States as it relates to evolution. By no means did my decision put a capstone on that, and it will proceed for generations I suspect."[47]

NOTES

1. "American Beliefs: Evolution vs. the Bible's Explanation of Human Origins," Gallup News Service, March 8, 2006, www.gallup.com/poll/21811/american -beliefs-evolution-vs-bibles-explanation-human-origins.aspx.
2. Jerry Adler, "In Search of the Spiritual," *Newsweek*, August 29/September 5, 2005, 49.
3. Henry M. Morris, ed., *Scientific Creationism* (San Diego: Creation-Life Publishers, 1974), 252.
4. G. Frederick Wright, "The Debt of the Church to Asa Gray," *Bibliotheca Sacra* 45, 1988, 527.

5. G. Frederick Wright, "The Divine Method of Producing Living Species," *Bibliotheca Sacra* 33, 1876, 455, 466.
6. Edward Humes, *Monkey Girl* (New York: Harper Collins, 2007), 45–46.
7. Tennessee Evolution Statutes, Chapter 27, House Bill No. 185, approved March 21, 1925, www.law.umkc.edu/faculty/projects/ftrials/scopes/tennstat.htm.
8. William Jennings Bryan, "William Jennings Bryan on the Subject of Evolution," *The Menace of Darwinism*, www.law.umkc.edu/faculty/projects/ftrials/scopes/bryanonevol .html.
9. Douglas O. Linder, University of Missouri—Kansas City (UMKC) School of Law, *Famous Trials in American History: Tennessee vs. John Scopes* (1925), www.law.umkc .edu/faculty/projects/ftrials/scopes/scopes.htm.
10. Ibid.
11. Ibid.
12. Ibid.
13. *John Thomas Scopes v. State of Tennessee*, opinion filed January 17, 1927, www.law .umkc.edu/faculty/projects/ftrials/scopes/statcase.htm.
14. *Epperson v. Arkansas*, 393 U.S. 97 (1968).
15. *Daniel v. Waters*, 515 F.2d 485 (1975).
16. Ibid.
17. Ibid.
18. Editorial, "Republican Candidate Picks Fight with Darwin," *Science*, September 12, 1980, 1214.
19. Ibid.
20. Jerry Bergman, "Presidential Support for Creationism," Institute for Creation Research, October 2006, www.icr.org/article/2942.
21. *Edwards v. Aguillard*, 482 U.S. 578 (1987).
22. Ibid.
23. Ibid.
24. Institute for Creation Research, "The Supreme Court's Decision and Its Meaning," *Impact*, no. 170, August 1987, www.icr.org/pubs/imp/imp-170.htm.
25. Bruce E. Johansen, *Silenced: Academic Freedom, Scientific Inquiry, and the First Amendment Under Siege* (Westport, CT: Praeger, 2007), 34.
26. Michael Behe, *Darwin's Black Box: The Biochemical Challenge to Evolution* (New York: The Free Press, 1996), 232–233.
27. Kenneth Miller, "Answering the Biochemical Argument from Design," available on Miller's Web site: www.millerandlevine.com/km/evol/design1/article.html.
28. Discovery Institute, "The Wedge Document: So What?" www.discovery.org/scripts/ viewDB/filesDB-download.php?id=109.
29. "Special Update: Evolution Opponents on the Offensive in Senate, House," American Geological Institute, Government Affairs Program, June 19, 2001, www.agiweb.org/ gap/legis107/evolution_update0601.html.
30. Ibid.
31. Ibid.
32. *No Child Left Behind Act of 2001*, Conference Report to accompany H.R. 1, www .discovery.org/scripts/viewDB/filesDB-download.php?command=download&id=113.
33. John Boehner, Judd Gregg, and Rick Santorum to the Discovery Institute, September 10, 2002, www.discovery.org/scripts/viewDB/filesDB-download .php?command=download&id=112.

34. Herbert Foerstel, *Banned in the USA: A Reference Guide to Book Censorship in Schools and Public Libraries*, revised and expanded edition (Westport, CT: Greenwood Press, 2002), xxv.

35. "Judgment Day: Intelligent Design on Trial," *NOVA*, PBS, November 13, 2007, www.pbs.org/wgbh/nova/transcripts/3416_id.html.

36. Ibid.

37. *Kitzmiller v. Dover Area School District*, opening statement, plaintiffs, September 26, 2005, quoted in National Center for Science Education, www2/ncseweb.org/kvd/trans/2005_0926_day1_am.pdf.

38. *Kitzmiller v. Dover Area School District*, opening statement, defense, September 26, 2005, quoted in National Center for Science Education, www2/ncseweb.org/kvd/trans/2005_0926_day1_am.pdf.

39. *Kitzmiller v. Dover Area School District*, expert witness, Kenneth Miller, September 26, 2005, quoted in National Center for Science Education, www2/ncseweb.org/kvd/trans/2005_0926_day1_pm.pdf.

40. *Kitzmiller v. Dover Area School District*, expert witness, Michael Behe, October 17, 2005, quoted in National Center for Science Education, www2/ncseweb.org/kvd/trans/2005_1017_day10_am.pdf.

41. Center for the Renewal of Science and Culture, "The Wedge Strategy," www.antievolution.org/features/wedge.html.

42. *Kitzmiller v. Dover Area School District*, closing arguments, plaintiff, November 4, 2005, quoted in National Center for Science Education, www2/ncseweb.org/kvd/trans/2005_1104_day21_pm.pdf.

43. *Kitzmiller v. Dover Area School District*, closing arguments, defense, November 4, 2005, quoted in National Center for Science Education, www2/ncseweb.org/kvd/trans/2005_1104_day21_pm.pdf.

44. *Kitzmiller v. Dover Area School District*, decision by Judge John Jones, III, December 20, 2005, quoted in The TalkOrigins Archive, www.talkorigins.org/faqs/dover/kitzmiller_v_dover_decision.html.

45. "Documentary Explores Key Case on 'Intelligent Design,'" *NewsHour with Jim Lehrer*, PBS, November 13, 2007, www.pbs.org/newshour/bb/education/july-dec07/evolution_11-13.html.

46. Ibid.

47. "Judgment Day: Intelligent Design on Trial," *NOVA*, PBS, November 13, 2007.

9

Science and the Politics of Xenophobia

The Statue of Liberty, in New York
Harbor, has been viewed as a symbol
of America's welcome for immigrants
"yearning to breathe free" since it was
erected in 1885. (National Park
Service.)

For years, American educators have warned that our students are underperforming in mathematics and science and are falling farther and farther behind the skill levels of students in other industrialized countries. At the same time, corporate and political leaders have decried the "brain drain," the loss of American scientists to overseas institutions and industries.

EXPORT CONTROLS ON SCIENCE AND SCIENTISTS

Understandably, the United States has sought to overcome its paucity of trained scientists by hiring foreign-born scholars and supporting foreign exchange students at our universities. Unfortunately, the politics of xenophobia has not only compromised our access to foreign scientists, but has prevented our homegrown scientists from working with their foreign colleagues.

To make matters worse, the federal government has been censoring its own scientific research in order to keep it from the prying of foreign eyes. In order to stop what is called "technology transfer," the government has restricted access to unclassified scientific research in American libraries and Web sites. The result has been a disaster for American science.

The legislative origins of our scientific xenophobia are a series of export laws and regulations that extended export restrictions beyond products to scientific and technical information and even to attendance at scientific seminars. The Arms Export Control Act (1976) and the Export Administration Act (1979) provide the authority to prevent foreign dissemination of scientific and technical data as described in a voluminous set of regulations, including the International Traffic in Arms Regulations (ITAR).

The ITAR were drafted so broadly that they extend beyond private commercial transactions to noncommercial expression or communication of technical information at scientific symposia attended by foreigners. The ITAR define "export" to have occurred "whenever technical data is inter alia, mailed or shipped outside the United States, carried by hand outside the United States, disclosed through visits abroad by American citizens (including briefings and symposia) and disclosed to foreign nationals in the United States (including plant visits and participation in briefings and symposia)."[1]

This network of broadly defined export controls has been extended to the point where the National Academy of Sciences has warned, "These new, more comprehensive technical data restrictions have had a chilling effect on some professional scientific and engineering societies."[2]

During the Reagan administration, Ruth Greenstein, former associate general counsel for the National Science Foundation, said export controls were deliberately written broadly in order to reach information that is, at best, remotely related to national security concerns. "[C]urrent export controls seek not merely to punish offending communication, but also to prevent communications before they take place," said Greenstein. "Courts have long found prior restraint more obnoxious than other forms of regulation of speech."

Nonetheless, President Reagan imposed export controls over scientific communication with such unrestrained zeal that Greenstein was led to declare, "A system that requires scientists to become entangled in government bureaucracies may discourage them from working in controlled areas of research. The effect may be to suppress not only the speech the controls are designed to suppress, but also speech beyond the scope of controls."[3]

The Export Administration Act of 1979 was scheduled to expire on September 30, 1983, leading Congress to prepare new legislation to replace it. Eventually, Congress failed to reach agreement on the language, and President Reagan invoked his emergency powers to extend the 1979 act indefinitely.

What is sensitive research and what is not? If information is not classified, why do we need to restrict it? The notion of "sensitive but unclassified" information was introduced in 1984 by President Ronald Reagan. Initially described as "unclassified but sensitive national security-related information," the Reagan directive (NSDD-145) left the details on what was truly sensitive to the various agency heads, but assigned enforcement authority to the highly secretive National Security Agency (NSA).[4]

Herbert S. White, dean of Indiana University's School of Library and Information Science, wrote, "If things are unclassified then they are presumably available to anyone, and everything in the general collections of public and academic libraries is unclassified. Phrases such as 'unclassified but sensitive' are oxymorons comparable to George Carlin's giant shrimp."[5]

When the details of Reagan's NSDD-145 became public, the scientific community made clear that an undefined, open-ended category of restricted information would be unworkable and unenforceable. John Poindexter, Reagan's national security adviser, attempted to create a definition. He said information would be considered sensitive if it "would adversely affect national security or other Federal government interests."[6] But what were those other government interests?

Poindexter wrote: "Other government interests are those related to, but not limited to, the wide range of government or government-derived economic, human, financial, industrial, agricultural, technological, and law enforcement information, as well as the privacy or confidentiality of personal or commercial proprietary information provided to the U.S. Government by its citizens."[7]

Upon considering Poindexter's comprehensive list of government interests, the Office of Technology Assessment (OTA) concluded, "It now appears that the definition of 'sensitive' could be applied to almost any information, or at least a very broad range of information, even if it is already published or available."[8]

In criticizing these restraints on scientific communication, physicist Robert Park, a former spokesperson for the American Physical Society, warned, "[T]he government is playing a dangerous game. The same actions that delay technology transfer to our military adversaries or economic competitors inevitably impede the transfer of information within our own borders. Whether the government likes it or not, the price of maintaining a free and informed society is that sometimes the neighbors listen in."[9]

Park feared that the federal government's attempts to keep unclassified scientific information from foreign-born scientists working in the United States would penalize American competitiveness. "In our open, democratic society, the practical result of citizen-based restrictions on information is to deny access to U.S. citizens and aliens alike. . . . The work force we propose to keep ignorant by citizenship restrictions is to a large extent our own."[10]

At a 1987 hearing on "sensitive but unclassified" information, Rep. Jack Brooks (D-TX), chairman of the House Government Operations subcommittee, described NSDD-145 as "one of the most ill-advised and potentially troublesome directives ever issued by a President. First, it was drafted in a manner which usurps Congress's role in setting national policy. Second, the directive is in conflict with existing statutes. . . . Finally, I seriously question the wisdom of the President's decision to give DOD the power to classify, hence control, information located in civilian agencies and even the private sector."[11]

Cryptography is another high-tech area within which private business chafes under federal export controls. In today's society, private encryption is used any time secure data is transmitted over telephone lines or any time a bank card is used in an ATM machine. Indeed, cryptography is fundamental to the entire advanced end of telecommunications. Yet export laws undercut the ability of America's private cryptography industry to compete internationally by allowing only weak algorithms to be exported.

D. James Bidzos, president of RSA Data Security, Inc., has complained publicly of the government's policy of restricting the private development of cryptography. "It's like saying that we shouldn't build cars because criminals will use them to get away," says Bidzos.[12]

The government's policies have been particularly hard on American data security companies, because foreign competitors have no such restraints on their cryptological software. Marshall Phelps, Jr., IBM vice president, told Congress, "[I]n formulating policy in this important area, it is essential that the government recognize the lawful uses of encryption technologies as well as the offerings of comparable products by non-U.S. firms on the global market."[13]

Eric Hirschhorn, an export control official in the Carter and Reagan administrations, and David Peyton, a policy analyst with the Information Technology Association of America, have attempted to explain how the federal government has been able to sustain such unrealistic policies for so long: "The reason is that when it comes to encryption, the Department of Defense won't yield to common sense unless compelled to do so. It fears that the availability of encryption-capable software will complicate its mission of listening in on foreign communications. . . . [T]he U.S. government treats all encryption-capable software as munitions and tightly restricts its export."[14]

Eventually, such complaints from government officials and business leaders brought a loosening of export controls during the 1990s, and international cooperation in science and technology grew accordingly—until 9/11. Suddenly, academia found itself a central target of old export control regulations and new national security laws.

"We're seeing a fundamental clash of values between university openness and national security interested in clamping down," said Eugene Skolnikoff, professor emeritus at MIT. "There's this push by government, saying, 'We've got to keep information out of the wrong hands.' Universities are essentially being asked to exclude foreign students from some projects."[15]

In March 2002, the State Department tightened ITAR export controls, limiting the higher-education exemption that had allowed scientists to communicate research data to their foreign colleagues from NATO countries. The new restrictions could subject researchers to fines or imprisonment for unauthorized discussions with foreign colleagues.

John Mester, a physicist at Stanford University, was collaborating with European researchers on a satellite-based experiment when the ITAR regulations were tightened. "I'm very concerned that they might restrict access to foreign nationals and to what research people can publish in open literature," he said.[16]

Mester recalled that two of his graduate students, a South Korean and a German, had helped produce a breakthrough in rocket-thruster research that allowed an aerospace company to build an important new research satellite. Unfortunately, the two graduate students were never allowed to see the actual thrusters in operation, or even to see their own designs, because they were barred under ITAR rules. "The students are really at the core of what we do here," said Mester. "If we were to restrict their access, it would have a huge impact. We couldn't even develop all the technology we've got now. We've been walking a fine line to satisfy both Stanford's openness requirement and the government restrictions."[17]

TURNING AWAY FOREIGN STUDENTS AND SKILLED WORKERS

A 2003 survey by the International Institute of Education (IIE) found that government policies were having measurable negative impact on foreign student enrollment. Marlene Johnson, executive director of the IIE, said, "I worry that what we're seeing is more than just another short-term response to an economic downturn. The survey suggests that, for the first time, US government policing are having the effect—although not the intent—of keeping legitimate students and scholars from accessing our schools."[18]

Bruce Alberts, president of the National Academy of Sciences, says, "Higher education has been one of our greatest exports. If we give foreign graduate students the impression they're not welcome or they are second-class citizens, then we'll repel a lot of that talent."[19]

Today, foreign students and skilled workers are more essential to America's scientific competitiveness than ever before. Yet a *Washington Post* editorial in June 2008 began: "Thanks to the nation's dysfunctional immigration system and the dysfunctional Congress that keeps it that way, tens of thousands of promising, intelligent, ambitious and highly skilled foreign professionals, including thousands receiving advanced degrees from American universities this month, will be denied a chance to contribute their expertise and energy to the American economy."[20]

The 2000 census showed that although immigrants accounted for only 12 percent of the U.S. workforce, they made up 47 percent of all scientists and engineers with doctorates. In addition, 67 percent of all those who entered the fields of science and engineering between 1995 and 2006 were immigrants. Vivek Wadhwa, a senior research associate at the Harvard Law School, describes the effect on America's competitive edge when these people return to their home countries: "Immigrants who leave the United States will launch companies, file patents and fill the intellectual coffers of other countries. Their talents will benefit nations such as India, China, and Canada, not the United States. America's loss will be the world's gain."[21]

Stuart Anderson, executive director of the National Foundation for American Policy and former executive associate commissioner at the Immigration and Naturalization Service, says, "Foreign graduate students, particularly those who study science or engineering, are a boon to the American economy and education system. They are critical to the United States' technological leadership in the world economy."[22]

Still, international student enrollment figures at American universities have been stagnating or declining since the 9/11 terrorist attacks. This has been attributed to restrictive visa policies, competition with other countries, the high cost of an American education, and the perception that the United States does not welcome foreign students. Indeed, foreign students pursuing advanced degrees in the United States must demonstrate that they will return to their home countries, or they will be denied a visa.

This protectionist attitude persists despite recent studies showing that for every 100 international students who receive science or engineering PhDs from American universities, the nation gains 62 future patent applications. The Association of American Universities estimates the monetary value of scientific research conducted by foreign workers in the United States at $12 billion a year, and foreign students educated in the United States have gone on to found some of America's most prominent technology companies, including Intel and Sun Microsystems.[23]

The United States makes it extremely difficult for foreign-born science and engineering doctorates to stay in this country, where they might work in private technology companies, conduct research in our laboratories, or teach at our universities. In 2006, the U.S. Labor Department had a backlog of 250,000 skilled-immigrant, permanent-residency applications, and the Immigration Service had a backlog of 180,000 cases. There was also a backlog of 71,000 applications for green cards, primarily because of per-country caps on the number of allowable green cards. Applications for the "skilled temporary-employment visas," or

H-1B, for fiscal year 2007 were exhausted in a few weeks, before the fiscal year even began.[24]

Yale University's global Web site concludes, "Without a doubt, skilled immigrants contribute to keeping the US a technology leader, yet increasing numbers look for jobs in Europe where citizenship is more readily available. With so many top scientists frustrated about US bureaucracy and quotas, analysts question whether the nation can maintain its technological and commercial status."[25]

Indeed, the Bush administration is trying to make it even more difficult. In 2005, the Defense and Commerce Departments proposed new rules that would further restrict the ability of foreign-born students and technicians to work in American research facilities.

Currently, an export license is required before a foreign national may work with "sensitive technology" in the United States. (The term "sensitive" in this context means unclassified but restricted by export regulations.) The new regulations would use *country of birth* rather than citizenship to determine whether export laws prevent employment. For example, a Canadian citizen born in Iran would now be regarded as an Iranian.

Barry Toiv, a spokesman for the Association of American Universities (AAU), said, "The impact on research could be very serious. The bottom line is that research that benefits both our economy and our national security just won't happen." Tobin Smith, a federal relations officer for the AAU, warns, "Our faculties don't want to say, 'Before you can work on this equipment I need to know where you were born.' That's not really realistic in a campus environment."[26]

As complaints about the proposed regulations mounted, the government was forced to back off. In 2006, the U.S. Bureau of Industry and Security (BIS) announced:

In response to 311 comments opposing the changes proposed . . . in March of 2005 the Bureau of Industry and Security determined that the current rules were adequate. The proposed rule would have required institutions of higher education to obtain export control licenses for many more of their foreign students and researchers, greatly increasing the already heavy regulatory burden in this area. . . . Numerous comments expressed concern that excessive and bureaucratic requirements would foster an impression among foreign students and researchers that the United States does not welcome foreign nationals in its high-technology research community. . . . Some comments noted that if forced to apply a country of birth criteria to their employees, companies might run afoul of both U.S. and foreign anti-discrimination and privacy laws.[27]

Even as it withdrew its 2005 proposed regulations, the BIS floated new proposals. In 2008, it requested public comments on "whether a more comprehensive assessment of foreign national affiliation should be used for purposes of making home country determinations in the deemed export licensing process."[28]

Recently, some of America's most prominent businessmen have begun complaining to Congress about the government's scientific xenophobia. In 2008,

Microsoft Chairman Bill Gates told the House Committee on Science and Technology that the nation needed more visas for skilled foreign workers.

Today, our university computer science and engineering programs include large numbers of foreign students," testified Gates. "In fact, the science and engineering indicators report showed that 59 percent of doctoral degrees and 43 percent of all higher ed degrees in engineering and computer science are awarded to temporary residents. But our current immigration policies make it increasingly difficult for these students to remain in the United States. At a time when talent is the key to economic success, it makes no sense to educate people in our universities, often subsidized by U.S. taxpayers, and then insist that they return home.

U.S. innovation has always been based, in part, on the contributions of foreign-born scientists and researchers. For example, a recent survey conducted by several universities showed that between 1995 and 2005, firms with at least one foreign-born founder created 450,000 new U.S. jobs. Moreover, as a recent study shows, for every H-1B holder that technology companies hire, five additional jobs are created around that person. But as you know, our immigration system makes it very difficult for U.S. firms to hire highly skilled foreign workers. Last year, at Microsoft, we were unable to obtain H-1B visas for over a third of our foreign-born candidates.

It's a total win-win situation for the economy and job creation to not force these people to be employed outside the United States. We at Microsoft, partly because of the current U.S. immigration policies, we created an office up in Vancouver, Canada, because that government, like virtually every government other than the United States, recognizes that competing for talent and encouraging talent, particularly talent educated in a foreign country, getting them to stay, that that's very, very important. And so just across the border you have quite a contrast in terms of how high-skilled workers are treated.[29]

Mr. Gates was clear and succinct on how American politics could ameliorate the problem. "There are a number of steps that Congress and the White House should take to address this problem, including extending the period that foreign students can work here after graduation, increasing the current cap on H-1B visas, clearing a path to permanent residency for high-skilled foreign-born employees, eliminating per-country green card limits, and significantly increasing the annual number of green cards," he said.[30]

Most members of the House subcommittee treated Gates's words with respect, but Representative Dana Rohrabacher (R-CA), a conservative advocate of tight controls on foreign workers, took exception to Gates's appeal for admitting more of the brightest foreign students to our universities. "Our goal isn't to replace the job of the [American] B student with A students from India," said Rohrabacher. "It's the B and C students that fight for our country and kept it free so that people like you would have the opportunity that you've had."[31]

"That's right," agreed Gates with patient understanding. "And what I've said here is that when we bring in these world class engineers, we create jobs around them."[32]

Bill Gates, Microsoft Corporation's cofounder, chairman, and chief software architect, introduces the Windows XP operating system in Seattle, February 13, 2001. (Waggener Edstrom/PR Newswire)

Craig Barrett, chairman of Intel Corporation, echoes Gates's concern about the politics of xenophobia. He notes that more than half of the advanced degrees in engineering granted by U.S. universities go to foreign students, yet "America shuts the door on many of these highly educated graduates, forcing them to look abroad for opportunities." Barrett concludes, "With Congress gridlocked on immigration, it's clear that the next Silicon Valley will not be in the United States. . . . The U.S. system forces thousands of valuable foreign-born professionals—including badly needed researchers, scientists, teachers and engineers—into legal and professional limbo for years. Not surprisingly, many are considering opportunities in competitor nations. . . . Europe has sent a message. It intends to aggressively pursue the professional talent necessary to compete on the global stage. The United States, on the other hand, seems intent on driving away the very same talent the European Union is rolling out the red carpet to welcome."[33]

It's not only Europe that is siphoning off these American-educated, foreign-born scientists. In recent years, Chinese scientists educated in American universities have begun returning to China in droves, lured by grants, tax breaks, looser regulations, and a scientific environment more open to areas of research such as stem cells. Back in 1978, Communist China first allowed students to go abroad for study, and in those days they seldom returned to China. But in recent years, more than 275,000 have gone back, many working for the Chinese

Academy of Sciences, the government-affiliated research institute, where 81 percent of the members are returnees; 50,000 of the returnees are starting their own companies.[34]

The anti-immigration politics of Republicans in Congress has infuriated business-oriented conservatives, including columnist George Will, who described U.S. policy toward foreign science students:

As soon as U.S. institutions of higher education have awarded you a PhD, equipping you to add vast value to the economy, get out. Go home. Or to Europe, which is responding to America's folly with "blue cards" to expedite acceptance of the immigrants America is spurning.[35]

Will notes that two-thirds of the doctoral candidates in science and engineering at U.S. universities are foreign born, yet only 140,000 employment-based green cards are available, leaving one million educated professionals waiting. He concludes, "Congress could quickly add a zero to the number [of green cards] available, thereby boosting the U.S. economy and complicating matters for America's competitors."[36]

In 2008, the *Washington Post* editorialized on America's policy of excluding foreign scientists: "Few policies match this one in terms of sheer irrationality, and few will do as much harm to this country's long-term prosperity and competitiveness. Yet Congress, mired in a political swamp of its own making when it comes to immigration, seems incapable of extracting itself."[37]

VISA RESTRICTIONS EXCLUDE FOREIGN SCIENTISTS

In his recent book *Age of Anxiety,* political analyst and author Haynes Johnson writes,

In Joe McCarthy's time, the nation paid a price for denying entry to distinguished scientists and technologists . . . because of misplaced concern over their political backgrounds or connections. Those refused visas included people with skills needed to develop missiles for the military. In our time, visas have been denied to writers and artists as well as to talented scientists who could redress a new "brain drain" in the United States. Moreover, the Patriot Act required that U.S. colleges and universities monitor their foreign students and scholars to determine that each student was "sufficiently engaged in course studies to dispel suspicion of terrorist activities."[38]

In the 1970s, the United States produced about half of the world's technical information. Today, it produces less than one quarter of such knowledge. When asked how the United States can prevent foreign interests from exploiting unclassified scientific information, physicist Robert Park answers, "[W]e can't. ... In our open, democratic society, the practical result of citizen-based restrictions on information is to deny access to U.S. citizens and aliens alike. ...

It is a dangerous myth that America's problems in competitiveness result from some one-sided flow of technical secrets."[39]

Park notes that the most fundamental requirement for a security clearance in the United States is becoming a U.S. citizen, despite the fact that almost half of all PhD engineers entering the U.S. work force are not U.S. citizens. He concludes, "The work force we propose to keep ignorant by citizenship restrictions is to a large extent our own."[40]

In 2002, Al Teich, director of science and policy programs for the American Association for the Advancement of Science, warned, "It's not just visas. Restrictions on publishing scientific papers—nonclassified basic research—are of great concern because then you're restricting the lifeblood of science and higher education."[41]

The number of prominent foreign scientists denied entry to the United States has risen sharply during the Bush administration, but the attitude of those scientists is indicative of the changing times. They are angry and offended, but not despondent. Knowing that the United States needs them more than they need the United States, they are confident of their professional success in the international market and contemptuous of the American visa system that excludes them.

A few examples may be instructive. Uvais Qidwai, an assistant professor of electrical engineering at Tulane University, returned to his village in Pakistan in the summer of 2002 to be married. When he attempted to return to his job at Tulane, the U.S. embassy told him he would require a security review from Washington. The review took five months, during which time the deadline for his National Science Foundation grant passed, resulting in sharp cuts in funding for his research in image processing, which included infrared surveillance that is of great value to U.S. homeland security programs. Even after successful completion of his security review, Qidwai was subject to lengthy questioning whenever he traveled abroad, often interfering with his research. In May 2005, he left the United States for good, taking a job in Qatar.

Tarek Aboul-Fadl, an Egyptian postdoctoral researcher, was invited in 2001 to join the laboratory of Dr. Arthur Broom at the University of Utah to work on an NIH project researching new anti-HIV drugs. The research went well and his grant was extended for a second year, but in May 2002 he had to return briefly to Egypt to allow his children to write exams in the Egyptian schools. On May 9, 2002, upon applying to reenter the United States, he was told that a security review would be required. The review took 18 months, ending his promising research. Before he could return, Dr. Broom closed the lab completely, saying, "I was mad as hell and I still am. It's impossible to know what would have been discovered and wasn't."[42]

In December 2003, Elena Casacuberta and her husband, Joan Roig, postdoctoral biologists at MIT and Stanford, flew home to Spain for a holiday visit with their families. While in Spain, they went to the U.S. embassy to renew their one-year visas, which allowed them to work and study in America. But embassy officials told them that because their occupation—molecular biologist—was on the Technology Alert List, their passports and visas would be withheld pending an extensive background check that would take about six weeks.

"I tried to explain my work, but the guy . . . knew nothing about biology," said Casacuberta. "I don't know how they could assess whether or not I was potentially dangerous."[43]

As the visa delays extended past the six-week period, Casacuberta and Roig communicated frantically with MIT and Stanford, trying to direct their graduate students from afar. Their important research projects were foundering. After five months, Casacuberta and her husband gave up and decided to work in Spain. "I was always the one saying, 'Maybe we shouldn't leave America,'" said Casacuberta. "Now, I don't say that anymore."[44]

Another example of American's exclusionary visa policies came in 2006, when professor Goverdhan Mehta, an internationally honored organic chemist, was denied entry to the United States as he attempted to attend a conference at the University of Florida. Mehta said U.S. consular officials accused him of hiding information that could be used for chemical weapons after he was unable to recall the details of his doctoral thesis.

"I did my PhD 40 years ago," recalls Mehta. "I told them I did not remember the topic. Science has progressed and changed completely since then."[45]

The International Council for Science (ICSU), an umbrella group of 133 national academies of science and international science unions, protested the U.S. treatment of Mehta, complaining, "The whole procedure is outrageous. He [Mehta] is not going to go on his knees and ask for a visa. Professor Mehta is a very well known scientist, but there are many lesser known scientists to whom this is happening. The bigger issue is important."[46]

The ICSU, which has coordinated major international research programs since 1931, expressed "grave concern" over the case, declaring, "It clearly illustrates that, despite some progress, all is far from well with regard to the visa policies and associated practices for scientists wishing to enter the U.S."[47]

Mehta seemed more shocked than angry about his treatment. "The issues are much more than giving me a visa," he said. "Humiliating experience apart, even the thought I could be denied a visa—I could not have imagined it."[48]

Mehta said he had canceled all plans to travel to the United States and had declined a visiting professorship at the University of Florida. He said a belated American willingness to issue him a visa would not change his decision.

The incident was particularly sensitive because it occurred just a week before President George W. Bush was scheduled to visit India to negotiate a civilian nuclear cooperation agreement. Then, to make matters worse, the United States denied a visa to still another Indian scientist, P. C. Kesavan, a geneticist specializing in radiation biology. He was refused entry when he failed to provide sufficient details about the potential applications of his work.

Kesavan said officials in the U.S. consulate treated him in a high-handed and rude fashion. "I felt humiliated about the whole process," he told a reporter. "If this is the case, I am not so keen on coming to your country."[49]

Wendy White at the National Academy of Sciences expressed concern that the United States was excluding scientists merely on the basis of their areas of expertise. "The question we need to ask is, 'Are we more secure?'" she said.[50]

At the heart of the visa problem is an arbitrary cap placed on the number of H-1B visas, those intended for skilled foreign workers. In 2008, H-1Bs were capped at 65,000, with another 20,000 available for foreign alumni of U.S. post-graduate programs. That same year, some 165,000 applicants vied for those visas. The U.S. immigration service was so swamped that it stopped accepting applicants after just five days. The disdain with which the government regards these skilled foreign workers can be seen in the fact that those visas that were awarded were selected at random by computer lottery.

"The cap keeps out doctors, engineers and other specialists—people who save lives and often create jobs for others in America," declared a *Washington Post* editorial. "One need only look at the national origins of founders of companies such as Google and Sun Microsystems to realize that foreign talent has helped to keep the U.S. economy on the cutting edge. Allowing the cap to stay so low effectively exiles not only the world's best and brightest but also the U.S. companies that employ them."[51]

A TIME FOR CHANGE

Near the end of President George W. Bush's second term, the president actually found himself to the left of his political base on the volatile issue of immigration. Conservatives were demanding that the nation build walls along our borders to keep foreigners out. Vigilante groups sprang into action, hunting down illegal aliens. Republicans in Congress exploited the nativism of the conservative base, but President Bush, fearing the loss of Hispanic votes in the upcoming 2008 election, remained silent on the more-extreme proposals.

In late 2007, a remarkable coalition arose from government, academia, the intelligence community, and the military, reaching a consensus that the nation's security required more, not less, skilled labor from abroad. Suddenly, it became difficult to cloak xenophobia in the flag.

On October 18, 2007, the National Academies released a report by their Committee on a New University-Government Partnership for Science and Security titled "Science and Security in a Post 9/11 World." The committee, made up of former national security leaders and university researchers, was cochaired by former U.S. Undersecretary of Defense for Acquisition, Technology, and Logistics Jacques Gansler and Lehigh University president Alice Gast. The committee recommended that the United States ensure the open exchange of unclassified research and welcome foreign-born scientists and science students.

Toward that end, the committee identified specific actions to be taken, including:

- Ensure that grants and contracts awarded to U.S. universities and research institutes do not restrict the publication of unclassified research. In addition, federal funding agencies should make clear that restrictive clauses governing publication or the participation of foreign scientists should not be passed down to universities.
- Review the number of research projects that are classified as "sensitive but unclassified." Numerous concerns have been raised about the increasing use of this designation, which limits the scientific community's right to publish the results of basic research and restricts participation of foreign researchers.
- Conduct regular government-wide reviews of export-control policy. Many of the restricted items are technologically outdated, widely available, or not controlled in other countries. In addition, reviews are needed to justify limits on "deemed exports," which refers to the transfer of information to a foreign national within the United States, such as a foreign-born scientist in a research library or a graduate student.
- Foster a productive environment for international science and engineering scholars in the United States. Foreign-born researchers are significant contributors to U.S. science and technology endeavors. The success of many U.S. universities and research institutions depends on attracting the best and brightest students both at home and abroad. After tighter visa restrictions were enforced following the September 11 attacks, international student enrollment decreased dramatically. The government and Congress should consider extending temporary visas for those working in high-demand research areas. The Technology Alert List— which restricts some non-U.S. students and scientists from working on legitimate technologies that could be misused to threaten national security—should be revised to include only areas of study that have explicit implications for national security.

Just two months later, an even stronger rejection of scientific xenophobia came in a report to the Secretary of Commerce by the Deemed Export Advisory Committee, chaired by former Under Secretary of the Army Norman Augustine and containing two former deputy directors of the CIA among its members.

The committee's report declared:

Although the United States has for many years been the beneficiary of significant contributions in the fields of science and engineering by foreign nationals, today's United States research enterprise would barely function without the foreign-born individuals, including foreign national, who contribute to it. . . . [T]he consequence of establishing barriers to the transfer of knowledge to foreign nationals is to make the United States a less desired partner in the global scientific and engineering communities and thus assign the United States to the fringes of the world's creative enterprise—with adverse consequences for both the nation's economy *and* national security. . . .

The seemingly inescapable conclusion from these evolving circumstances is that the erection of high "walls" around large segments of the nation's science and engineering knowledge base has become not only increasingly impracticable, but that attempts to build such walls are likely to prove counterproductive—*not only to America's commercial prowess but also, in balance, to America's ability to defend itself.*[52]

The report concluded, "An entirely new approach to Deemed Exports, and perhaps to exports in general, is, in the unanimous view of the members of this Committee, warranted based upon the above considerations and the seismic changes which have engulfed the planet since the current Deemed Export regime was first promulgated years ago."[53]

There was more to come. On January 8, 2009, just days before the inauguration of President-elect Barack Obama, a panel of the National Research Council, the research arm of the National Academy of Sciences, issued a bold report calling on Obama to remove Cold War–era restrictions on high-tech exports and immigration of foreign scientists and engineers. The report, "Beyond Fortress America: National Security Controls on Science and Technology in a Globalized World," contained recommendations that had been explicitly designed for immediate implementation through a presidential executive order.

The panel, cochaired by John Hennessy, president of Stanford University, and Brent Scowcroft, retired air force general who served as national security adviser to Presidents Gerald Ford and George H. W. Bush, declared, "The export controls and visa regulations that were crafted to meet conditions the United States faced over five decades ago now quietly undermine our national security and economic well-being. The entire system of export controls needs to be restructured and the visa controls on credentialed foreign scientists and engineers should be further streamlined to serve the nation's current economic and security challenges."[54]

The National Research Council report listed four findings:

- The current system of export controls now harms our national and homeland security, as well as our ability to compete economically.
- The system of export controls on the international flow of science, technology, and commerce is fundamentally broken and cannot be fixed by incremental changes below the presidential level.
- U.S. national security and economic prosperity depend on full global engagement in science, technology, and commerce. The best scientific talent from outside the United States has been and remains critical to the U.S. research and development enterprise. Maintaining access to this talent depends on visa policies that are welcoming to legitimate and qualified students and researchers.
- A new system of export controls can be more agile and effective, recognizing that, under current global conditions, risks to national security can be mitigated but not eliminated.[55]

Among its recommendations, the report said:

The President should maintain and enhance access to the reservoirs of human talent from foreign sources to strengthen the U.S. science and technology base. Traditionally, the

U.S. had to worry about science and technology flowing out of the country. In today's conditions, the U.S. must make sure that advanced science and technology will continue to flow into the country. For this reason, the U.S. visa regulations as applied to credentialed foreign scientists should ensure that the U.S. has access to the best talent.[56]

The report concluded:

Visa regulations and export controls are not issues that provoke the attention of the nation's citizens. . . . Nonetheless, the combined effect of these controls over the past 20 years has been to corrode the very institutions they were developed to protect—our national security and well-being. . . . Almost all of these serious problems can be corrected with one Executive Order from the President. . . . The committee recommends the issuance of an Executive Order that implements the recommendations it has outlined as one of the first orders of business in January 2009.[57]

The response of the new Obama administration to this formal request has been shaped by the disastrous recession it inherited, during which more than 5 million jobs were lost. As a result, Obama's stimulus package included a provision that prohibits U.S. companies that take federal bailout money from hiring H1-B visa holders for two years if they have laid off American workers during the previous six months. "This is part of the broader story of the unwinding of globalization in the current economic crisis," explained Edward Alden at the Council of Foreign Relations. "As goods have moved more freely around the world, so did people, but now that's ending."[58]

Sen. Bernie Sanders (I-VT) was more explicit in support of American workers. "The H1-B program is a sweetheart deal for employers in many instances, to be able to gain cheap labor from abroad," he said. "I don't think anyone is going to tell me with a straight face that they can't find some of that American talent right here on the unemployment lines."[59]

NOTES

1. House of Representatives, hearings before a Subcommittee of the Committee on Government Operations, *The Government's Classification of Private Ideas,* 96th Cong., February 28, March 20, August 21, 1980 (Washington, DC: US GPO, 1981), 270.
2. House Committee on Science, Space, and Technology, staff report, *Export Controls, Competitiveness, and International Cooperation: A Critical Review,* 101st Cong., 1st sess., February 1989 (Washington, DC: US GPO, 1989), 24.
3. Ruth Greenstein, "National Security Controls on Scientific Information," *Jurimetrics Journal,* Fall 1982: 80–82.
4. "Computer Security Mandates and Legislation," Code Idol. Accessed August 30, 2009. http://codeidol.com/security/csb2/Some-Security-History/Computer Security -Mandates-and-Legislation
5. Herbert S. White, "White Papers," *Library Journal,* October 15, 1988, 55.

6. "Computer Security Mandates and Legislation," Code Idol. http://codeidol.com/security/csb2/Some-Security-History/Computer-Security-Mandates-and-Legislation.

7. Ibid.

8. Office of Technology Assessment, *Science, Technology and the First Amendment: Special Report* (Washington, D.C.: US GPO, January 1988), 8.

9. Robert L. Park, "Restricting Information: A Dangerous Game," *Issues in Science and Technology,* Fall 1988, 62.

10. Ibid., 55, 65.

11. *Critical Infrastructure Protection and the Endangerment of Civil Liberties,* Washington, D.C.: Electronic Privacy Information Center, 1998, 9. http://epic.org/ security/infowar/epic-cip.html.

12. "Intelligence Community in Breach with Business," *Washington Post,* April 30, 1992, A8.

13. "The Threat of Foreign Economic Espionage to U.S. Corporations," Marshall C. Phelps, Jr., IBM vice president, statement before the House Subcommittee on Economic and Commercial Law, House Committee on the Judiciary, April 29, 1992, 8–9. www.loc.gov/law/find/nominations/gates/011_excerpt.pdf.

14. Eric Hirschhorn and David Peyton, "Uncle Sam's Secret Decoder Ring," *Washington Post,* June 25, 1992, A23.

15. "Academia Becomes Target for New Security Laws," *Christian Science Monitor,* September 24, 2002, www.csmonitor.com/2002/0924/p11s02-lehl.htm.

16. Ibid.

17. Ibid.

18. Jeffrey Nachtigal, "Access Denied," Berkeley Science Review, issue 6, Spring 2004, http://sciencereview.Berkeley.edu/articles.php?issues=6&article=students.

19. "Academia Becomes Target for New Security Laws," *Christian Science Monitor,* September 24, 2002, www.csmonitor.com/2002/0924/p11s02-lehl.htm.

20. Editorial, "A Recipe for Weakness," *Washington Post,* June 4, 2008, A18.

21. Vivek Wadhwa, "They're Taking Their Brains and Going Home," *Washington Post,* March 8, 2009, B2.

22. Stuart Anderson, "America's Future Is Stuck Overseas, *New York Times,* November 16, 2005, www.nytimes.com/2005/11/16/opinion/16anderson.html.

23. Ibid.

24. June Kronholz, "For Dr. Sengupta, Long-Term Visa Is a Long Way Off," *Wall Street Journal,* June 27, 2006. http://online.wsj.com/article/SB115135331760891063.html.

25. Ibid.

26. Scott Shane, "Universities Say New Rules Could Hurt U.S. Research," *New York Times,* November 26, 2005, www.nytimes.com/2005/11/26/education/26research.html.

27. The Catholic University of America, "Summary of Federal Laws: Research," 2008, http://counsel.cua.edu/FEDLAW/EAA.cfm.

28. Ibid.

29. Bill Gates, testimony before the Committee on Science and Technology, U.S. House of Representatives, March 12, 2008, quoted on Microsoft Web site, www.microsoft.com/Presspass/exec/billg/speeches/2008/congress.mspx.

30. Ibid.

31. Ibid.

32. Ibid.

33. Craig Barrett, "A Talent Contest We're Losing," *Washington Post,* December 23, 2007, B7.

34. "Opportunities in China Lure Scientists Home," *Washington Post,* February 20, 2008, B1.

35. George F. Will, "Building a Wall Against Talent," *Washington Post,* June 28, 2008, A19.

36. Ibid.

37. Editorial, "A Recipe for Weakness," *Washington Post,* June 4, 2008, A18.

38. Haynes Johnson, *The Age of Anxiety: McCarthyism to Terrorism* (New York: Harcourt, 2005), 478.

39. Robert L. Park, "Restricting Information: A Dangerous Game," *Issues in Science and Technology,* Fall 1988, 62.

40. Ibid., 66.

41. "Academia Becomes Target for New Security Laws," *Christian Science Monitor,* September 24, 2002, www.csmonitor.com/2002/0924/p11s02-lehl.htm.

42. Edward Alden, "The Closing of the American Border: Terrorism, Immigration, and Security Since 9/11" (New York: HarperCollins, 2008), 198.

43. Whitehead Institute for Biomedical Research, "Visa Denied," 2004, www.wi.mit.edu/news/archives/2004/cpa_1104c.html.

44. Ibid.

45. "Science Group Slams U.S. Visa Stance," Silicon.com, February 24, 2006, http://management.silicon.com/government/0,39024677,39156744,00.htm.

46. Ibid.

47. Ibid.

48. "U.S. Approves Visa for Indian Scientist," *Washington Post,* February 24, 2006, A12.

49. Ibid.

50. Ibid.

51. Editorial, "Visas Needed," *Washington Post,* March 25, 2008, A14.

52. The Deemed Export Advisory Committee, "The Deemed Export Rule in the Era of Globalization," submitted to the Secretary of Commerce, December 20, 2007, 12, 14, http://tac.bis.doc.gov/2007/deacreport.pdf.

53. Ibid., 3.

54. National Research Council, "Beyond 'Fortress America': National Security Controls on Science and Technology in a Globalized World," National Academy of Sciences, 2009, 1, www.nap.edu/catalog.php?record_id=12567.

55. Ibid., 3–4.

56. Ibid., 8.

57. Ibid., 61.

58. Emily Wax, "U.S. Visa Limits Hit Indian Workers," *Washington Post,* April 6, 2009, A8.

59. Ibid.

10

The Promise of Political Change and Scientific Redemption

President Barack Obama signs an executive order reversing the restrictions on stem cell research imposed by President George W. Bush as well as a presidential memorandum on scientific integrity, March 9, 2009. (AP Photo/Gerald Herbert)

Promises come easily during a presidential campaign, but delivering on them takes political skill and a bit of luck. The severe economic recession facing President Barack Obama during his first term made things particularly difficult, but Obama also inherited an unprecedented number of anti-environmental regulations pushed through in the final days of the Bush administration.

OBAMA OFFERS PROMISES; BUSH ISSUES LAST-MINUTE REGULATIONS

Early in his 2008 presidential campaign, Senator Barack Obama (D-IL) and his running mate, Senator Joseph Biden (D-VT), issued a position paper titled "Promoting a Healthy Environment" that detailed the environmental policies of an Obama administration. It placed heavy emphasis on combating global warming through reduced carbon emissions, energy efficiency, increased fuel economy standards, forest protection, and carbon sequestration. The paper itemized an aggressive plan to protect and restore our environment, including:

- **Clean Up Our Water:** Barack Obama and Joe Biden will reinvigorate the drinking water standards that have been weakened under the Bush administration and update them to address new threats.
- **Restore the Wetlands:** Barack Obama is an advocate for conserving our wetlands and supports a broad range of traditional conservation programs, including the North American Wetlands Conservation Act and the Wetland Reserve Program.
- **Restore the Great Lakes:** As president, Barack Obama will push for the passage of the Great Lakes Collaboration Implementation Act, which will move us past playing defense against environmental problems and toward a comprehensive restoration of the Great Lakes.
- **Control Superfund Sites and Data:** As president, Obama will restore the strength of the Superfund program by requiring polluters to pay for the cleanup of contaminated sites they created.
- **Protect National Parks and Forests:** Barack Obama fought efforts to drill in the Arctic National Wildlife Refuge. Obama supports the Roadless Area Conservation Rule to keep over 58 million acres of national forests pristine.
- **Conserve New Lands:** Barack Obama is a strong supporter of increased funding for the Land and Water Conservation Fund, which supports land acquisition and maintenance of parks. As president, Barack Obama will lead efforts to acquire and conserve new parks and public lands, focusing on ecosystems such as the Great Plains and Eastern forests, which do not yet have adequate protection.
- **Partner with Landowners to Conserve Private Lands:** As a U.S. Senator, Barack Obama has supported conservation programs that serve as a resource to landowners and assist them with sustainable environmental planning and best land management practices. As president, he and Joe Biden will put an unprecedented level of emphasis on the conservation of private lands.[1]

As a companion to the environmental position paper, Obama issued another document, titled "The Change We Need/Technology," which promised to restore scientific integrity to the White House. It declared, "Good policy in Washington depends on sound advice from the nation's scientists and engineers and decision-making based on the needs of all Americans. Obama and Biden will restore the basic principle that government decisions should be based on the best available, scientifically-valid evidence and not on the ideological predispositions of agency officials or political appointees."[2]

The paper discussed a number of recommendations, including making math and science education a national priority, improving and prioritizing science assessments, pinpointing college aid for math and science students, and investing in the sciences and university-based research.

A November 2008 editorial in the *Washington Post* began, "Using the waning days of power to ram through rules and regulations to burnish a legacy or preempt a successor is a time-honored tradition of outgoing administrations. That President Bush's White House is no exception was demonstrated by last week's announcement by the Bureau of Land Management (BLM) that it would authorize the sale of oil and gas leases on 360,000 acres of public land in Utah."[3]

The land at issue is clustered around three prominent national parks, making previous administrations reluctant to approve industrial development. Not so with the Bush White House. In another departure from past practice, the Bush administration did not bother to consult the National Park Service in reaching its decision. In fact, the lands designated for leasing were actually proposed by the oil and gas industry.

The leases are focused primarily on about 500 square miles of public land in eastern Utah, sparking protests from environmental groups and National Park Service officials who fear air and land pollution in the adjoining national parks.

"The Bush administration started its energy policy in back rooms with oil lobbyists, and it's fitting that's how they want to end it," said Bobby McEnaney at the Natural Resources Defense Council. "They're destroying the whole process that is designed to protect these lands."[4]

David Garbett, a staff attorney for the Southern Utah Wilderness Society, says the Bush administration finalized other last-minute resource management plans that will allow the auction of larger areas in the future. "It's a final attempt by the administration to set in stone guidance for these lands for the long term, in a way that will not protect resources," he said.[5]

The new Obama administration will have to decide whether to honor these contracts or pay millions in scarce taxpayer dollars to buy them back, if the companies that own them are willing to sell. Kathleen Sgama, director of government affairs for the Independent Petroleum Association of Mountain States, says it will be difficult to reverse these deals. "Once you get a lease out, it's a contract and you can't renege on a contract," said Sgama, adding that "it would be very expensive to buy that out."[6]

In an attempt to leave an indelible stamp on the federal government, the Bush White House approved 61 new regulations in November 2008, many of them benefiting key industries with ties to the Bush administration, including oil and gas companies. The new regulations assist industries that feel burdened by pollution controls or wilderness-protection laws. For example, one rule, adopted just three days after Obama's election victory, eases restraints on environmentally damaging oil-shale development throughout the West. Colorado governor Bill Ritter (D) called the new regulation "not just premature, it's hasty and I would even argue reckless."[7]

Other newly approved, industry-friendly rules include a restriction on the ability of Congress to halt logging, mining, and oil and gas extraction on public lands as well as a rule allowing federal agencies to conduct development projects without undergoing independent scientific review under the Endangered Species Act. The latter regulation, issued by Interior Secretary Dirk Kempthorne, would remove the decades-old requirement that agencies consult with the Fish and Wildlife Service to determine whether a project is "likely to adversely affect" an endangered species.

Representative Nick Rahall (D-WV), chairman of the House Natural Resources Committee, said, "I am deeply troubled by this proposed rule, which gives federal agencies an unacceptable degree of discretion to decide whether or not to comply with the Endangered Species Act. Eleventh-hour rulemakings rarely, if ever, lead to good government."[8]

Senator Barbara Boxer (D-CA), who chairs the Environment and Public Works Committee, called the rule "another in a continuing stream of proposals to repeal our landmark environmental laws through the back door."[9]

Despite such warnings and complaints, the new rule on endangered species took effect before President Obama's inauguration, leaving him with little recourse other than the courts. The *Washington Post* editorialized, "No doubt environmental groups will sue to stop the regulation. By settling out of court on terms that are favorable to the plaintiff and that match the new president's philosophy, Interior Secretary designate Ken Salazar and the Obama administration could nullify Mr. Kempthorne's ill-advised rule much faster than by undertaking the long process of issuing new regulations."[10]

On December 2, 2008, at the behest of the mining industry, the Bush administration finalized a rule making it easier for mountaintop mining companies to dump their waste near rivers and streams, replacing a 25-year-old prohibition. A spokesman for the National Mining Association explained, "We had sought clarification on the rule because there had been various court decisions that put a halt to surface mining. This put jobs at risk and mining activities at risk."[11]

Cindy Rank of the West Virginia Highlands Conservancy said, "With this rule change, the outgoing Bush administration is poised to eliminate forever more of our headwater streams—the very lifeblood of our mountains and the source of healthy water resources that future generations will depend upon."[12]

On December 12, 2008, Bush's EPA issued a new regulation exempting an estimated 118,500 tons of hazardous waste annually from federal incineration controls. The rule, approved three weeks after Obama's election victory, allows companies that create hazardous wastes to burn them as fuel in their own incinerators.

Ben Dunham, legislative counsel for Earthjustice, said, "[E]verything about this rulemaking is flawed," including "the logic that says, 'If you can burn it, it's not a hazardous waste.'"[13]

Even in early January 2009, the Bush administration was still pushing through changes in resource management regulations. Mark E. Rey, a former timber lobbyist serving as head of the U.S. Forest Service, announced his intention to change Forest Service rules to allow more mountain forests to be converted to housing subdivisions. Rey vowed to formalize the controversial change before the inauguration of President-elect Obama, who had campaigned against the measure, and he negotiated the policy shift behind closed doors with Plum Creek, the nation's largest private landowner.

Robert Dreher, a lawyer with Defenders of Wildlife, said, "There's been a lot of concern about the nature of the process and the lack of inclusiveness. You've got the county government in Montana angry over it. If they do this walking out the door, they're kind of ramming it down their throats."[14]

What can the new Obama administration do about these eleventh-hour regulations? Any of them that the Office of Management and Budget (OMB) believes will have major economic impact take legal effect after 60 days, meaning that some will become effective before President-elect Obama's inauguration. Less economically significant regulations take effect in 30 days or less. Once new regulations take effect, they can be undone only through complicated means such as: (1) new regulatory rule-making procedures that could take years; (2) congressional amendments to underlying laws; (3) special, fast-track resolutions of disapproval by the House and Senate.

Brendan Daly, spokesman for House Speaker Nancy Pelosi (D-CA), said the House leadership "will review what oversight tools are at our disposal regarding last minute attempts to inflict severe damage to the law in the waning moments of the Bush administration."[15]

HIGH EXPECTATIONS AND AMPLE ADVICE
FOR THE NEW PRESIDENT

Anticipating a more sympathetic administration, both the scientific community and the general public were quick to offer advice to President-elect Obama. Just days after Obama's victory in the presidential elections, the environmental group Earthjustice released a brief statement titled "Six Easy Things the Obama Administration Can Do to Heal Our Environment."

Referring to the last-minute regulations pushed through by the Bush administration, the statement begins:

Some of the Bush/Cheney anti-environmental policies will outlast this presidency. Even with the election of Barack Obama, there will be plenty of work to do to reverse the most damaging of the anti-environmental rules and restore balance to the environment. … Earthjustice has identified six critical areas where the new Obama administration can take fairly quick and easy steps to stop or reverse some of the environmental damage wrought by the Bush administration. They are:

1. Limit CO_2 emissions under the Clean Air Act
2. Restore the Endangered Species Act
3. Restore the Roadless Area Conservation Rule
4. Restore Protections for America's Rivers, Streams, Lakes, and Wetlands
5. Address Arctic Oil and Gas Development
6. Adopt Stronger Energy Efficiency Standards[16]

Other organizations quickly followed suit. A coalition of 20 national environmental organizations, including Earthjustice, Greenpeace, the Sierra Club, and the Union of Concerned Scientists, issued a massive, 340-page document subtitled "Environmental Transition Recommendations for the Obama Administration." The report's introduction states, "We urge the agency transition teams to use this document in the first crucial days of the Obama administration and look forward to working with the administration to develop policies that will both revitalize our economy and protect the planet."[17]

The outline of recommendations includes:

GUIDING PRINCIPLES

Economic Vitality, Clean Energy, and Climate Solutions Go Hand-in-Hand

We can lift ourselves out of this economic crisis through investing in clean energy solutions that solve global warming.

Social Justice Requires Environmental Justice

We believe that an economic plan built around green-collar job training and strengthened environmental safeguards will . . . provide a path out of poverty and a more just society.

Science Should Have a Primary Role in Safeguarding Our Environment

At the base of the best environmental regulations rests not politics but science. Yet science has been under siege at federal agencies for the last eight years. . . . This situation needs to be reformed across federal agencies now.

Integrity Must Be Returned to Environmental Governance

To fully hold itself accountable, government must become more transparent and citizens must be invited back into decisions about their own air, water, and lands. Above all, agencies must be allowed to use their regulatory tools to advance the public interest, not serve special interests.

TOP AREAS FOR PRIORITY ACTION

Clean Energy and Climate Change

The top priority of the environmental community remains addressing climate change and creating the new clean energy economy, key to America's economic revitalization. . . . Successfully tackling this issue will require: (a) using existing executive authority; (b) working with Congress to pass legislation; (c) and showing real leadership internationally on the issue.

The Federal Budget and Stimulus Legislation

This is now a critical time for the nation to reinvest in the budgets of federal agencies with responsibilities for clean energy, human health, and environmental protection while redirecting those resources to the best possible use.

The White House as a Leader on Clean Energy and the Environment

The job of restoring environmental protection in the federal government needs to start at the top in the White House. This includes having the President's advisors focus on energy and climate as a top priority. . . . Furthermore, the broken regulatory process should be fixed, with the Office of Management and Budget's role properly defined so that the mission of the federal government becomes again protecting the public's health, safety and environmental assets.

Putting the Right People in the Right Jobs

In this document we have tried to identify some of the most important government policy posts. Filling these positions with individuals who have integrity, are highly qualified, and have an appreciation of the value of environmental protection is essential to the success of these agencies.[18]

In December 2008, the Union of Concerned Scientists (UCS) issued its own detailed recommendations in the form of a report: "Federal Science and the Public Good: Securing the Integrity of Science in Policy Making." Subtitled "Presidential Transition Update," the report provided analysis of the Bush administration's science policies and concrete steps to remedy those policies. Among its conclusions the report states:

During the first 100 days of his administration, we urge President Obama to:

- Appoint a widely respected scientist to be a cabinet-level assistant to the president for science and technology.
- Instruct agency heads to refrain from retaliating against whistle-blowers.
- Publicly commit to the principles of open government and create policy-making processes that presume all government information is public knowledge, to be withheld only when necessary.
- Instruct the heads of scientific and regulatory agencies to issue memos to their staffs indicating their commitment to open government and stating that scientific integrity is a crucial component to achieving their missions.
- Issue an executive order outlining his regulatory process that reverses the three major tenets of executive order 12422 and restricts the role of the OMB in reviewing the scientific work of the executive branch agencies.[19]

Accompanying its larger report, UCS issued its "New Year's Resolutions for the New Administration," recommending that the incoming Obama administration should take these ten New Year's Resolutions to start off on the right foot:

1. Defend Americans from unsafe drugs, toys, and other products by requiring that federal agency leaders protect employees who blow the whistle when science is misused.
2. Allow the public access to tremendous scientific resources by letting government scientists tell us what they know.
3. Protect the air we breathe by obeying the law and setting air pollution standards based on science.
4. Restore our faith in government by providing more information to the public about how science-based policy decisions are made.
5. Use science to conserve our natural heritage for future generations.
6. Collect enough information to give us flexibility to meet future challenges and keep tabs on current problems.
7. Hold your administration accountable to high scientific integrity standards.
8. Keep politics out of science by reigning in the power of the White House to tamper with purely scientific analyses.
9. Safeguard our health by putting the Environmental Protection Agency back in charge of evaluating the potential dangers of chemicals without interference from other agencies.
10. Protect us by shining a bright light on all agency meetings held with special interests so we can understand their influence.[20]

As if this were not enough, UCS also issued separate "Scientific Integrity Recommendations" for the Food and Drug Administration (FDA), Environmental Protection Agency (EPA), and Department of the Interior. How could any new president sift through all of this advisory material and the volumes that would follow?

The general public seemed to have its own suggestions for Obama. A *Washington Post-ABC News* poll in December 2008 asked:

Do you think Obama should or should not?

Require companies to increase the use of renewable sources of energy?

Should: 84%   Should Not: 14%

Implement policies to try to reduce global warming?

Should: 75%   Should Not: 20%

Expand federal funding of stem-cell research?

Should: 52%   Should Not: 42%

Only on the issue of stem-cell research did the responses break down along partisan political lines, with a majority of Republican respondents opposing expanded federal funding, whereas Democrats and Independents strongly supported it. On renewable energy and global warming, strong support for increased federal intervention cut across party lines.[21]

A later Washington Post-ABC News poll judged Obama's first 100 days in office, characterizing it as Obama's "First-Quarter Report Card." The poll found a 69 percent public confidence in his ability to make the right decisions for the country's future. Obama's highest ratings were on the Iraq war and international affairs, but he also earned a 61 percent approval rating on global warming.[22]

OBAMA'S SCIENCE TEAM

During the first three months of his administration, President Obama's choices for key cabinet positions and science advisers demonstrated a new respect for science, elevating expertise over politics. As Obama said in his March 9, 2009, statement on stem-cell research:

Promoting science isn't just about providing resources—it's also about protecting free and open inquiry. It's about letting scientists like those who are here today do their jobs, free from manipulation or coercion, and listening to what they tell us even when it's inconvenient—especially when it's inconvenient. It is about ensuring that scientific data is never distorted or concealed to serve a political agenda—and that we make scientific decisions based on facts, not ideology. . . . And that's why today I'm also signing a Presidential Memorandum directing the head of the White House Office of Science and Technology Policy to develop a strategy for restoring scientific integrity to government decision-making to ensure that in this new administration we base our public policies on the soundest science; that we appoint scientific advisors based on their credentials and experience, not their politics or ideology; and that we are open and honest with American people about the science behind our decisions.[23]

Obama's personnel choices have reflected this approach. Lisa P. Jackson, the new head of the Environmental Protection Agency (EPA), had worked for the EPA from 1987 to 2002, after which she became chief of New Jersey's Department of Environmental Protection. She is credited with helping to pass the state's Global Warming Response Act. During her confirmation hearing, Jackson said she would take a more active approach toward protecting the environment. "Science must be the backbone of what EPA does," said Jackson, promising that the EPA would serve Americans who have suffered from "environmental negligence." Such people, she said, "are my conscience."[24]

Obama's choice to head the Food and Drug Administration (FDA) was Margaret A. Hamburg, a physician and former New York City health commissioner. A graduate of Harvard Medical School, she served in the U.S. Office of Disease Prevention and Health Promotion from 1986 to 1988 and in the National Institute of Allergy and Infectious Diseases from 1989 to 1990. As an assistant health secretary in the Clinton administration, she helped lay the groundwork for the government's bioterrorism and pandemic preparations. She takes over an agency in chaos after a series of scandals involving food-borne illnesses and unsafe imported goods.

Environmental Protection Agency Administrator Lisa Jackson speaks at a National League of Cities conference, March 16, 2009. (AP Photo/Manuel Balce Ceneta)

Diana Zuckerman, president of the National Research Center for Women and Families, says Hamburg faces a daunting challenge. "She had a very impressive track record in New York, and the question is: Can she bring that to this under-funded, dysfunctional agency?" asked Zuckerman.[25]

President-elect Barack Obama introduces Steven Chu, 1998 Nobel Prize in Physics co-winner, as his nominee for Secretary of Energy, December 15, 2008. (AP Photo)

Steven Chu, a Nobel Prize–winning physicist who headed the Lawrence Berkeley National Laboratory, is Obama's new secretary of energy. Chu won the Nobel Prize for his work on laser light, but in recent years his focus has been energy and climate change. In his remarks before the Senate Energy and Natural Resources Committee, Chu said, "It is now clear that if we continue on our current path, we run the risk of dramatic, disruptive changes to our climate in the lifetimes of our children and grandchildren."[26]

Obama's cabinet choices have impressive résumés, but not all of them are known for their environmental activism. Interior Secretary Ken Salazar is known as a centrist who advocates traditional energy development with environmental safeguards. "He's going to be an honest broker, and there are going to be competing interests in this job," said Bill Meadows, president of the Wilderness Society. "He's trying to manage conflicts in a way that reaches resolution."[27]

Still, Salazar brings significant change to the Interior Department. "There was a mess that was left here by the prior administration," said Salazar, "And it essentially revolves around a perspective . . . that the laws were to be skirted, and the consequences of that is that we're dealing with many decisions that have had to be revisited. . . . There were many decisions that were made which essentially, I think, were a reckless abandonment of the law and environmental considerations."[28]

Tom Vilsack, Obama's choice for secretary of agriculture, is another centrist with a reputation as a friend to corporate agriculture and ethanol producers. Nonetheless, Vilsack declared, "I absolutely see the constituency of this department as broader than those who produce our food—it extends to those who consume it."[29]

Perhaps the most troubled of all the federal agencies has been the Federal Emergency Management Agency (FEMA), the much-criticized U.S. disaster-response arm. Blamed for the Bush administration's bungled response to Hurricane Katrina, FEMA will now be led by one of the nation's most experienced hurricane hands, W. Craig Fugate. As director of the Florida Division of Emergency Management since 2001, Fugate led the hurricane response to four major storms in 2004 and 2005. Obama said, "I'm confident that Craig is the right person for the job and will ensure that failures of the past are never repeated."[30]

Just days before the White House was scheduled to convene a summit on health reform, Obama nominated Kansas governor Kathleen Sebelius to become secretary of health and human services. After her nomination, Sebelius

Kathleen Sebelius, Secretary of Health and Human Services, at a press conference following her remarks at the 62nd World Health Assembly, held at UN headquarters in Geneva, May 19, 2009. (AP Photo/Keystone/ Salvatore Di Nolfi)

told Obama, "I share your belief that we can't fix the economy without fixing health care."[31] Sebelius had overseen the Medicaid program for the poor during her tenure as governor, but she had endured fierce criticism from anti-abortion activists after she vetoed a bill that would have required doctors who perform late-term abortions to report a reason for the procedure. "Abortion is a personal decision made by a woman in consultation with her doctor, her family and her clergy," said Sebelius, a Roman Catholic.[32]

Because of her support for abortion rights, Sebelius suffered drawn-out confirmation hearings that ended only after the outbreak of swine flu and the threat of a global pandemic. Faced with the need for a functioning Department of Health and Human Services (HHS), the Senate confirmed Sebelius on April 28 by a vote of 65 to 31.

Along with Sebelius, Obama named Nancy-Ann DeParle, former commissioner of the Department of Human Services in Tennessee, as director of the White House Office of Health Reform. DeParle, who attended Harvard Law School and was a Rhodes scholar at Oxford, had earlier overseen Medicare and Medicaid in the Clinton administration's Health Care Financing Administration. Together, Sebelius and DeParle will help craft and sell the administration's plan to revamp the nation's health care system.

"Nancy-Ann Deparle and Governor Sebelius are an outstanding team not only for the president but for the nation," said Frederick Graefe, a health care lawyer and lobbyist. "They each have unique, complementary skills."[33]

In July 2009, Obama named Regina M. Benjamin as the nation's new Surgeon General. Benjamin, an Alabama family physician, founded and ran a rural health clinic in Bayou La Batre, Alabama, where more than 40 percent of residents have no health insurance. She served as head of the Medical Association of Alabama and received a "genius" award from the MacArthur Foundation.

Louis Sullivan, a former Secretary of Health and Human Services, described Benjamin as "a person of outstanding scientific qualifications and excellent communications skills."[34]

Also in July, Obama picked Francis Collins, a physician and scientist who helped guide the Human Genome Project to completion, as his director of the National Institutes of Health. Rare among world-class scientists, Collins is a born-again Christian, but he nonetheless declared, "The NIH director needs to focus on science. I have no religious agenda for the NIH."[35]

Collins, who helped formulate Obama's policy on embryonic stem cells, was confirmed unanimously by the Senate on August 9.

Obama chose Seattle police chief R. Gil Kerlikowske as his new drug czar. The administration removed the job's cabinet designation but said Kerlikowske would have full access and a direct line to the president and vice president. Kerlikowske had earlier served as police chief in two Florida cities, police commissioner in Buffalo, New York, and worked for the Clinton Justice Department as director of the Office of Community Oriented Policing Services. General Barry McCaffrey, former drug czar in the Clinton administration, said

Kerlikowske's background as a street cop would serve him well: "I tell people, 'If you want to understand the drug issue, talk to any cop at random with more than 10 years on the force.'"[36]

Carol M. Browner, EPA administrator for eight years in the Clinton administration, has been named as the first-ever assistant to the president for energy and climate. As EPA administrator under Clinton, she pushed for tougher air-pollution standards, which the agency defended against industry lawsuits. Called the "energy czarina," Browner will oversee energy, environmental, and climate policies.

Nancy Sutley, a deputy mayor of Los Angeles for energy and environment, will chair the White House Council on Environmental Quality. She will head a group that will work with Browner to help shape the administration's policies on climate change and the environment. Sutley had been a top aide to Browner at the EPA and had earlier served as an energy adviser to California governor Gray Davis.

Other Obama appointees to key science positions include Harvard physicist John Holdren, who will lead the White House Office of Science and Technology Policy, and Jane Lubchenco, who heads the National Oceanic and Atmospheric Administration (NOAA). In 2007, as chairman of the board of the American Association for the Advancement of Science (AAAS), Holdren oversaw approval of the board's first endorsement of "concerted action" to curb global warming. In February 2009, Lubchenco told a Senate committee, "I believe very strongly that the role of science is to inform our understanding and inform our decisions."[37]

In 2008, Lubchenco said public attitudes toward global warming were changing, even among conservatives. "The Bush administration has not been respectful of the science," she said. "But I think that's not true of Republicans in general."[38]

Both Holdren and Lubchenco have argued for a mandatory limit on greenhouse gas emissions. Michael Hirshfield, chief scientist for the advocacy group Oceana, says, "Climate change damages our oceans more every day we fail to act. We need these two supremely qualified individuals on the job yesterday."[39]

Kevin Knobloch, president of the Union of Concerned Scientists, said, "Holdren's appointment will be a stark contrast to what we've seen over the last eight years. He is knowledgeable about the greatest threats facing our nation and the world—global warming, energy insecurity, and nuclear weapons proliferation—and has deep expertise in both science and public policy."[40]

OBAMA'S FIRST SEMESTER REPORT CARD

In its first hours, the Obama administration ordered work halted on all federal regulations left unfinished after President Bush's departure. A memo directed all agencies and departments to stop pending rules until the new administration conducts a "legal and policy review" of each rule. The memo did not apply to the last-minute Bush administration rules that had already taken effect. To reverse those rules would require an act of Congress or special executive action.

On his first full day in office, Obama signed two executive orders and three presidential memoranda laying out strict new guidelines on ethics and openness in government. Within the next few days, he issued a memorandum lifting Bush's ban on U.S. funding for international family planning groups that perform abortions, directed his administration to implement new fuel-efficiency standards, and ordered the EPA to reconsider California's request for a waiver to impose tougher standards for car emissions.

Kevin Knobloch, president of the Union of Concerned Scientists, said, "Reconsidering the waiver denial is a clear indication that the new administration is ready to lead on energy and global warming. . . . By directing the Department of Transportation to revisit federal fuel economy standards, Obama has an opportunity to make even greater gains in cutting our oil consumption and saving consumers money at the pump. If the Obama administration grants the waiver, more than a dozen states will be able to exercise their right to have cleaner cars on their roads."[41]

Within the next two months, the administration issued a proposal to create a national greenhouse gas registry, filed a lawsuit charging a coal-fired plant in Louisiana with violating the Clean Air Act, and notified electric utilities that they may have to account for their greenhouse gas pollution.

The proposal for a greenhouse gas registry would cover about 13,000 facilities that account for 85 to 90 percent of the nation's greenhouse gas output. It had surfaced during the Bush administration but stalled when the White House expressed opposition to the EPA's use of authority under the Clean Air Act. Obama's EPA administrator, Lisa Jackson, quickly approved the registry proposal, saying, "Through this new reporting, we will have comprehensive and accurate data about the production of greenhouse gasses. This is a critical step toward helping us better protect our health and environment."[42]

On February 17, 2009, EPA Administrator Jackson said the agency would consider regulating carbon-dioxide emissions from coal-fired power plants, setting aside a Bush administration memorandum that declared the EPA would not limit such emissions. Though not explicitly issuing a stay on the Bush memo, Jackson said the states "should not assume the [Bush] memorandum is the final word on the appropriate interpretation of the Clean Air Act."[43]

On February 24, Obama advocated a mandatory cap on greenhouse gas emissions through a cap-and-trade system that would put a price on carbon and allow industries to trade pollution allowances.

Also in February, the Obama administration reversed Bush policy by agreeing to a binding international pact to reduce the use of mercury. "The United states will play a leading role in working with other nations to craft a global, legally binding agreement that will prevent the spread of mercury into the environment and improve the health of workers, pregnant women, and children throughout the world," said Nancy Sutley, chair of the White House Council on Environmental Quality.[44]

In March 2009, the Obama administration reversed a 2006 regulation enacted by President Bush that eased the reporting requirements for nearly 600 toxic chemicals, including arsenic, benzene, and cadmium. The change was accomplished through a little-noticed provision in the massive spending bill signed by Obama on March 11. It compels all plants and facilities to inform the public of any chemical releases that total 500 pounds a year or more, lowering the 2,000-pound threshold adopted by Bush.

Daniel Rosenberg, attorney for the National Resources Defense Council, said, "The Bush administration was never able to offer a credible defense for reducing public information about chemical emissions, and reversing this rule will allow EPA to give people information about chemicals in their neighborhoods."[45]

On April 15, the EPA announced that for the first time the agency will require pesticide manufacturers to test 67 chemicals contained in their products to determine whether they disrupt the endocrine system. EPA Administrator Lisa Jackson said, "Endocrine disruptors can cause lifelong health problems, especially for children. Gathering this information will help us work with communities and industry to protect Americans from harmful exposure."

Even the pesticide industry seemed to agree. "If we do learn something about our products that raises a cause for concern, our industry will be at the table, ready and willing to step forward and take action to mitigate risk," said Jay Vroom, CEO of CropLife America.[46]

On March 20, the EPA submitted a finding to OMB that would allow the federal government to limit greenhouse gas emissions under the Clean Air Act, reversing one of the Bush administration's landmark decisions on global warming. Just a month later, the EPA officially concluded that carbon dioxide and other greenhouse gas emissions pose a danger to the public's health and welfare, a position that could trigger federal regulations on everything from vehicles to coal-fired power plants. The EPA's finding stated: "In both magnitude and probability, climate change is an enormous problem. The greenhouse gases that are responsible for it endanger the public health and welfare within the meaning of the Clean Air Act."[47] The Bush administration had opposed mandatory limits on greenhouse gas emissions on the grounds that they might hurt business, and Bush's EPA refused to invoke the Clean Air Act as a basis for action. Despite the EPA's new assumption of authority, Obama expressed a preference for a legislative solution to greenhouse gas regulation. If Congress does not act, Obama is likely to press ahead with EPA curbs.

On May 19, 2009, the Obama administration proposed tough new standards for tailpipe emissions and fuel efficiency. New passenger vehicles and light trucks would have targets of 35.5 miles per gallon by 2016 and tailpipe emissions would have a standard of 250 grams per mile, roughly the equivalent of what would be emitted by vehicles meeting the mileage standards.

On June 26, 2009, the House passed a climate bill that would significantly change the way energy is created, sold, and used, imposing new costs on electricity from fossil fuels and directing billions of dollars to "clean power" from sources like wind and the sun. President Obama said he would look at the final product and, if it met broad environmental criteria, "it's a bill I'm going to embrace."[48]

The new Obama administration has also moved quickly to reverse Bush administration policies on land and water pollution, wilderness, and wildlife. In February 2009, Interior Secretary Salazar canceled 77 oil and gas leases in Utah, reversing the Bush administration's decision to allow drilling near pristine areas like Nine Mile Canyon and Dinosaur National Monument. A few weeks later, Salazar scrapped leases for oil-shale development in Colorado and Wyoming, once more reversing a Bush administration decision.

On March 24, the EPA challenged a Bush administration policy that eased restrictions on mountaintop-removal mining, saying that the agency would henceforth review the impact of such mining on local streams and wetlands before approving permits. In particular, EPA Administrator Lisa Jackson sent letters to the Army Corps of Engineers objecting to proposed operations in West Virginia and Kentucky, saying the two projects posed a serious threat to "aquatic resources of national importance."

Jackson said, "I have directed the agency to review other mining permit requests. EPA will use the best science and follow the letter of the law in ensuring we are protecting our environment."[49]

Robert F. Kennedy, Jr., senior attorney for the National Resources Defense Council, said, "The Obama administration's decision to suspend these permits and take a fresh look at mountaintop removal is consistent with Obama's commitment to science, justice and transparency in government and his respect for America's history and values. . . . Thanks to yesterday's decision, hope, not mining waste, is filling the valleys and hollows of Appalachia."[50]

On April 27, Interior Secretary Salazar instructed the Justice Department to seek a court order to overturn the Bush administration regulation allowing waste from mountaintop mining to be dumped near rivers and streams. Calling the Bush regulation "legally defective," Salazar said the nation's coal reserves should not be developed "without appropriately assessing the impact such development might have on local communities and natural habitat and the species it supports."[51]

On June 11, 2009, the Obama administration announced plans to tighten scrutiny of permit applications for mountaintop removal mining. (See Chapter 6.)

On March 30, the president signed sweeping land conservation legislation protecting more than two million acres of wilderness and creating a national system of land conservation. At the signing ceremony, Obama said, "This legislation guarantees that we will not take our forests, rivers, oceans, national parks, monuments and wilderness areas for granted, but rather we will set them aside and guard their sanctity for everyone to share."[52]

Also in March, Obama issued a presidential memorandum restoring a requirement that federal agencies consult with either the Fish and Wildlife Service or National Oceanic and Atmospheric Administration to determine whether their projects might harm threatened or endangered species. The Bush administration had allowed agencies to waive such reviews if they felt no harm would come from their projects.

House Natural Resources Committee chairman Nick Rahall (D-WV) said the Obama decision was "one more indication that the new administration truly represents change for the better and is committed to the protection of our natural resources and our environment."[53]

In May, Agriculture Secretary Tom Vilsack issued a temporary order increasing federal scrutiny of all projects in "roadless areas" of national forests. Vilsack said that while the temporary order is in effect, the Obama administration would work with Congress to try to create a permanent policy on roadless regions.[54] (See Chapter 6.)

Also in May, Obama reversed the controversial Bush administration rule known as "preemption" that used federal regulations to override state laws on the environment, health, public safety, and other issues. In a May 20 memo to federal agency heads, Obama said his administration would undertake regulations preempting state laws only in rare instances and "only with full consideration of the legitimate prerogatives of the states and with a sufficient legal basis for preemption."[55]

Obama ordered department heads to review all regulations issued in the past ten years that are designed to preempt state law to determine whether they are justified. Doug Kendall, president of the Constitutional Accountability Center, said, "It's environmental law, it's drug law, it's mortgage law, it's a whole host of areas where the Bush administration was really aggressive about using regulatory action to clear state and local laws that businesses and corporations didn't like."[56]

President Obama has also taken early action in support of medical science and public health. In February 2009, Obama moved to rescind the Bush administration's last-minute regulation that cut off federal funding for hospitals, clinics, and other entities if they did not allow employees to opt out of any health service that violated their personal or religious beliefs. The regulation was presumably intended to discourage abortion or contraceptive drugs like Plan B, but it was interpreted broadly by the Bush administration. An HHS official explained that the White House was open to a new rule that explicitly addressed abortion:

We recognize and understand that some providers have objections to providing abortions. We want to ensure that current law protects them. But the Bush rule goes beyond current law. . . . We've been concerned that the way the Bush rule is written, it could make it harder for women to get the care they need. It is worded so vaguely that some have argued it could limit family planning counseling and even potentially block transfusions and end-of-life care.[57]

On March 14, as Obama named Margaret Hamburg as his FDA commissioner, he also announced the formation of a Food Safety Working Group to "upgrade our food safety laws for the 21st century." Accusing the Bush administration of having created a "hazard to public health" by failing to curb food contamination, Obama said he would ask Congress for funds to add food inspectors and modernize laboratories.

"There are certain things only a government can do," said Obama. "And one of those things is ensuring that the food we eat and the medicines we take are safe and do not cause us harm."[58]

On March 23, U.S. District Judge Edward Korman overruled the Bush administration's restrictions on the availability of the "morning-after pill," Plan B, ordering the FDA to make the pill available to 17-year-olds and to review whether it should be available to all ages without a doctor's order. The judge said the Bush administration's handling of the issue was "arbitrary and capricious" and influenced by "political and ideological" considerations.[59]

Susan Wood, who had resigned from the FDA because of the Bush administration's restrictions on Plan B, said, "I think FDA is now in a position to make science-based decisions. This is a chance for the agency to demonstrate it is back on track."[60]

Indeed, the following month the FDA announced that it would allow the sale of Plan B without a prescription to women as young as 17. The agency notified Barr Pharmaceuticals, Plan B's manufacturer, that it would approve such sales at the manufacturer's request.

On April 7, Obama announced his Act Against AIDS program, a five-year, multimedia project of HHS and the Centers for Disease Control and Prevention created to inform the public on the AIDS epidemic, how people can protect themselves, and where they can seek testing and treatment. Obama also charged his Office of National AIDS Policy to craft a national AIDS strategy with three goals: lower the rate of HIV infections, increase the number of people in care, and reduce disparities in care.[61]

The most contentious change in federal science policy introduced by President Obama, his executive order increasing federal support for embryonic stem-cell research, was also the most elaborately staged. The announcement came before an audience containing not just scientists and members of Congress but also people in wheel chairs or led by guide dogs. The message was clear: the sick and infirm would no longer be denied the promise of embryonic stem-cell therapy.

The new executive order would overturn a Bush administration restriction limiting federal funding to what amounted to just 21 available cell lines. In announcing the change, Obama began: "Today, with the executive order I am about to sign, we will bring the change that so many scientists and researchers, doctors and innovators, patients and loved ones have hoped for, and fought for, these past eight years. We will lift the ban on federal funding for promising embryonic stem cell research. And we will aim for America to lead the world in the discoveries it one day may yield."[62]

In acknowledging the concerns of religious conservatives, Obama stated:

In recent years, when it comes to stem cell research, rather than furthering discovery, our government has forced what I believe is a false choice between sound science and moral values. In this case, I believe the two are not inconsistent. . . . I believe we have been given the capacity and will to pursue this research—and the humanity and conscience to do so responsibly. . . . I can also promise that we will never undertake this research lightly. We will support it only when it is both scientifically worthy and responsibly conducted. We will develop strict guidelines which we will rigorously enforce, because we cannot ever tolerate misuse or abuse.[63]

On April 17, the promised strict guidelines began to emerge in a National Institutes of Health statement limiting government-sponsored embryonic stem-cell research to excess fertility clinic embryos, prohibiting the creation of embryos for research purposes. The guidelines also specified that the donation of embryos must be voluntary, without pressure or financial inducement. The creation of stem-cell lines from such embryos would still have to be done with private funds, but federally funded research could use those cell lines.

Lawrence Soler of the Juvenile Diabetes Research Foundation said, "This is what the patient community, the scientific community and the medical community has been asking for. We need to give credit to the administration for living up to their promise to keep politics out of science."[64]

On July 6, 2009, the National Institutes of Health issued new rules concerning embryonic stem cell research. The new guidelines permit federal funding for research using the approximately 700 embryonic stem cell lines currently in existence so long as they meet the following ethical requirements:

- The embryo that was destroyed to create a line must have been discarded after an in vitro fertilization procedure
- The donors must have been informed that the embryo would be destroyed for stem cell research and made fully cognizant of their choices, including donating the embryo to another couple who want a baby
- No donors may have been paid for an embryo
- No threats or inducements may have been used to nudge couples toward making a donation

R. Alta Charo, an ethicist at the University of Wisconsin, described the new guidelines as a huge step forward. "They are making it absolutely possible to move this field forward and fund the research in a responsible way."[65]

NOTES

1. Barack Obama and Joe Biden, Environment Fact Sheet, 2008, www.barackobama .com/pdf/issues/EnvironmentFactSheet.pdf.
2. Barack Obama and Joe Biden, "The Change We Need/Technology," position paper, 2008, www.barackobama.com/issues/technology.

3. Editorial, "Drilling in Utah," *Washington Post*, November 13, 2008, A22.
4. "U.S. Moves Ahead on Oil, Gas Leases on Public Land," *Washington Post*, November 29, 2008, A1.
5. Ibid., A5.
6. Ibid.
7. "At the Last Minute, A Raft of Rules," *Washington Post*, November 30, 2008, A4.
8. "Endangered Species Act Changes Give Agencies More Say," *Washington Post*, August 12, 2008, A5.
9. Ibid.
10. Editorial, "Protections in Peril," *Washington Post*, December 27, 2008, A14.
11. "Rule Would Ease Mining Debris Disposal," *Washington Post*, December 3, 2008, A6.
12. Ibid.
13. "EPA Issues Exemptions for Hazardous Waste, Factory Farms," *Washington Post*, December 13, 2008, A4.
14. "U.S. Forest Policy Is Set to Change, Aiding Developer," *Washington Post*, January 4, 2009, A2.
15. Ibid.
16. Earthjustice, "Six Easy Things the Obama Administration Can Do to Heal Our Environment," press release, November 12, 2008, www.earthjustice.org/news/press/2008/six-easy-things-the-obama-administration-can-do-to-heal-our-environment.
17. "Transition to Green: Leading the Way to a Healthy Environment, a Green Economy, and a Sustainable Future," Environmental Transition Recommendations for the Obama Administration, November 2008, iii, www.saveourenvironment.org/assets/transition-to-green-full-report-1.pdf.
18. Ibid., iv–vi.
19. Union of Concerned Scientists, "Federal Science and the Public Good: Securing the Integrity of Science in Policy Making," December 2008, ucsusa.org/integrity/Federal-Science-and-the-Public-Good-Exec-Sum-12-08-Update.pdf.
20. Union of Concerned Scientists, "New Year's Resolutions for the New Administration," December 2008, www.ucsusa.org/New-Years-Resolutions.pdf.
21. "Optimism, Hopes High for Obama White House," *Washington Post*, December 21, 2008, A12.
22. Jon Cohen, "Obama Off to Solid Start, Poll Finds," *Washington Post*, April 26, 2009, A1.
23. Barack Obama, "Transcript: Obama's Remarks on Stem Cell Research," *New York Times*, March 9, 2009, www.nytimes.com/2009/03/09/us/politics/09text-obama.html.
24. "Nominee Signals Big Changes for EPA," *Washington Post*, January 15, 2009, A8.
25. "FDA Pick Was NYC Health Chief," *Washington Post*, March 12, 2009, A2.
26. "At Hearing, Chu Tempers Comments on Gas Tax, Coal," *Washington Post*, January 14, 2009, A9.
27. "Obama to Name Salazar As Secretary of Interior," *Washington Post*, December 17, 2008, A3.
28. Lois Romano, "Bush Administration Left a 'Mess,' Interior Secretary Says," *Washington Post*, May 19, 2009, A17.
29. "Vilsack: USDA Must Serve Eaters As Well As Farmers," *Washington Post*, February 5, 2009, A4.

30. "Fla. Official Chosen to Run FEMA," *Washington Post*, March 5, 2009, A17.
31. "Sebelius, DeParle Named to Health-Care Posts," *Washington Post*, March 3, 2009, A4.
32. "Sebelius's Record Raises Ire of Antiabortion Activists," *Washington Post*, February 25, 2009, A17.
33. "Sebelius, DeParle Named to Health-Care Posts," *Washington Post*, March 3, 2009, A4.
34. Alexi Mostrous, "Obama Names Surgeon General," *Washington Post*, July 14, 2009, A4.
35. Lauran Neergaard, "New NIH Chief Sees 'Bold,' Practical Agenda," *Washington Post*, August 18, 2009, A13.
36. "Choice of Drug Czar Indicates Focus on Treatment, Not Jail," *Washington Post*, March 12, 2009, A4.
37. "Some Easy Nominations, " *Washington Post*, February 13, 2009, A15.
38. "Advocates for Action on Global Warming Chosen As Obama's Top Science Advisers," *Washington Post*, December 19, 2008, A6.
39. "Nominations on Hold for 2 Top Science Posts," *Washington Post*, March 3, 2009, A3.
40. Union of Concerned Scientists, "John Holdren Could Strengthen Federal Science," press release, December 19, 2008, www.ucusa.org/news/press_release/john-holdren-could-strengthen-0180.html.
41. Union of Concerned Scientists, "Obama Opens the Door to States Implementing Clean Car Law," statement, January 26, 2009. www.ucusa.org/news/press_release/obama-opens-the-door-to-0186.html.
42. "EPA Plans U.S. Registry of Greenhouse Gas Emissions," *Washington Post*, March 11, 2009, A2.
43. "EPA May Reverse Bush, Limit Carbon Emissions from Coal-Fired Plants," *Washington Post*, February 8, 2009, A2.
44. "Nations to Write Treaty Cutting Mercury Emissions," *Washington Post*, February 21, 2009, A2.
45. "Reporting Rules for Chemical Releases Toughened," *Washington Post*, March 12, 2009, A2.
46. "EPA Will Mandate Tests on Pesticide Chemicals," *Washington Post*, April 16, 2009, A3.
47. "EPA Says Emissions Are Threat to Public," *Washington Post*, April 18, 2009, A4.
48. Steven Mufson, "Obama Praises Climate Bill's Progress but Opposes Its Tariffs," *Washington Post*, June 29, 2009, A5.
49. "EPA to Scrutinize Permits for Mountaintop Removal Mining," *Washington Post*, March 25, 2009, A13.
50. Robert F. Kennedy, Jr., "Hope in the Mountaintop," *Washington Post*, March 25, 2009, A15.
51. "Salazar Seeks to Vacate Bush-Era Mining Rule," *Washington Post*, April 28, A3.
52. "2 Million Acres Gain Wilderness Protection," *Washington Post*, March 31, 2009, A3.
53. "Obama Reverses Bush on Species Protection Measure," *Washington Post*, March 4, 2009, A4.
54. David Fahrenthold, "'Roadless' Forest Areas Now under Vilsack," *Washington Post*, May 29, 2009, A15.

55. Philip Rucker, "Obama Curtails Bush's Policy of 'Preemption,'" *Washington Post,* May 22, 2009, A3.
56. Ibid.
57. "Plan Reignites Debate over 'Conscience' Rule," *Washington Post,* February 28, 2009, A2.
58. "Obama Targets Food Safety," *Washington Post,* March 15, 2009, A2.
59. "FDA Ordered to Rethink Age Restriction for Plan B," *Washington Post,* March 24, 2009, A2.
60. Ibid.
61. Editorial, "AIDS at Home," *Washington Post,* April 14, 2009, A16.
62. Barack Obama, "Obama's Remarks on Stem Cell Research," transcript, *New York Times,* March 9, 2009. www.nytimes.com/2009/03/09/us/politics/09test-obama.html.
63. Ibid.
64. "Scientists Applaud Decision to Roll Back Stem Cell Rules," *Washington Post,* March 7, 2009, A9.
65. Shankar Vedantam, "Rules on Stem Cell Research Are Eased," *Washington Post,* July 7, 2009, A1.

APPENDIX

A Survey of Private Organizations Involved in Science and Politics

This appendix lists and describes the major private organizations and associations that influence science through the political process, including lobbying, litigation, publishing, media relations, and research. Some of these groups may have an overtly political agenda—conservative or liberal—but, more often, what distinguishes and divides them is whether they challenge or endorse "mainstream" science.

Liberal organizations will usually accept evidence presented by the scientific community through its peer-reviewed research, regardless of the social or economic implications. Conservative organizations tend to challenge the accuracy of scientific research when it conflicts with economic, social, or religious values. When judging the technological applications of scientific research, conservative and liberal organization are often in agreement on the need for moral and budgetary restraints, but when it comes to matters such as political censorship or manipulation of scientific research, there is fundamental disagreement.

The following alphabetical, annotated list of organizations is necessarily selective and, for the most part, current. If a particular organization has been discussed in the earlier chapters of this book, reference to that chapter will be included in the organization's description.

ADVANCEMENT OF SOUND SCIENCE CENTER

Originally known as The Advancement of Sound Science Coalition (TASSC), the organization was founded in 1993 by Steve Milloy, publisher of the Web site JunkScience.com, to challenge the scientific basis for regulatory action against private industry. Describing itself as a "grassroots-based, not-for-profit watchdog group of scientists and representatives from universities, independent organizations, and industry that advocates the use of sound science in the public policy arena,"[1] TASSC played a major role in the "sound science" campaign that questioned the scientific basis for federal regulation. The original seed money for TASSC came primarily from Philip Morris, after which TASSC conducted an aggressive public relations campaign to downplay the dangers of second-hand smoke. (See Chapter 6.)

In its early heyday, TASSC claimed a membership of over 400 corporations representing chemical, agricultural, manufacturing, oil, dairy, timber, paper, and mining interests, including Amoco, Chevron, and Occidental Petroleum, as well as industry trade associations. TASSC also had a science advisory panel of over 200 members, primarily made up of "science skeptics" who questioned the scientific community's assessment of environmental and public-health threats. (See Chapter 6.)

In September 1994, TASSC released a poll of scientists suggesting that politicians were abusing science on issues such as asbestos, pesticides, dioxin, environmental tobacco smoke, and water quality. A TASSC newsletter directly challenged an EPA report on second-hand smoke and questioned the scientific credibility of the EPA generally. (See Chapter 7.)

In an October 1994 speech, TASSC chairman Gary Carruthers, former governor of New Mexico, endorsed a regulatory reform proposal in Congress, stating, "We want to offer information on how scientific issues are communicated to the public as another means of ensuring that only sound science is used in making public policy decisions."[2]

Partly as the result of its failed campaign on the issue of second-hand smoke, TASSC no longer wields the political power it once had, but Steve Milloy continues to operate TASSC from his home in Potomac, Maryland.

AMERICAN ASSOCIATION FOR THE ADVANCEMENT OF SCIENCE

The American Association for the Advancement of Science (AAAS) was founded in 1848 and serves some 262 affiliated societies and academies of science. Its Web site (www.aaas.org) describes AAAS as "an international non-profit organization dedicated to advancing science around the world by serving as an educator, leader, spokesperson and professional association." To fulfill this mission, the AAAS board has set the following goals:

- Enhance communication among scientists, engineers, and the public
- Promote and defend the integrity of science and its use
- Strengthen support for the science and technology enterprise
- Provide a voice for science on societal issues
- Promote the responsible use of science in public policy
- Strengthen and diversify the science and technology workforce
- Foster education in science and technology for everyone
- Increase public engagement with science and technology
- Advance international cooperation in science

The AAAS has played a major role in defending peer-reviewed scientific research from political or religious challenges. It has provided important friend-of-the-court briefs in creationist lawsuits against the teaching of evolution and has been particularly effective in exposing Intelligent Design (ID), the most recently proposed form of creationism, as a religious doctrine. In a 2002 resolution, the AAAS declared that "to date, the ID movement has failed to offer credible scientific evidence to support their claim that ID undermines the current scientifically accepted theory of evolution."[3] In the landmark 2005 case *Kitzmiller v. Dover School District*, the AAAS brief helped convince the court that ID was religion, not science. (See Chapter 8.)

AMERICAN CIVIL LIBERTIES UNION (ACLU)

The American Civil Liberties Union (ACLU) was founded in 1920 by Roger Baldwin, Crystal Eastman, Albert DeSilver, and other civil liberties advocates. The ACLU Web site (www.aclu.org) describes its mission as the protection of:

- Your First Amendment rights—freedom of speech, association and assembly; freedom of the press, and freedom of religion.
- Your right to equal protection under the law—equal treatment regardless of race, sex, religion or national origin.
- Your right to due process—fair treatment by the government whenever the loss of your liberty or property is at stake.
- our right to privacy—freedom from unwarranted government intrusion into your personal and private affairs.

The Web site further declares: "We are nonprofit and nonpartisan and have grown from a roomful of civil liberties activists to an organization of more than 500,000 members and supporters. We handle nearly 6,000 court cases annually from our offices in almost every state."[4]

In 2005, the ACLU represented parents in Dover, Pennsylvania, who challenged the required teaching of Intelligent Design (ID), a recent creationist doctrine, alongside evolution. The case, *Kitzmiller v. Dover School District*, concluded that Intelligent Design is a religious doctrine whose teaching in public school violated the Establishment Clause. (See Chapter 8.)

AMERICAN ENTERPRISE INSTITUTE

The American Enterprise Institute (AEI), founded in 1943, is a private, nonpartisan, not-for-profit institution dedicated to research and education on issues of government, politics, economics, and social welfare. Its Web site (www.aei.org) states:

AEI's purposes are to defend the principles and improve the institutions of American freedom and democratic capitalism—limited government, private enterprise, individual liberty and responsibility, vigilant and effective defense and foreign policies, political accountability, and open debate. Its work is addressed to government officials and legislators, teachers and students, business executives, professionals, journalists, and all citizens interested in a serious understanding of government policy, the economy, and important social and political developments.

AEI came to prominence in the 1970s, playing an important role in the congressional debate over the supersonic transport (SST). Its release of a positive report on the SST convinced conservative icon Paul Weyrich of the importance of building the plane and actually motivated Weyrich to form the Heritage Foundation, a major conservative think tank.

During the Bush administration, AEI was a prominent voice opposing embryonic stem-cell research. (See Chapter 4.)

ANNAPOLIS CENTER FOR SCIENCE-BASED PUBLIC POLICY

The Annapolis Center, based in Annapolis, Maryland, was begun by a group of scientists, former policy-makers, and economists who were frustrated by the decision-making process in environmental, health, and safety areas. The center's Web site (www.annapoliscenter.org) says the basic premise of the center is based on the summary of the 1990 report from the EPA's Science Advisory Board:

There are heavy costs involved if society fails to set environmental priorities based on risk. If infinite resources are expended on lower-priority problems at the expense of higher-priority risks, then society will face needlessly high risks. If priorities are established based on the greatest opportunities to reduce risk, total risk will be reduced in a more efficient way, lessening threats to both public health and local and global ecosystems.

In 1997, the center held a workshop on the EPA's decision to lower the National Ambient Air Quality Standard on particulate matter (PM), questioning the risk to public health posed by PM.

More recently, the center has been a leader in the sound science movement, which seeks to limit government regulation on environmental matters. In 2003, when Republican members of Congress led by Representative Chris Cannon (UT) announced the formation of a Sound Science Caucus, the center honored Cannon at its annual dinner, citing his sound science initiative. In 2004, the center feted conservative Senator James Inhofe (R-OK) for his support of "rational science-based thinking and public policy." Inhofe had gained national attention for his Senate speech declaring that global warming may be "the greatest hoax ever perpetrated on the American people."[5]

CENTER FOR REGULATORY EFFECTIVENESS

The Center for Regulatory Effectiveness (CRE) was established in 1996, after the passage of the Regulatory Review Act, which would provide Congress with independent analyses of agency regulations. Headed by Jim Tozzi, CRE subsequently grew into a clearinghouse for methods to improve the federal regulatory process. Its Web site (www.thecre.com) declares:

The CRE has two paramount goals:

- To ensure that the public has access to data and information used to develop federal regulations, and
- To ensure that information which federal agencies disseminate to the public is of the highest quality

The only business of the Center for Regulatory Effectiveness is regulation. CRE staff have served at OMB and other federal agencies, so they possess both a technical understanding of substantive regulatory issues in addition to the procedural mechanisms which can be used to modify or halt regulations with serious problems. . . . CRE's mode of operation is to undertake work on a range of issues for a number of firms, so the Center does not represent *per se* any particular member of an industry. CRE is supported by a number of trade associations and private firms, usually in the form of a monthly contribution to support the Center's activities.

In 2000, the center's Jim Tocci drafted the so-called Data Quality Act, which was passed as part of an appropriations bill. As subsequently interpreted by the Bush administration, the act created a cumbersome process through which businesses could challenge not only government regulations but also scientific information that could lead to regulations. As soon as the act took effect, the CRE joined the Kansas Corn Growers Association to challenge an EPA risk assessment concerning the use of the herbicide atrazine, claiming that the risks posed by atrazine were not based on sound science.

In 2002, CRE challenged the Clinton-era national assessment on climate change and the Bush-era *Climate Action Report*, charging that the documents relied on "junk science." (See Chapter 5.)

In 2003, the CRE again invoked the Data Quality Act, submitting a petition on behalf of the food industry that challenged the authority of the Department of Agriculture to rely on a World Health Organization report in its 2005 U.S. dietary guidelines that included the well-known "Food Guide Pyramid."

DISCOVERY INSTITUTE

The Discovery Institute is a conservative organization located in Seattle, Washington, best known for its examination of issues related to religion and government. Its Web site (www.discovery.org) declares:

The Institute discovers and promotes ideas in the common sense tradition of representative government, the free market and individual liberty. Our mission is promoted through books, reports, legislative testimony, articles, public conferences and debates, plus media coverage and the Institute's own publications and Internet website. Current projects explore the fields of technology, science and culture, reform of the law, national defense, the environment and the economy, the future of democratic institutions, transportation, religion and public life, government entitlement spending, foreign affairs and cooperation within the bi-national region of "Cascadia."

The institute was founded in 1990 by Bruce Chapman, a Harvard graduate and conservative Episcopalian who ran unsuccessfully as a Republican candidate for governor of Washington. Chapman would later direct the U.S. Census Bureau and serve as a deputy assistant to President Ronald Reagan. Chapman invited political scientist John West and science philosopher Stephen Meyer to create a unit within the institute called the Center for the Renewal of Science and Culture (CRSC) that was dedicated to overthrowing "scientific materialism" and fomenting "nothing less than a scientific and cultural revolution."[6]

The center soon became the most prominent anti-evolution think tank in the country, introducing a new version of creationism called Intelligent Design. ID claimed that the complexity of living organisms could not have occurred through the randomness of Darwin's natural selection, but would require an intelligent designer. Although ID proponents seldom mentioned God in their form of creationism, the "designer" was clearly a supernatural force. (See Chapter 8.)

The Discovery Institute played a leading role in the landmark 2005 case *Kitzmiller v. Dover Area School District*, which ruled that a Dover, Pennsylvania, law requiring the teaching of Intelligent Design alongside evolution was a violation of the Establishment Clause.

The institute has also entered the stem-cell controversy, with senior fellow Wesley Smith leading the call for adult stem-cell research rather than embryonic stem-cell research.

FEDERATION OF AMERICAN SCIENTISTS

The Federation of American Scientists (FAS) was founded in 1945 by scientists who had worked on the Manhattan Project to develop the first atomic bombs. On its Web site (www.fas.org), FAS states:

These scientists recognized that science had become central to many key public policy questions. They believed that scientists had a unique responsibility to both warn the public and policy leaders of potential dangers from scientific and technical advances and to show how good policy could increase the benefits of new scientific knowledge. . . . With 70 Nobel Laureates on its Board of Sponsors, FAS provides timely, nonpartisan technical analysis on complex global issues that hinge on science and technology. Priding itself on agility and an ability to bring together people from many disciplines and organizations, the organization often addresses critical policy topics that are not well covered by other organizations.

The FAS has a long history of opposing political manipulation of scientific research. It was the major restraint on the unsupported claims of the Reagan administration with respect to its "Star Wars" missile defense system, and it fought Reagan's dismantling of the watchdog Office of Technology Assessment (OTA). (See Chapter 2.)

When Congress did away with the respected Office of Technology Assessment (OTA) in 1995, the FAS warned that the OTA had been "a sacrificial victim" of the resurgent Republican Congress, with grave implications for scientific integrity within the federal bureaucracy. The growing politicization of science during the following years proved the FAS warning to be prescient. The FAS then advocated a strengthening of the White House Office of Science and Technology Policy (OSTP), calling for increased influence and a greater public role.

The 2004 FAS report *Flying Blind: The Rise, Fall, and Possible Resurrection of Science Policy Advice in the United States* documents the disastrous results that occur when political policy ignores scientific input. The report proposed solutions involving both Congress and the White House, few of which have been implemented.

FRONTIERS OF FREEDOM INSTITUTE

The Frontiers of Freedom Institute (FOF) was founded in 1994 by U.S. Senator Malcolm Wallop. Its Web site (http://ff.org) states: "FOF is an educational institute (or think tank) whose mission is to promote conservative public policy based on the principles of individual freedom, peace through strength, limited government, free enterprise, and traditional American values as found in the Constitution and the Declaration of Independence."

Among the "Ten Tenets" listed on the Web site is one that declares: "To remove sound science from public policy is legislative and regulatory malpractice. To employ junk science in public policy is unethical and irresponsible."

The terms "sound science" and "junk science" were introduced more than a decade ago by conservative skeptics on climate change, endangered species, and the dangers of smoking. As employed by FOF, they reflect a suspicion of all government regulation, particularly on environmental issues. (See Chapter 5.)

The FOF's Center for Science and Public Policy (CSPP) has primary responsibility for the institute's campaign against "junk science." CSPP's science director, Dr. Willie Soon, has written several reports challenging the science of global warming, and he has questioned the need for regulating mercury emissions from power plants. In 2003, CSPP issued a report claiming that the EPA's attempt to regulate mercury contamination was not based on sound science.

GEORGE C. MARSHALL INSTITUTE

The George C. Marshall Institute (GMI) is a nonprofit organization founded in 1984 "to improve the use of science in making public policy about important issues for which science and technology are major considerations." The GMI Web site (www.marshall.org) says its current programs emphasize national security and the environment, and it explains:

Decisions and conclusions about many public policy matters are shaped by advances in science and technology. For that reason, unbiased and scientifically accurate assessments of the meaning of these advances for policy are critical. Where science is misused and distorted to promote special interests, GNI works to improve the situation:

- By communicating scientific information clearly,
- By identifying key linkages between science and policy issues, and
- By providing balanced and accurate assessments on specific science-based policy issues.

The Institute's accurate and impartial analyses are designed to help policy makers distinguish between opinion and scientific fact so that decisions on public policy issues can be based on solid, factual information, rather than opinion or unproven hypotheses.

The Marshall Institute established its influence on public science policy during the Reagan administration, when it became the most prominent defender of Reagan's Strategic Defense Initiative (SDI), known as Star Wars. (See Chapter 2.) Indeed, the institute's first published pamphlet defended the scientific basis for the controversial Star Wars program.

GMI later became heavily involved in the debate over climate change, publishing a number of reports between 1989 and 1992 that cast doubt on the scientific basis for global warming. GMI has received significant funding from the petroleum industry, which has consistently challenged the connection between carbon emissions and global warming. (See Chapter 5.) In 1998, the *New York Times* exposed an internal American Petroleum Institute memo implicating GMI in an industry strategy to "maximize the impact of scientific views consistent with ours with Congress, the media, and other key audiences." The full memo, available at www.environmentaldefense.org, indicates that a representative of GMI helped develop the industry plan.

In 2003, GMI published a book, *Politicizing Science: The Alchemy of Policymaking*, charging that the Clinton administration used junk science to justify its policy on global warming. The scientific community was unconvinced, and in 2004 the Union of Concerned Scientists (UCS) released a highly publicized report indicting the Bush administration for its politicization of science. The Marshall Institute came to the administration's defense in a press conference held at the National Press Club, at which it rejected the UCS report as part of a liberal political agenda.

GUTTMACHER INSTITUTE

The Guttmacher Institute was founded in 1968 as the Center for Family Planning Program Development. The center was originally constituted as a semiautonomous division of Planned Parenthood Federation of America. Alan Guttmacher, an eminent obstetrician-gynecologist, teacher, and writer, nurtured the early development of the center, which was renamed in his memory. The Guttmacher Institute became an independent, not-for-profit corporation in 1977.

The Institute's Web site (www.guttmacher.org) states:

The Guttmacher Institute advances sexual and reproductive health through an inter-related program of social science research, policy analysis and public education designed to generate new ideas, encourage enlightened public debate, promote sound policy and program development and, ultimately, inform individual decision making. . . .
The Institute regards sexual and reproductive health as encompassing a wide range of people's needs from adolescence onward. The Institute works to protect, expand and equalize access to information, services and rights that will enable women and men to

- avoid unplanned pregnancies;
- prevent and treat sexually transmitted infections, including HIV;
- exercise the right to choose abortion;
- achieve health pregnancies and births; and
- have healthy, satisfying sexual relationships.

The institute envisions a world in which all women and men have the ability to exercise their rights and responsibilities regarding sexual behavior, reproduction, and family formation freely and with dignity. Essential to this vision are societal respect for and protection of personal decision-making with regard to unwanted pregnancies and births, as well as public and private-sector policies that support individuals and couples in their efforts to become responsible and supportive parents, maintain stable family structures, and balance parenting with other roles. (See Chapter 3.)

The institute played a major role in the controversy over Plan B, the emergency contraceptive, or morning-after pill, monitoring and documenting the political process that denied FDA approval for over-the-counter sales of Plan B. The institute's published estimate that, despite being available only through prescription, Plan B prevented more than 100,000 unintended pregnancies and 51,000 abortions was instrumental in getting eventual FDA approval.

HERITAGE FOUNDATION

The Heritage Foundation was founded in 1973 as a conservative research and education institution. Its Web site (www.heritage.org) says its mission is "to formulate and promote conservative public policies based on the principles of free enterprise, limited government, individual freedom, traditional American values, and a strong national defense."

The foundation's Web site explains, "Our expert staff—with years of experience in business, government and on Capitol Hill—don't just produce research. We generate solutions consistent with our beliefs and market them to the Congress, the Executive Branch, the news media and others. These solutions build on our country's economic, political and social heritage to produce a safer, stronger, freer, more prosperous America."

Among the science-related events advertised on the Heritage Foundation's Web site are lectures and conferences that challenge mainstream science. A lecture on May 24, 2007, titled "The Politically Incorrect Guide to Science," is summarized as follows:

A lot of what passes for science these days is pseudo-science, and a lot of scientific fact is hidden from public view because it's not politically correct. Science has been politicized—not by the Right, but by the Left, which sees global warming, Darwinism, stem cell research, and innumerable other issues as tools to advance its agenda (and in many cases expand the reach of government).

An earlier lecture, titled "Science but not Scientists," states,

Public policy on science increasingly has little to do with science and much to do with ideological warfare, distorted constitutional arguments, and crass politics. Litigants use the federal courts to impose their own views of what constitutes valid science. Scientist and educated laypersons whose interpretation of the available evidence falls outside of the "mainstream" (whatever that is) are increasingly shunned from the public debate and subjected to *ad hominem* attacks.

More on this can be found in Chapter 2.

INSTITUTE FOR CREATION RESEARCH

The Institute for Creation Research (ICR) was established by Dr. Henry M. Morris in 1970 as the research division of Christian Heritage College (now San Diego Christian College). ICR became autonomous in 1981. Its mission statement on its Web site (www.icr.org) says:

ICR equips believers with evidence of the Bible's accuracy and authority through scientific research, educational programs, and media presentations, all conducted within a thoroughly biblical framework.

ICR says its programs focus on "research, communication, and education in those fields of science particularly relevant to the study of origins." (See Chapter 8.)

ICR's founder, Henry Morris, is best known as coauthor of *The Genesis Flood*, a book claiming that the geologic evidence suggesting that the Earth was billions of years old could be better explained as the result of the biblical flood involving Noah's ark. Morris was uncomfortable with the growing preference for Intelligent Design (ID) among creationists. He feared that many Christians would embrace ID as a way to avoid "having to confront the Genesis record of a young earth and global flood."[7] He was particularly dismissive of the notion that the intelligent designer in ID need not be God.

NATIONAL CENTER FOR SCIENCE EDUCATION

The National Center for Science Education (NCSE) was founded in 1981 and incorporated in 1983. Its Web site (www.natcenscied.org) states that NCSE

is a not-for-profit, membership organization providing information and resources for schools, parents and concerned citizens working to keep evolution in public school science education. We educate the press and public about the scientific, educational, and legal aspects of the creation and evolution controversy, and supply needed information and advice to defend good science education at local, state, and national levels. Our 4000 members are scientists, teachers, clergy, and citizens with diverse religious affiliations.

NCSE is religiously neutral, though it cooperates nationally and locally with religious organizations, as well as scientific and educational organizations like the National Academy of Sciences, the National Association of Biology Teachers, and the National Science Teachers Association.

NCSE was originally organized by groups of scientists, teachers, parents, clergy, and interested citizens who opposed the teaching of "scientific creationism" in public school science classes. They regarded scientific creationism as a restatement of biblical literalist religious doctrine and believed that its teaching would violate the separation of church and state.

NCSE sometimes works with organization that have broad concerns about civil liberties or public education, but only when evolution education is involved. When relevant legislation is introduced, NCSE informs its members of how evolution would be affected but does not advocate a particular position regarding civil liberties or the schools. (See Chapter 8.)

NCSE may have been the most important player in the celebrated evolution case *Kitzmiller v. Dover Area School District*. Despite the fact that the ACLU is commonly regarded as the moving force in the suit against the Dover school board, the truth is that the ACLU had insufficient staff, litigation funds, and scientific expertise to conduct the case, so the ACLU's Vic Walczak called the NCSE before accepting the case.

NCSE provided biologists, paleontologists, philosophers of science, mathematicians, and a host of other consultants and expert witnesses. The NCSE also granted the ACLU full access to its archives, covering more than two decades of creationism cases and Intelligent Design arguments. Most important, NCSE referred Walczak to an attorney, Eric Rothschild, at the prestigious international law firm Pepper Hamilton. After Pepper Hamilton's *pro bono* panel endorsed entering the case, Rothschild and his colleague, Steve Harvey, entered the case as lead attorneys, along with the ACLU's Wolczak.

NATIONAL COALITION AGAINST CENSORSHIP

The National Coalition Against Censorship (NCAC), founded in 1974, is an alliance of 50 national nonprofit organizations, including literary, artistic, religious, educational, professional, labor, and civil liberties groups. Its Web site (www.ncac.org) says:

United by a conviction that freedom of thought, inquiry, and expression must be defended, we work to educate our own members and the public at large about the dangers of censorship and how to oppose them.

In recent years, NCAC has forcefully addressed the censorship and manipulation of science by the Bush administration. In particular, it created The Knowledge Project: Censorship and Science, which examines the clash between First Amendment principles of free expression and government suppression or distortion of scientific information.

On February 6, 2007, NCAC issued its "Joint Statement on Censorship and Science: A Threat to Science, the Constitution, and Democracy," endorsed by the American Association of University Professors, American Civil Liberties Union, American Library Association, American Booksellers Foundation for Free Expression, Association of American Publishers, National Center for Science Education, PEN American Center, and People for the American Way.

The introduction to the joint statement describes a congressional hearing that "revealed a widespread pattern of political interference in the operations of federal scientific activities, including censorship of federal scientists' speech and writing, the distortion and suppression of research results, and retaliation against those who protest these acts."[8]

The joint statement then analyzes examples of political interference with science and concludes: "In sum, what is at stake is the integrity of government sponsored science, the ability of government scientists to adhere to the highest professional standards, their right to contribute to debates on matters of pressing concern, and the public's access to information created by public servants that is necessary to make informed judgments and hold officials accountable for their actions."[9]

NCAC's influential 2007 report, "Political Science: A Report on Science and Censorship," summarized the work of the Knowledge Project in a cogent and comprehensive document that concluded:

Science should inform politics, not the reverse. As the public, members of Congress, and public officials debate the implications of restricting the free speech of its scientists, certain basic principles should be considered:

- Scientific speech deserves and requires the full measure of constitutional protection envisioned by the Framers . . .
- Government scientists are entitled to function according to the highest professional standards, and to discuss their research freely with each other, members of Congress and state legislatures, other public officials, and interested members of the press and the public . . .
- anging scientific information, and government scientists should be permitted to do so without unreasonable constraints . . . [10]

NATURAL RESOURCES DEFENSE COUNCIL

The Natural Resources Defense Council (NRDC) was founded in 1970 as a not-for-profit, tax-exempt environmental action group and membership organization. Its Web site (www.nrdc.org) says its mission is "to safeguard the Earth: its people, its plants and animals and the natural systems on which all life depends." (See Chapter 6.)

In October 2008, the U.S. Supreme Court heard oral arguments on an important environmental case brought by the NRDC. *Winter v. Natural Resources Defense Council* involved a dispute over whether the Navy's use of sonar in training exercises off the California coast endangers whales and other marine mammals.

The NRDC charged that the Navy violated federal law by failing to produce an environmental impact statement before starting its sonar exercise and that, in the absence of injunctive relief, there was the possibility of irreparable harm to marine life. A lower court agreed, ordering the Navy to power off the sonar if a marine mammal came within 2,200 yards of the sonar source and to reduce sonar power by 75 percent if the Navy detected marine mammal activity. The Navy appealed, claiming that the restrictions imposed on its exercises would damage its ability to protect the national security. A U.S. appeals court upheld the decision granting the injunction, and the case was then appealed to the Supreme Court.

The Supreme Court held in a 5-4 decision that the standard for granting a preliminary injunction is not the "possibility" of irreparable harm to marine life, but rather that "irreparable injury is likely."[11]

OMB WATCH

OMB Watch is a nonprofit research and advocacy organization formed in 1983 to oversee the work of the White House Office of Management and Budget (OMB). Its Web site (www.ombwatch.org) says:

OMB Watch exists to increase government transparency and accountability; to ensure sound, equitable regulatory and budgetary processes and policies; and to protect and promote active citizen participation in our democracy. OMB Watch envisions a more just and democratic society, one in which an open, responsive government protects people's health, safety, and well-being, safeguards the environment, honors the public's right to information, values an engaged and effective citizenry, and adequately invests in the common good.

OMB Watch says it was formed "to lift the veil of secrecy shrouding the White House Office of Management and Budget," which oversees federal regulation, the budget, information collection and dissemination, proposed legislation, testimony by agencies, and a host of other federal activities.

OMB Watch currently concentrates on four main areas:

- Budget, taxation, and government performance
- Access to government information
- Nonprofit action, advocacy, rights, and policy
- Regulatory policy

OMB Watch has criticized the Bush administration's attempts to "stack" scientific advisory committees on the basis of ideology rather than scientific credentials. Its 2004 publication, *Special Interest Takeover: The Bush Administration and the Dismantling of Public Safeguards*, examines the administration's regulatory record and concludes: "Special interests have launched a sweeping assault on protections for public health, safety, the environment, and corporate responsibility—and, unfortunately, the Bush administration has given way. Crucial safeguards have been swept aside or watered down; emerging problems are being ignored; and enforcement efforts have been curtailed."[12]

Other OMB Watch publications include: *Polluted Logic: How EPA's Ozone Standard Illustrates the Flaws of Cost-Benefit Analysis* (2007); *A Failure to Govern: Bush's Attack on the Regulatory Process* (2007); and *Regulation and Competitiveness* (2005).

PACIFIC LEGAL FOUNDATION

ThePacific Legal Foundation (PLF), established March 5, 1973, is a nonprofit corporation that functions as a public interest legal advocate. Its Web site (http://community.pacificlegal.org) says it "fights for limited government, property rights, individual rights and a balanced approach to environmental protection." It declares:

Pacific Legal Foundation is devoted to a vision of individual freedom, responsible government, and color-blind justice. Like America's founders, we believe that the blessings of liberty are beyond measure. And like them, we believe that each generation must defend those blessings against government encroachment. . . . PLF's litigation focuses on three major projects: to defend the fundamental human right of private property; to promote sensible environmental policies that respect individual freedom and put people first; and to create a nation in which people are judged by the content of their character. In addition, PLF's Economic Liberty and Free Enterprise Projects are devoted to protecting the right to earn a living, and protect businesses against unfair burdens.

Among its featured cases are the following:

- Challenging regulatory abuses under the Clean Water Act
- Endangered Species Act abuse
- Opposing environmental injustices by government and activists
- Ensuring responsible management of public lands and natural resources[13] (See also Chapter 6.)

In 1999, the PLF brought suit against the federal government, challenging the listing of the Oregon coho salmon under the Endangered Species Act. PLF claimed that the National Marine Fisheries Service had used junk science when it excluded hatchery fish in its count of coho salmon. A district court judge agreed with the PLF, and the ruling opened the door to challenges of the endangered status of many other animal populations.

Scientists complained that the court ruling ignored important biological distinctions between wild and hatchery fish, including genetic adaptations to domestication that make hatchery fish less viable in the wild.

In January 2005, PLF brought suit again, this time challenging the endangered status of Klamath coho salmon. The same district judge who ruled in favor of PLF on the Oregon coho did much the same with respect to the Klamath coho, but he postponed delisting the Klamath coho pending the issuance of a new hatcheries policy by the fishery service. Meanwhile, PLF has threatened a sweeping lawsuit to overturn a wide range of salmon protections.

RUTHERFORD INSTITUTE

The Rutherford Institute's Web page (www.rutherford.org) states:

Founded in 1982 by constitutional attorney and author John W. Whitehead, The Rutherford Institute is a civil liberties organization that provides free legal services to people whose constitutional and human rights have been threatened or violated. . . . The Institute's mission is twofold: to provide legal services in the defense of religious and civil liberties and to educate the public on important issues affecting their constitutional freedoms.

John Whitehead founded the Rutherford Institute in the wake of his 1981 book *The Second American Revolution*, which advocates political and judicial activism on the part of conservative Christians. The institute was named after Samuel Rutherford, a 17th-century Scottish theologian who argued that kings must be subordinate to the law because the rule of kings is derived from men, whereas the rule of law is derived from God. Rutherford was known for being an opponent of the experiment with religious liberty in the American colonies, warning that the apostles "had but one Religion" and "toleration of many Religions [is] not . . . a part of the New Testament liberty."[14]

Early members of the Rutherford Institute's board of directors included prominent Christian fundamentalists Francis Schaeffer and R. J. Rushdoony, and the institute's activities reflected this influence. In cases involving public schools, the institute attempted to stop condom distribution, sex education, AIDS prevention programs, and programs that taught tolerance of homosexuality.

Surely, the case that attracted the most public attention to the Rutherford Institute came with the Paula Jones lawsuit against President Bill Clinton. John Whitehead, the institute's founder, acted as co-counsel for Jones. The case was eventually settled out of court.

The institute's most recent high-profile case was *Kitzmiller v. Dover*, the landmark evolution case. In *Kitzmiller*, three sets of parents formally petitioned the federal court to join the suit, claiming that if the ACLU suit against teaching Intelligent Design in the Dover high school succeeded, it "will have the effect of censoring . . . and shielding ninth graders from all criticism of the theory of biological evolution," in violation of their First Amendment rights.[15] The Rutherford Institute represented the petition by the Dover parents, but the judge ultimately ruled that there was no fundamental parental right to have any particular subject taught, or denied, in public school. That, said the court, was a matter determined by state education standards and the local school district. (See Chapter 8.)

In recent years, the Rutherford Institute has moved toward a more mainstream constitutional position, taking a strong stand against the Patriot Act, opposing student drug testing, and arguing that terrorist suspect Yaser Hamdi deserved due process. Still, the institute's primary focus remains on religion and government.

THOMAS MORE LAW CENTER

The Thomas More Law Center, headquartered in Ann Arbor, Michigan, is a not-for-profit public interest law firm founded in 1999. Its Web site (www.thomasmore .org) says it is

dedicated to the defense and promotion of the religious freedom of Christians, time-honored family values, and the sanctity of human life. Our purpose is to be the sword and shield for people of faith, providing legal representation without charge to defend and protect Christians and their religious beliefs in the public square. We achieve this goal principally through litigation, seeking out significant cases, consistent with our mission, where our expertise can be of service to others.

The center plays an important role in the debate over religion and politics, and its Web site acknowledges,

Our ministry was inspired by the recognition that the issues of the *cultural war* being waged across America, issues such as abortion, pornography, school prayer and the removal of the Ten Commandments from municipal and school buildings, are not being decided by elected legislatures, but by the courts. These court decisions, largely insulated from the democratic process, have been inordinately influenced by legal advocacy groups such as the American Civil Liberties Union (ACLU) which seek to systematically subvert the religious and moral foundations of our nation.

The center was launched by the billionaire founder of Domino's Pizza, and it was led by Tom Monaghan, a prominent business and Christian leader, and Richard Thompson, a former Michigan prosecutor who is best known for his role in the prosecution of Jack Kevorkian, of assisted-suicide fame. The center says it is currently handling over 259 legal matters in 43 different states.

The center's most recent high-profile case came in the 2005 landmark case *Kitzmiller v. Dover Area School District*, in which Richard Thompson served as the lead attorney for the school board. In that case, the court found that the board had unconstitutionally introduced a religious doctrine, Intelligent Design, into Dover science classes.

UNION OF CONCERNED SCIENTISTS

The Union of Concerned Scientists (UCS) began as a collaboration between students and faculty members at the Massachusetts Institute of Technology in 1969 and later became an alliance of more than 250,000 citizens and scientists. The UCS Web site (www.ucsusa.org) states:

> The Union of Concerned Scientists is the leading science-based nonprofit working for a healthy environment and a safer world. UCS combines independent scientific research and citizen action to develop innovative, practical solutions and to secure responsible changes in government policy, corporate practices, and consumer choices. . . . UCS members are people from all walks of life: parents and businesspeople, biologists and physicists, teachers and students. Our achievements over the decades show that thoughtful action based on the best available science can help safeguard our future and the future of our planet.

During the Reagan administration, UCS joined with other scientific organizations to challenge the science behind the Star Wars missile defense system. (See Chapter 2.) More recently, the UCS has confronted the Bush administration on the misuse of science in areas like embryonic stem-cell research, global warming, mercury pollution, condom use, and abortion.

On February 18, 2004, the UCS held a press conference to announce that over 60 leading scientists and former government officials, including 20 Nobel laureates, had signed on to a UCS document, "Scientific Integrity in Policymaking," denouncing the Bush administration for misrepresenting and suppressing scientific information. Examples included distorting the science of climate change, quashing government scientific reports, and stacking scientific advisory panels. The document stated, "Other administrations have, on occasion, engaged in such practices, but not so systematically nor on so wide a front."[16]

Eventually, thousands of other scientists, including 48 Nobel laureates, 62 National Medal of Science recipients, and 135 members of the National Academy of Sciences, would sign on to the UCS document.

UCS then conducted a poll that showed broad public support for scientific integrity, fairness, and transparency in governmental processes. Some 83 percent of U.S. citizens polled believed it was important for America's leaders to gather information and scientific advice from experts, including those they might not agree with. Seventy-nine percent of those surveyed said it was unacceptable to subject candidates for scientific advisory committees to political litmus tests. An overwhelming majority also considered it unacceptable for government officials to suppress research results or remove scientific information.[17]

In 2005, UCS joined with Public Employees for Environmental Responsibility to send surveys on the politicization of science to more than a thousand scientists at the Fish and Wildlife Service. Almost half of the respondents working on endangered species said they had been directed, for nonscientific reasons, to refrain from recommending the protection of species. Twenty percent of respondents said they had been directed to inappropriately alter or exclude technical information from agency documents. (See Chapter 6.)

NOTES

1. "National Watchdog Organization Launched to Fight Unsound Science Used for Public Policy Comes to Denver," Highbeam Research, November 24, 1993. www.highbeam.com/doc/1P2-18839157.html.
2. Chris Mooney, "The Fraud of Sound Science: A History of a Conservative Term of Art," The River Speaks, May 10, 2004. http://theriverspeaks.blogspot.com/2004-06-01-archive.html
3. AAAS, Resolution on Intelligent Design Theory, October 18, 2002, www.aaas.org/news/releases/2002/1106id2.shtml.
4. www.aclu.org
5. James Inhofe, Senate floor speech, July 28, 2003, http://inhofe.senate.gov/pressreleases/climate.htm.
6. Ronald L. Numbers, The Creationists: From Scientific Creationism to Intelligent Design (Cambridge: Harvard University Press, 2006), 382.
7. Ibid., 377.
8. "Joint Statement on Censorship and Science: A Threat to Science, the Constitution, and Democracy," National Coalition Against Censorship, February 6, 2007, www.ncac.org/Censorshiop_and_Science_Threat_To_Science_Constitution_Democracy.
9. Ibid.
10. National Committee Against Censorship, "Political Science: A Report on Science and Censorship," 2007, www.ncac.org/ncacimages/political_science.pdf.
11. Winter v. Natural Resources Defense Council, Inc., Oyez: U.S. Supreme Court Media, November 12, 2008, www.oyez.org/cases/2000-2009/2008/2008_7_1239.
12. OMB Watch, "Special Interest Takeover," www.ombwatch.org/article/archive/260.
13. "Featured Cases," Pacific Legal Foundation, http://community.pacificlegal.org/Page.aspx?pid=258.
14. "Samuel Rutherford Refutes Roger Williams Regarding Toleration, Sectarianism and Peace," from the 1649 edition of Rutherford's *Free Disputation Against Pretended Liberty of Conscience,* Still Water Revival Books, www.swrb.com/newslet/actualNLs/ruthrefwil.htm.
15. Edward Humes, *Monkey Girl* (New York: HarperCollins, 2007), 222.
16. Union of Concerned Scientists, "Restoring Scientific Integrity in Policymaking," February 18, 2004, www.ucsusa.org/global_environment/rsi/page.cfm?pageID=1320.
17. Union of Concerned Scientists, "Attitudes Toward Science and Politics," survey conducted for the Integrity of Science Working Group, September 20, 2004, www.ucusa.org/scientifi_integrity/abuses_of_science/poll-the-public's-belief-in.html.

Index

Abortion, 57, 59–62, 68
Abraham, Spencer, 93
Abrahamson, James, 41
Abstinence, xvi, 49–54, 137–138
Abul-Fadl, Tarek, 183
Acosta, Dean, 91
Adolescent Family Life Act, 50
Adult stem cells, 66, 74–76
Advancement of Sound Science Coalition
   (TASSC), 43, 215–216
AIDS (Acquired Immune Deficiency Syndrome)
   Bush, George W., on, 51
   McIlhaney, Joe, on, 54
   needle exchange programs, 138–139
   Obama's Act Against AIDS program, 209
   Reagan, Ronald, on, xi, 130, 136–137
Air pollution, 116
Alberts, Bruce, 177
Albright, David, 18
Alden, Edward, 188
Aldrin, Edwin "Buzz," Jr., 25
Allen, George, 73
American Association for the Advancement
   of Science (AAAS), xv, 216–217
American Civil Liberties Association
   (ACLU), 165–166, 217
American Enterprise Institute, 217–218
American Physical Society, x
Anderson, Stuart, 178
Annapolis Center for Science-Based Public
   Policy, xiii, 218
Arms Export Control Act, 174
Aspin, Les, 44

Atala, Anthony, 67
Atomic bomb, viii, 1–3
Atomic Energy Act, vii, xv, 3, 13,16
Atomic Energy Commission (AEC), 3–6,
   9–12
Augustine, Norman, 186

Baltimore, David, xv
Barrett, Craig, 181
Barton, Joe, 144
Bauer, Gary, xi, 136
Becker, S. William, 119
Beggs, James, 31
Behe, Michael, 162, 167
Bell, Griffin, 14–15
Benjamin, Regina M., 133, 203
Berg, Paul, 70, 77
Bertin, Joan, xiv
Bethe, Hans, 12
Biden, Joseph, 192–193
Bidzos, D. James, 176
Bird, Kai, 11
Bishop, J. Michael, 72
Bisphenol-A (BFA), 135
Blackburn, Elizabeth, 75
Blair, Tony, 100
Blumenthal, Richard, 60
Boehner, John, 164
Boisjoly, Roger, 31–33
Bonsell, Alan, 165, 168, 70
Borden, William Liscum, 4–5, 9
Born classified, vii, xv
Bowen, Gregory, 45

Boxer, Barbara, 113–115, 120, 194
Breaux, John, 147
Brind, Joel, 61
Briscoe, Andrew, 147
Brooks, Connie, 121
Brooks, Jack, 176
Broom Arthur, 183
Brown, George, Jr., xii, 42
Brownback, Sam, 72–73, 75
Browner, Carol M., 204
Bryan, William Jennings, 155–157
Buchanan, Pat, 137
Buckingham, Bill, 165, 168, 170
Burnett, Jason, 119
Burney, Leroy E., 140
Bush, George Herbert Walker, xii, 43, 59,
    107, 130
Bush, George W.
    abortion, 59–61
    abstinence-only programs, 49, 51
    AIDS, 138–139
    air pollution, 116–117
    atomic energy, 16–21
    Carmona, Richard, on, 131
    Challenger disaster, 35
    condoms, 54–55
    drug safety, 133–134
    export controls, 179
    global warming, 85–87, 89–93, 96, 98
    Intelligent Design, 166
    last-minute regulations, 191–195,
        205–206
    missile defense, 44–45
    mountaintop removal, 110–111
    politicized science, 106
    sound science, xii-xiii
    stem cells, 69–70, 72–74, 76–77
    tobacco industry, 144
    visas, 183–187
    Vision for Space Exploration, 38
    water pollution, 114–115
    wilderness and wildlife, 121–125
Bush, Vannever, 8
Butler Act, 155–156, 158
Butler, John, 155–156
Byrnes, James, 2

California Institute for Regenerative Medicine
    (CIRM), 77–78
Campbell, William, 143
Cannistraro, Vincent, 20
Card, Andrew, 87, 93
Carmona, Richard, 130, 132–133, 143–144, 147

Carruthers, Gary, 216
Casacuberta, Elena, 183–184
Center for Progressive Regulation, xiii
Center for Regulatory Effectiveness,
    218–219
Challenger disaster, xvi, 29–35, 37–38, 40
Chapman, Bruce, 220
Charo, R. Alta, 210
Cheney, Dick, 16–19, 87, 92–93, 107–108
Chertoff, Michael, 109
Chiang, John, 77
Christie, Thomas, 45
Chu, Steven, 201
Clapp, Philip, 85
Clark, Richard, 21
Claussen, Eileen, 85–86
Clean Air Act, 117–118, 120, 205–206
Clinton, Bill
    abortion, 59
    Elders, Joycelyn, resignation, 130
    endangered species, 123
    global warming, 85–86, 90
    health care reform, 149
    Lewinski, Monica, 131
    missile defense, 44
    Shalala, Donna, 139
    stem cells, 68–69
    tobacco industry, 141
    wilderness policy, 121
Clinton, Hillary Rodham, 57
Cloning, 71–74
Coburn, Tom, 54
Coker, Robert, 146
Collins, Francis, 203
Columbia Accident Investigation Board
    (CAIB), 35–38
Columbia disaster, 35–38
Commonsense Consumption Act, 148
Competitive Enterprise Institute (CEI), 89
Condoms, xi, 50, 54–55, 136
Contraception, 54
Contract with America, xiii
Conyers, John, Jr., 44
Cook, Ken 136
Cook, Richard, 30–31
Corzine, Jon, 78
Coyle, Philip, 44–45
Craig, Larry, 147
Crawford, Lester, 57
Creationism, xi, xvii-xviii, 154, 158–161,
    167
Crichton, Michael, 96
Cryptography, 176

D'Souza, Dinesh, 60
Daly, Brendan, 195
Danforth, John, xvi, 73, 79
Daniel v . Waters, 159
Darrow, Clarence, 155–157
Darwin, Charles, 153–157, 166
Daugherty, Rebecca, 109
Davidoff, Frank, 56
Davis, Gray, 77, 204
DeLauro, Rosa, 135
DeMint, Jim, 149
DeParle, Nancy-Ann, 203
Department of Energy, 14–15
Devine, Donald, 58
Devine, Tom, 134
DeWitt, Hugh, 42
Dickey, Nancy, 59
Dickey-Wicker Amendment, 68
Dioxin, 115–116
Discovery Institute, 162–68, 219–220
Discovery space shuttle, 38
Doerflinger, Richard, 76
Dreher, Robert, 195
Dulles, Allan, 27
Dunham, Ben, 195
Dwyer, Timothy, 108

Earthjustice, 195
Ebling, Bob, 32
Ecker, Allan, 6
Edwards v. Aguillard, 160–161, 167
Eggan, Kevin, 79
Einstein, Albert, 7, 12
Eisenhower, Dwight D., viii-ix, 5, 7, 26–27
Elders, Joycelyn, 130
Emanuel, Rahm, 76
Embryonic stem cells, xvi, 65–70, 191, 199, 209–210
Endangered Species Act, xvii, 122, 124–125
Englehardt, Irl, 92
Environmental Protection Agency (EPA)
    air pollution, 117–120
    carbon dioxide regulation, 98–99, 101
    climate change report, 90
    Hurricane Katrina, 105, 112
    mountaintop removal, 111
    Obama's EPA appointments, 199–200
    Obama's EPA initiatives, 205–207
    Reagan, Ronald, xi
    tobacco industry, 143
    Union of Concerned Scientists, report on, 106–107, 198
    water pollution, 113–116

Enzi, Michael, 133
Epperson, Susan, 158
Epperson v. Arkansas, 158–159
Evans, Donald L., 93
Evans, Ward, 6, 9–10
Evolution, xi, xvii-xviii, 153–170
Executive Order 12356, ix-x
Export Administration Act, 174–175
Export controls, xviii, 174–179, 188

Falwell, Jerry, 58
Federal Emergency Management Agency (FEMA), 106, 108–110, 112, 202
Federation of American Scientists (FAS), 30, 44, 220–221
Feinstein, Diane, 120
Fermi, Enrico, 3
Feynman, Richard, 31, 33
Fish and Wildlife Services, see U.S. Fish and Wildlife Services
Fleischer, Ari, 52
Food and Drug Administration (FDA)
    condom use, 55
    drug safety, 134
    food additives, 146
    Obama appointments to, 199, 209
    Plan B, 133, 156–157
    smoking, 144
    Union of Concerned Scientists, recommendations, 198
Ford, Carl W., Jr., 20
Ford, Gerald, 187
Forrest, Barbara, 167–168
Fortas, Abe, 158
Fossett, James, 80
Francis, Donald, 137
Frist, Bill, 148
Frontiers of Freedom Institute (FOF), 221
Fugate, W. Craig, 202

Gade, Mary, 116
Gag rule, 58–60
Gainen, Hal, 35
Galson, Steven, 133
Gansler, Jacques, 185
Garbett, David, 193
Garrison, Lloyd K., 6, 9
Gasper, Jo Ann, 58
Gast, Alice, 185
Gates, Bill, 180–181
Gelbspan, Ross, 92
George C. Marshall Institute, 221–222
Gillen, Patrick, 166

Gingrich, Newt, xii-xiii, 44
Glenn, John, 15
Global warming, xii, xvii, 83–99, 199
Golden, K. C., 99
Gordon, Asa, 33–34
Gordon, Bart, 107
Gore, Al, xvii, 44, 83–87, 93
Gorsuch, Anne, xi
Gottlieb, Michael, 137
Government Accountability Project (GAP), 97
Graefe, Frederick, 203
Graham, David, 134–135
Graham, William, 31
Gray, C. Boyden, 11
Gray, Gordon, 6, 9, 11
Greenstein, Ruth, 174–175
Greer, Joyce Hens, 58
Gregg, Judd, 164
Griles, J. Stephen, 110–111
Grove J. W., viii
Groves, Leslie R., 2, 4–5
Grumbles, Benajmin, 113
Grunwald, Michael, 112
Guttmacher Institute, 222–223

Hager, W. David, 56
Hall, Dick, 124
Hall, Zach, 77
Ham, Linda, 36
Hamburg, Margaret A., 199, 209
Hansen, Charles, 15
Hansen, James, 84–85, 91–92
Harvey, John, 42
Hatch, Orrin, 73
Hecker, Jim, 111
Hennessy, John, 187
Henrich, C. E., 9
Heritage Foundation, 223–224
Herold, Eve, 73
Heslep, Charter, 9
Hirschhorn, Eric, 176
Hirshfield, Michael, 204
Hitchens, Theresa, 45
HIV. See AIDS
Holdren, John, 204
Holmstead, Jeffrey R., 117–118
Holsinger, James, 133
Hoover, J. Edgar, 4, 7, 9
Hubbell, Scott, 35
Hussein, Saddam, 16–21
Huwaish, Abdul, 20
Hydrogen bomb, iv, xv, 8, 10, 12–15

Inhofe, James, 95–96, 149, 218
Inslee, Jay, 122
Institute for Creation Research, 161, 224
Intelligent Design, xvii-xviii, 161–164,
    167–170, 220
Intercontinental ballistic missiles, 27–28, 40
Intergovernmental Panel on Climate Change
    (IPCC), 85–87, 93
International Atomic Energy Agency (IAEA),
    19–20
International Space Station, 38–39
International Traffic in Arms Regulations,
    174, 177
Iraq, 16–21

Jackson, Lisa P., 199–200, 205–207
Janssen, Sarah, 135
Johnson, Harvey, 109
Johnson, Haynes, 182
Johnson, Lyndon, 120
Johnson, Marlene, 177
Johnson, Phillip E., 163
Johnson, Stephen, 114, 116, 119
Jones III, John E., 166–167, 170
Jones, Alex, 109
Jong-wook, Lee, 147

Kaine, Tomothy, 53
Kass, Leon, 72
Katrina hurricane, xvii, 105, 108–110, 112,
    115, 202
Kay, David, 22
Kempthorne, Dirk, 194–195
Kendall, Doug, 208
Kennedy, Donald, 91
Kennedy, John F., ix, 28, 140
Kennedy, Robert F., Jr., 96, 207
Kerlikowske, R. Gil, 204
Kesavan, P.C., 184–185
Keyworth, George, xi, 41, 160
Kidder, Ray, 42
Kierstead, Hans, 67
Killian, James, viii, 26
Kitzmiller, Tammy, 165
Kitzmiller v. Dover Area School District,
    xviii, 164–170, 217, 225, 230
Kline, Robert, 78
Knobloch, Kevin, 204–205
Koop, C. Everett, xi, 60, 129–130, 137,
    140–141
Koplan, Jeffrey, 55
Korman, Edward, 209

Krepon, Michael, 45
Kyoto treaty, xvi, 86, 89, 94

Labaton, Vivien, 133
Landay, Jonathan, 17
Launius, Roger, 27
Lay, Kenneth, 108
Leahy, Patrick, 120, 148
Leavitt, Michael, 52, 121, 144
Leon, Judy, 135
Lewinski, Monica, 131
Libby, Lewis, 17, 19, 21
Library Awareness Program, x
Lilienthal, David L., 7
Littell, David, 102
Logsdon, John, 28, 38–39
Lubchenco, Jane, 204
Luntz, Frank, 94–95
Lynch, Patrick, 98

MacDonald, Julie, 123–124
Manhattan Project, viii, 4
Manson, Craig, 123
Marks, Herbert, 6
Matzke, Nick, 167
Matzner, Franz, 121
McAuliffe, Christa, 29
McCaffrey, Barry, 203
McCarthy, James, xv
McCarthy, Joseph, 5–6, 182
McCloy, John, 7
McConnell, Mitch, 148
McCormack, Don, 36
McCurdy, Howard, 28, 35
McEnaney, Bobby, 193
McFarlane, Robert, 41
McGarity, Thomas, xiii
McIlhaney, Joe, 54–55
Meacher, Michael, 96
Meadows, Bill, 201
Mehta, Goverdhan, 184
Melamine, 135
Merlo, Ellen, 143
Mester, John, 177
Metcalf, Maynard, 157
Miller, George, 42
Miller, Judith, 17
Miller, Kenneth, 162, 166
Milloy, Steve, 215
Mooney, Chris, vii, 71
Moonwalk, 25, 28
Morgan, Thomas A., 6

Morgan, W. Lowell, 43
Moritsugu, Kenneth, 133
Morland, Howard, 13–16
Morrison, Philip, vii
Morton Thiokol, 31–34
Mosholder, Andrew, 133–134
Mountaintop removal, 110, 207
Mukerji, Chandra, viii
Mulhern, Joan, 111
Mulloy, Larry, 31
Murphy, Richard, 78
Murray, Patty, 57
Musgrave, Story, 36
Myers, Matthew, 145

Nagin, Ray, 105
National Academy of Sciences (NAS), xii
National Aeronautics and Space Administration (NASA), xvi, 28, 31–39, 91
National Center for Science Education (NCSE), 225
National Coalition Against Censorship (NCAC), xiv, 70, 225–226
National Institutes of Health (NIH), 68–71, 210
National Science Foundation, viii
National security, viii–ix, xiv, 28, 177
National Security Agency, x
National Security Decision Directive 145 (NSDD-145), x, 175
Natural Resources Defense Council (NRDC), 108, 118, 121, 227
Nazzaro, Robin, 124
Needle exchange program (NEP), 138–139
Nelson, Don, 28
Neufeld, Michael, 26
Nichols, Kenneth, 6
Nitze, Paul, 41
Nixon, Richard M., ix, 28
Norton, Gale, 93, 121

O'Keefe, Sean, 35
O'Reilly, Patrick, 46
Obama, Barack
    Benjamin, Regina, appointment of, 133
    early administration policies, 191–208
    export controls, 187–188
    health care reform, 149
    smoking, 145
    space shuttle, 39
    wilderness policy, 122
Obesity, xvii, 145–149

Office of Censorship, 2
Office of Technology Assessment (OTA), xii
OMB Watch, 227–228
Oppenheimer, J. Robert, xv, 3–12
O-rings, 30–33

Pacific Legal Foundation, 228–229
Palmer, Fred, 92
Park, Robert, x, 175–176, 182–183
Patriot Act. 182
Paulison, R. David, 110
Pelosi, Nancy, 39, 195
Perchlorate, 113–114
Perry, Whit, 99
Peyton, David, 176
Phelps, Marshall, Jr., 176
Philip Morris, 141, 143, 216
Phillips, Howard, 60
Piel, Gerard, 12–13
Pike, John, 30, 44
Pillar, Paul, 19
Piltz, Rick, 90
Pitts, Joe, 62
Plan B, 55–56, 133, 208–209
Planned Parenthood, 58, 60
Poindexter, John, 175
Pombo, Richard, 122
Powell, Colin, 17, 21
Powell, Keri, 118
Prentice, David, 75
President's Science Advisory Council
    (PSAC), ix
Progressive, 13–16
Public health, 129

Qidwai, Uvais, 183

Rahall, Nick, 122, 124, 194, 208
Randol, Randy, 86, 93
Rappaport, Jamie, 125
Rathjeans, George, 14
Raulston, John T., 156–157
Raynolds, Ned, 102
Reagan, Ronald
    abortion, 57–58, 60
    abstinence-only education, 50
    AIDS policies, 130, 136–137
    Challenger disaster, 29, 34
    Creationism, 159–60
    environmental policies, 117
    Environmental Protection Agency, xi-xii
    export controls, 174–175

Star Wars, 40–41, 46
    tobacco industry, 140
Reardon, David, 62
Regan, Donald, 30
Reid, Harry, 39
Reilly, William, xii, 85, 99
Remnick, David, 96
Rexwood, Caird E., 72
Rey, Mark E.. 195
Rice, Condoleezza, 18, 87, 93
Richards, Cecile, 54
Ritter, Bill, 194
Roadless rule, 121–122, 208
Robb, Roger, 6, 9, 11
Roberts, James, 44
Roe v. Wade, 57–59, 68
Rogers, William P., 30
Rogers Commission, 31–35
Rohrabacher, Dana, xii, 180
Roig, Joan, 183–184
Rolphe, Trish, 122
Romm, Joseph, 90
Roose, Rebecca, 123
Roosevelt, Frederick Delano, vii
Rosenbaum, Janet, 54
Rosenberg, Daniel, 206
Rothschild, Eric, 166–167
Rouse, James T., 108
Rowland, Alex, 38
Rubin, Donn, 79
Ruckelshaus, William, xi
Rumsfeld, Donald, 17–18
Russo, Nancy Felipe, 62
Rutherford Institute, 229–230

Salazar, Ken, 201, 207
Sanders, Bernie, 188
Santorum, Rick, 163, 166
Satcher, David, 130–131
Saucier, Aldric, 43–44
Scalia, Antonin, 160–161
Schaeffer, Eric, 107, 117–118
Schwarzenegger, Arnold, 77–78, 100–101,
    119
Scopes, John, 156–157, 161
Scopes trial. See Tennessee v. John
    Scopes
Scowcroft, Brent, 187
Sebelius, Kathleen, 202–203
Second-hand smoke, 142–144
Secular humanism, 96
Sensitive but unclassified, 175, 186

Sex education, 49–50, 53
Sexually transmitted diseases (STDs), 50, 52, 54–55
Sgama, Kathleen, 193–194
Shalala, Donna, 68–69, 139
Shattuck, John, x
Sherwin, Martin, 11
Shultz, Lexi, 123
Simon, Bob, 18
Skolnikoff, Eugene, 177
Smith, Tobin, 179
Smith, Wesley, 75
Smith, William, 54
Smoking, xvii, 129, 139, 141–145
Smyth, Henry, 10
Soler, Lawrence, 210
Sonder, Mark, 52
Sound science, xii-xiii, 147
Soviet Union, viii, xv, 26–27, 41, 43
Space shuttle, 28–29
Speakes, Larry, 137
Sputnik, viii, xv, 26–28
Spy satellites, 26, 28
Star Wars, xvi, 40–41, 43–46, 222
Steiger, William, 132, 147
Steitz, David, 39
Stem cells. *See* Adult stem cells; Embryonic stem cells
Stevens, John Paul, 118
Stowars, Jim, 79–80
Strategic Defense Initiative (SDI), 40, 42–46
Strauss, Lewis, 4–5, 7, 9–11
Strickland, Ted, 54
Sullivan, Louis, 68, 203
Superman, 2
Supersonic transport
Sutley, Nancy, 111, 204, 206
Symons, Jeremy, 90

Tamminen, Terry, 100
Technology transfer, x, xviii, 174
Teich, Al, 183
Teller, Edward, 8, 11, 13, 15, 40–42
Tenet, George, 19–20
Tennessee v. John Scopes, 155–58
Terry, Luther, 140
Thaxton, Charles, 167
Thielman, Gregory, 18
Thomas More Law Center, 165–66, 230–231
Thompson, Tommy, 147
Thomson, James, 65–67, 71, 75–76

Tibbot, Cindy, 110
Tobacco industry, xii, 140–145
Toiv, Barry, 179
Tozzi, Jim, 218–219
Trounson, Alan, 67
Truman, Harry S., vii, 2, 4

Union of Concerned Scientists (UCS)
    auto emissions, comments on, 205
    Bush political appointees, xv
    endangered species 122–123
    Holdren, John, evaluation of, 204
    missile defense, 46
    organizational history, 231–232
    political interference in science, report on, 97, 106–107
    recommendations to new Obama administration, 196–198
U.S. Army Corps of Engineers, 112
U.S. Fish and Wildlife Services (FWS), 124–123

Varmus, Harold, 66, 72
Vilsack, Tom, 122, 202, 208
Vioxx, 134–135
Visas, 178–188
Volpe, Joe, 6–7
Von Braun, Werner, 26–28
Von Eschenbach, Andrew, 144

Wadhwa, Vivek, 178
Walczak, Vic, 165
Walling, Richard, 132
Wallop, Malcolm, 221
Warren, Robert, 14, 16
Watson, Robert, 86, 93
Watt, James, xi, 160
Waxman, Henry, xiv, 51–53, 119–120, 130–132
Weapons of Mass Destruction (WMDs), xv, 16, 19–22
Webster, Lee, 27
Wedge document, 162, 168
Weissman, Irving, 74, 77
Weldon, Dave, 39, 61
Werner, Michael, 79
White, Herbert S., 175
White, Wendy, 185
White House Council on Environmental Quality (CEQ), 111
White House Office of Science and Technology, ix, xi

Whitehouse, Sheldon, 116
Whitman, Christine Todd, 87–89, 107
Wiesner, Jerome, xi
Wilderness, 120–122
Wilderness Act, 120
Wiles, Richard, 113
Will, George, 182
Wilmut, Ian, 71
Wilson, Joseph, 19–20
Wilson, Shari, 102
Wilson, Woodrow, 155
Wirth, Timothy, 84

Wolfle, Dael, 10
Wood, Lowell, 41–42
Wood, Samuel, 74
Wood, Susan, 56–57, 209
Woodruff, Roy, 40–42
Wright, David, 46
Wright, G. Frederick, 154

Xenophobia, xviii, 173–188

Zerhouni, Elias, 71
Zuckerman, Diana, 200

About the Author

HERBERT N. FOERSTEL is the former Head of Branch Libraries at the University of Maryland, board member at the National Security Archive, and former editor of Maryland Library Association's newspaper. He is the author of many books on First Amendment issues, including *Secret Science: Federal Control of American Science and Technology* (Praeger, 1989) and *Killing the Messenger: Journalists at Risk in Modern Warfare* (Praeger, 2006).